IELTS Intensive

A short course for IELTS success

Louis Rogers and Nick Thorner

Download the free DELTA Augmented app onto your device

Start picture recognition and scan this page

Download files and use them now or save them for later

1st edition 1 5 4 3 2 | 2024 23 22 21

Delta Publishing 2020
www.deltapublishing.co.uk
www.klett-sprachen.de/delta

Edited by Catriona Watson-Brown
Designed by Caroline Johnston
Cover design by Greg Sweetnam
Printed by RR Donnelley, China

Photo acknowledgements
All photos by Shutterstock except page 13, right-hand photo (Nick Thorner).
page 24a: maoyunping / Shutterstock.com; page 38 (volunteering): City of Angels / Shutterstock.com; page 42 (shopping): 501room / Shutterstock.com; page 42 (eating out): Alexander Mazurkevich / Shutterstock.com; page 70(1): Hadrian / Shutterstock.com;
page 70(2): JuliusKielaitis / Shutterstock.com; page 70(3): TungCheung / Shutterstock.com; page 70(4): chrisdorney / Shutterstock.com; page 70(5): ricochet64 / Shutterstock.com;
page 70(6): JuliusKielaitis / Shutterstock.com

Illustration acknowledgements
Kathy Baxendale (pages 9, 16, 21, 28, 34, 36, 42, 48, 56, 62, 74, 76, 90, 91, 92, 93, 94, 95 and 114)
Oxford Designers and Illustrators (pages 10 and 14)

Text acknowledgements
We are grateful to the following for permission to reproduce copyright material:
page 31: *The Science of Laughter* by Robert Provine adapted from https://www.psychologytoday.com/articles/200011/the-science-laughter; reproduced by permission of Psychology Today © Copyright 2000 www.Psychologytoday.com
page 34: Privacy Policy Analysis graph from *The Current State of Web Privacy, Data Collection, and Information Sharing* by Joshua Gomez, Travis Pinnick and Ashkan Soltani from http://www.knowprivacy.org/; reproduced by permission of Know Privacy and the authors
page 36: chart of smartphone usage from https://wwwstatista.com/chart/3666/frequency-of-smartphone-usage/; reproduced by permission of Statista
page 39: adaptation of *Is travel good for you?* by Art Markman from https://www.psychologytoday.com/blog/ulterior-motives/201309/extended-travel-affects-personality; reproduced by permission of Art Markman
page 51: extract from *How moods affect our health* by Anastasia Stephens http://www.independent.co.uk/life-style/health-and-families/healthy-living/how-moods-affect-our-health-764289.html; reproduced by permission of *The Independent*
page 90 (Task 1): graph of American time use survey from http://www.bls.gov/tus/charts/students.htm; source Bureau of Labor Statistics USA
page 91 (Task 3): graph from http://www.gfkmri.com/ConsumerInsights/MediaHabits.aspx; reproduced by permission of GfK MRI
page 91 (Task 4): data from http://w3techs.com/technologies/overview/content_language/all; reproduced by permission of W3Techs
page 94 (Task 9): graph *Urban and Rural Populations by Development Group 1950–2050* from http://www.un.org/en/development/desa/publications/world-urbanization-prospects-the-2011-revision.html; source United Nations
page 94 (Task 10): graph *Monthly Voice and Text Usage by Age*, Nielsen Company April 2009 – March 2010; reproduced by permission of Nielsen

In some instances we have been unable to trace the owners of copyright material and we would appreciate any information that would enable us to do so.

ISBN 978-3-12-501580-7

INTRODUCTION

IELTS Intensive is a short course in IELTS (academic) training and test practice. It's designed for students aiming to achieve an IELTS band score of between 5.5 and 6.5.

TO THE STUDENT

IELTS Intensive is ideal if you're approaching the standard of academic English you require to achieve your target IELTS band score, but you need a short course to help you become familiar with the tasks in the test and the techniques needed to tackle them. *IELTS Intensive* offers thorough training and realistic practice to give you the confidence and skills you need for the IELTS test.

The IELTS quiz

How well do you know the IELTS test? If you're familiar with the format of IELTS tasks, try the quiz on pages 6–9 before you start. If not, follow the references to this quiz throughout the course (look for the Test check icon ➤). They appear at the start of each skill section and help familiarise you with the task types that appear in each unit.

TO THE TEACHER

IELTS Intensive is designed to help you strike a balance between training in test techniques and practice in all four skills areas. For short courses, we recommend using only the main lessons in Units 1–8. This will provide approximately 40 hours of teaching material. The Test files and Writing task bank can then be set for homework. For longer courses, you can incorporate the Test files and Writing task bank into the main lessons. This will provide approximately 20 hours of additional classroom-based materials.

Reading

In each Reading section, the *Skills focus* section introduces a new question type, providing a strategy for each task, and reviews a question type introduced in previous units. Because candidates often find it challenging to complete 40 questions in one hour, each question is accompanied by a target time to help students maintain an adequate reading speed. Students are also given an opportunity to set a target score.

Listening

Each Listening section has a *Prepare to listen* task to help students predict possible answers and avoid some of the most common mistakes. As with the Reading sections, students are asked to set a target score before each task to help them monitor their progress towards their required band level. (See *IELTS quiz: Listening* question 2 for assistance in target setting.)

Speaking

The Speaking sections have a vocabulary task to make students aware of higher-level vocabulary they might exploit. They then study tasks from the test and analyse extracts from two candidates' answers. Students use the *You're the examiner* boxes to help them think about marking criteria. This is then followed by either a *Fluency focus* or a *Pronunciation focus* – important marking criteria that students are often less familiar with. *Boost your band score* boxes provide students with tips to help them apply these skills in the test. The section ends with an opportunity for realistic test practice.

For Part 1 and Part 3 Speaking tasks (in both the main units and the Test files), students have the choice of either using the audio transcripts to work in pairs, asking and answering the questions, or listening to the questions on the audio and replying individually. The latter option is a better simulation of the IELTS Speaking test, but the former is more interactive in the classroom environment. If students are working with the audio, there is a 15-second pause for them to answer each Part 1 question and a 25-second pause for them to answer each Part 3 question.

Writing

Most Writing sections focus on a particular genre of writing task. Students analyse tasks in depth and, as with the Speaking sections, assess sample answers with help from the *You're the examiner* feature. This is followed by a *Language focus* section to help students acquire language that is particularly useful to the task genre. The tips in the *Boost your band score* box suggest how students can use the language to gain higher band scores. Lessons end with an authentic writing task or a reference to a related task in the Writing task bank (see pages 90–97).

Test files

After every two units there's an opportunity to practise the skills that students have developed. The tasks in the Test files are presented in a format that closely reflects the IELTS test, and students are encouraged to attempt them under test conditions.

Writing task bank

In addition to the Task 1 questions from Units 1, 3, 5 and 7 plus the Test files, this provides four further Task 1 questions and eight further Task 2 questions for students to practise. Each of these tasks features a set of questions to help guide students through the stages of task planning.

Sample answers

For each *Over to you* writing task in the main units and the Writing tasks in the Test files, there's a sample answer at the back of the book. Students are encouraged to attempt the task by themselves before comparing the sample answer with their own. The samples are accompanied by questions to help students compare them with their own writing and there's also a tip that may help students increase their band scores.

CONTENTS

Reading

Time: 60 minutes

Format:

- 40 questions
- Three long passages (from books, journals or newspapers)
- Can include diagrams, graphs and pictures

1 Choose the correct options to complete the paragraph.

The three reading texts contain a total of around two and a half [1]*thousand / hundred* words. They are of [2]*general / specialist* interest, and any technical vocabulary is explained in a glossary. There are [3]*eleven / seven* common question types.

2 Approximately how many marks do you need to get out of 40 for each of these band scores?

Band score	Mark out of 40
5	________
6	________
7	________
8	________

3 Are these statements about matching tasks true or false?

1 The two lists of items you have to match are equal in length, for example, seven letters to seven numbers.
2 Sometimes the options can be used more than once. The instructions will tell you if this is possible.
3 When matching sentence endings, the answer to the first question will be found in the text before the answer to the second and so on.

4 Choose the correct options in these sentences about *True / False / Not Given* and *Yes / No / Not Given* tasks.

1 True / False / Not Given tasks test whether the candidate can identify *facts / opinions* in a text. Yes / No / Not Given tasks test the candidates' ability to identify *facts / opinions*.
2 Any prior knowledge that candidates have from outside the text *can / cannot* be relied on when answering the questions.

5 Are these sentences about gap-completion tasks true or false?

1 Spelling and grammar are not important.
2 If candidates write more than the number of words asked for, they'll lose the mark.
3 Contracted words are not tested.
4 Hyphenated words count as single words.

6 Complete the paragraph about multiple-choice questions with a number from 1 to 5.

In multiple-choice tasks, candidates select either the best answer from [1]________ alternatives, the best two from [2]________ alternatives, or the best [3]________ from six. Multiple-choice questions can test specific parts of the passage or the main ideas of the text. Questions that focus on one part of the text usually come in the same order as the information in the text.

7 Are these sentences about matching-headings tasks true or false?

1 You'll be given more headings than paragraphs.
2 You'll have to match headings to all paragraphs.
3 One of the headings may already be matched as an example.

8 Summary tasks may or may not include a word pool. Are these statements true for summaries *with* pools (P) or *without* pools (WP)?

1 Choose words from the reading passage so that the summary and passage have the same meaning.
2 Select words that have similar meanings to words in the reading passage.
3 The instructions tell you how many words to write.
4 There are often a lot of options in the list (but only a few will fit each gap).

9 Choose the correct options to complete the information about matching-information tasks.

In matching-information questions, sections of the text have [1]*numbers / letters*. You [2]*have to / may not have to* find information in every paragraph or section of the text. There [3]*may / won't* be more than one piece of information in a given paragraph or section.

10 At the end of the Reading test, do you have time to transfer your answers to an answer sheet?

Listening

Time: 30 minutes + 10 minutes to write answers on answer sheet

Format:

- 40 questions
- Four recordings (two monologues, two dialogues)

1 Complete the gaps with the correct number.

The questions and the corresponding information you need from the recordings come in the same order. The first [1]________ recordings focus on everyday social contexts. The final recordings focus on academic contexts. In Sections [2]________ and [3]________, candidates listen to a single speaker. The recordings are heard [4]________ time(s) only.

2 Approximately how many answers will you need to get correct out of 40 to attain each of these band scores?

Band score	Mark out of 40
5	________
6	________
7	________
8	________

3 In which way will Section 2 differ from Section 1 (A, B, C or D)?

A You will hear more speakers.
B The task will be more challenging.
C The topic will be more academic.
D You will have more questions to answer.

4 Answer these questions about Section 3 of the Listening test.

1 Are you likely to hear a conversation about holidays?
2 Where will the recording probably be set?
3 In what context might you hear a third speaker?

5 Which of these topics might the speaker discuss in Section 4?

A The local area
B Binomial theorem
C A famous scientific discovery

6 Which type of multiple-choice question does *not* appear in the Listening test?

A Choose one answer from four possible answers.
B Choose three options from a longer list.
C Choose one answer from three possible answers.
D Choose a category (A, B or C) for each question.

7 Match the question types (1–4) with the type of information they test (a–d).

1 a form	**a** Used to summarise information which relates to clear categories, eg place/time/price.
2 a set of notes	**b** Used to summarise a process which has clear stages.
3 a table	**c** Often used to record factual details such as names.
4 a flow chart	**d** Used to summarise any type of information.

8 Are these sentences about gap-completion tasks true or false?

1 You don't have to change the words you hear in any way.
2 You can lose points for incorrect spelling.
3 Grammar is not important.

9 Complete the information about marking using the words from the box.

answer	band	hour	mark	minutes	mistakes

In total, you listen for half an hour and then have ten [1]________ to transfer your answers to your [2]________ sheet. It's important to do this carefully because any [3]________ will be penalised. All questions carry one [4]________. A different table converting your score to an IELTS [5]________ score is produced for each test.

10 At the end of the Listening test, do you have time to transfer your answers to an answer sheet?

Speaking

Time: 11 to 14 minutes

Format: A face-to-face interview comprising three parts:

- short questions
- speaking at length on a familiar topic ('long turn')
- a structured conversation

1 Choose the correct options to complete the paragraph.

Part 1 of the Speaking test is about [1]*you / global issues*. It deals with [2]*general / academic* topics. In Part 2, you're given a task card which asks you to [3]*talk about / choose* a particular topic. It includes points to cover in your talk. You speak for [4]*one minute / between one and two minutes*. In Part 3, the examiner asks you about [5]*a new topic / the topic from Part 2*.

2 During the Speaking test, you're graded in four areas. In which area(s) (1–4) are the following tested?

high-level words   word stress   linking words
speech rate   complex sentences

1 Fluency and coherence
2 Lexical resource
3 Grammatical range and accuracy
4 Pronunciation

3 Are these statements about Part 2 of the Speaking test true or false?

1 You have 60 seconds to prepare and speak.
2 You should stop when you think you've said enough.
3 You can write notes to help you speak.
4 You should ask the examiner if you don't understand the task.

4 Look at these descriptions of what a candidate can be expected to do. What band score do you think all three apply to?

1 Can generally be understood throughout, though mispronunciation of individual words or sounds reduces clarity at times.
2 May make frequent mistakes with complex structures, though these rarely cause comprehension problems.
3 Has a wide enough vocabulary to discuss topics at length and make meaning clear in spite of inappropriacies.

5 Which of these *must* you do if you want to get a Band 7 in the Speaking test?

1 Speak without obvious effort.
2 Use sentences that are generally free of errors.
3 Be easy to understand at all times.

6 Are these statements about the Speaking test true or false?

1 You should speak for as long as you can in Parts 1 and 3.
2 You should try to speak in a formal academic style.
3 You can ask the examiner how you did after the test.

7 Do these pieces of advice apply to Parts 1, 2 or 3 of the Speaking test?

1 Keep going – don't stop!
2 Don't talk about yourself!
3 Answer the question, then add one more piece of information.

8 Are these statements about Part 2 true or false?

1 You can write on the task card.
2 After two minutes, the examiner will stop you speaking.
3 After you finish, you're asked a further question on the topic.

9 In which sections of the Speaking test can you ask the examiner to ...

1 clarify the meaning of a word?
2 explain the task again?
3 ask the question in completely different words?

10 Which of these problems is it possible to have and still get a Band 6?

A Mispronounce words frequently.
B Make frequent grammar mistakes.
C Give rather short answers to questions.

Writing

Time: 60 minutes

Format:

- Task 1 (150 words): summarise a table, graph, chart or diagram
- Task 2 (250 words): a short essay

1 Match these features with the two tasks in the Writing test.

20 minutes 40 minutes paragraphs not needed
an introduction needed including data
including examples opinions facts

Task 1	Task 2

2 Which of these statements is *not* true about the Writing test?

A Part 1 is worth 66% of the Writing mark.
B Candidates should only describe the information. They don't need to use their knowledge to explain it.
C Candidates should only describe the important features.

3 In addition to grammar and vocabulary, examiners give a score for the following criteria. Match each criterion (1–4) with a definition (a–d).

1 Coherence
2 Cohesion
3 Task response (Task 2 only)
4 Task achievement (Task 1 only)

a How closely you respond to the question
b How well you connect ideas
c How logically you order your ideas
d How well you represent data

4 Look at these three types of chart. Which ones are usually used to a) compare data, b) show trends?

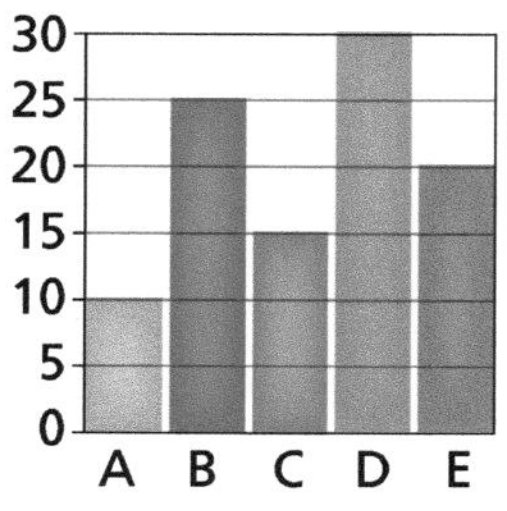

bar chart

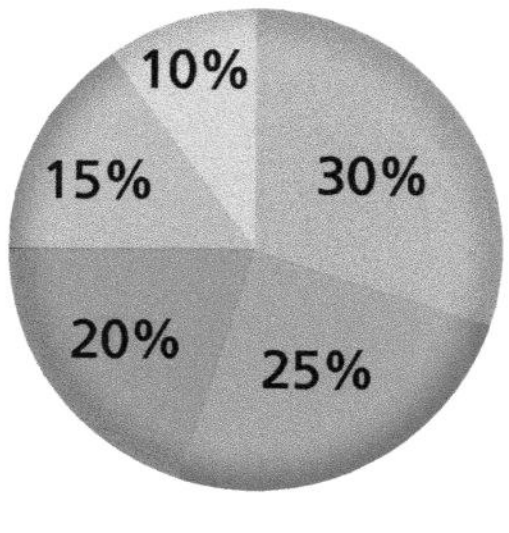

pie chart

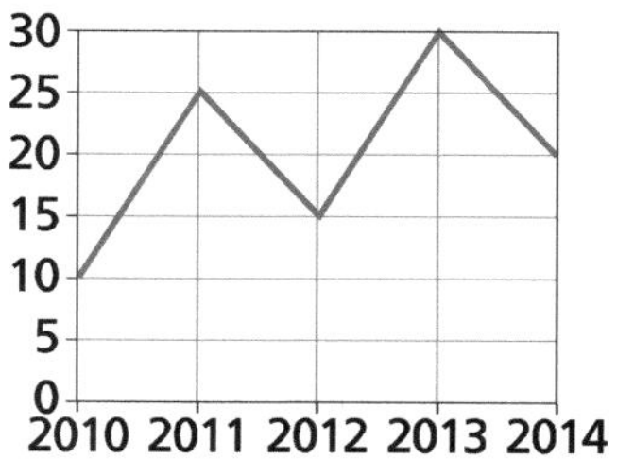

line graph

5 Answer these questions about Task 2.

1 Can you write more than 250 words?
2 Is it important to write paragraphs?
3 What should you include to support your opinion?

6 Which of these aspects of language is useful for describing processes?

A Past tenses
B Sequence markers: *first, second*, etc
C Markers of addition: *furthermore, moreover*, etc
D Conclusions

7 Are these statements about essay writing true or false?

1 You should write down as much as you can about the question topic.
2 You should write in a neutral or academic style.
3 You will lose marks if you copy words from the task prompt.

8 When describing maps and diagrams, which *one* of these statements is true?

A Candidates must describe all the features they see.
B It's not necessary to write an overview statement (eg *In general, we can see* ...).
C You should try to *explain* the features you see.
D When describing a diagram, you may not need to refer to numbers.

9 Which of these describes a Band 6 candidate, and which describes a Band 7 candidate?

A Presents a clear central topic in each paragraph.
B Attempts to use less common vocabulary.
C Addresses some parts of the task more fully than others.
D Only makes occasional errors in spelling.
E Has good control of punctuation.

UNIT 1 Education

TOPIC FOCUS

1 Look at the images. Complete the name of the subject for each one.

1 l________

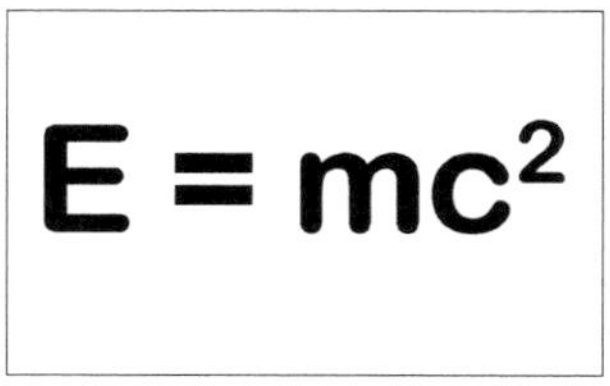

2 ph_____

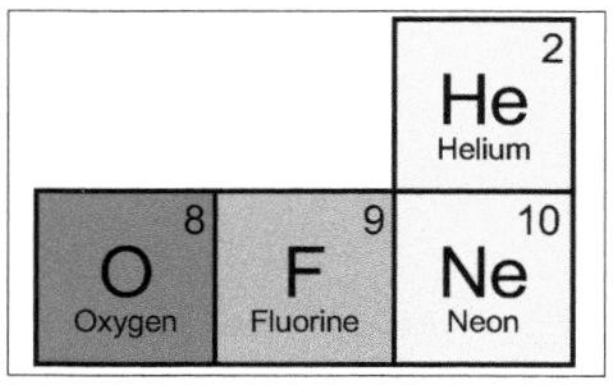

3 ch_______

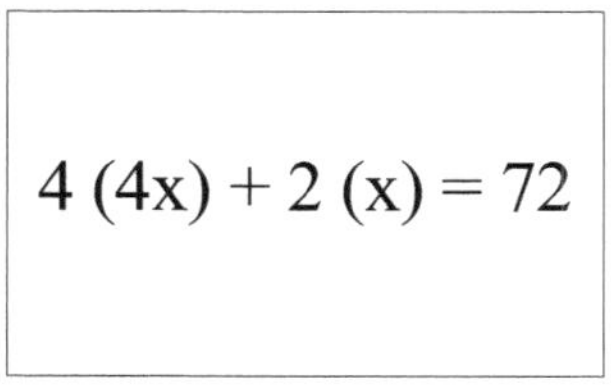

4 m____

5 li________

6 ec_______

7 bu______

8 s_____ sc_____

2 Which of the subjects in Exercise 1 are:

a most interesting for you?
b most useful for a career?
c most important to study?

➤ **IELTS quiz** page 6, questions 1 and 3

READING

LESSON AIMS

- Academic reading skills
- Matching features
- Matching sentence endings

1 What subject have you chosen to study, and why? Tell a partner and discuss other reasons for choosing a subject.

Skills focus

2 Tell a partner how you might read differently in each of these situations.

a Looking for a specific programme in a TV guide
b Reading a test question
c Deciding whether to read a news article in detail or not

3 Different reading tasks require different strategies. Match the strategies (1–3) with the reading tasks (a–c).

1 Scanning	a Read for gist and to understand the main ideas.
2 Skimming	b Look for specific information.
3 Reading intensively	c Understand precise meaning.

4 Match these IELTS question types (a–c) with the most appropriate strategies in Exercise 3 (1–3).

a Matching a list of headings to paragraphs in a text (eg Questions 7–14, page 52)
b Multiple choice (eg page 40)
c Matching people to their opinion (eg Questions 1–7, page 12)

What should you study?

In America, high-school students study compulsory subjects such as science, mathematics, English and physical education, but from the second year they can also study other subjects that they want to focus on. However, students often find themselves wondering whether they've chosen the right subjects, or if the class they're in is relevant. The impact on people's lives can be significant. In America, one in four students who start high school fail to graduate.

One explanation may be poor course design. Take maths, for example. According to Andrew Hacker, a professor of political science, the type of maths taught in high school – algebra, geometry and calculus – is not only too challenging but arguably of little use in real life. John P. Smith III, an educational psychologist at Michigan State University, has found that mathematical reasoning in the workplace is significantly different from that taught in schools. He believes we need to review how some subjects are taught.

For others, the debate is not limited to individual subjects. Many believe that we need to change the entire curriculum. Cognitive scientist Roger C. Shank argues that we need to change a number of academic disciplines. He believes chemistry is a subject most people study but forget as soon as they leave school. Other subjects, such as physics, are relevant to life, but we needn't study them as academic subjects. Inventions such as planes or cars do not come from learning theories; people simply try ideas until they work. The theory comes afterwards to explain it.

But these arguments assume that relevance is important. For some academics, the key to a good education is for students to learn to transfer skills to other areas. Professor Daniel Willingham contends that economic growth does not come from creativity and inventors. He points to research by economists which shows that cognitive skills — especially maths and science — are good predictors of individual income, of a country's economic growth, and of the distribution of income. He believes well-educated workers are more likely to see the potential for using an innovation in a new context and generating money from this.

The debate about the right things to study is not limited to high school. When we go to university, we have more choice than ever, but many end up making the wrong decisions. Among the most popular degree programmes are business courses, perhaps because they seem most relevant to students' ambitions, but choosing the course that seems most relevant isn't always a guarantee of success. In their book *Academically Adrift*, Richard Arum and Josipa Roksa argue that nearly half of all students do not improve their writing and analytical skills in the first two years. Interestingly, students on business degrees are often the worst, whereas students studying subjects in science, maths and social science make good progress in these skills. One reason for this may be that vocational courses are sometimes chosen for career reasons, rather than because students like them. When you study something you do not like, you are less likely to be successful, professionally and financially.

What's more, vocational degrees may not be the only courses that develop the right skills for the workplace. An employer survey by the National Association of Colleges and Employers (NACE) shows companies want good communication skills, analytical skills and teamwork skills, which you can acquire in a liberal arts degree programme. In fact, 89% of the employers surveyed said they would be happy to accept students with an arts background. It seems you do not necessarily need a degree in business to work in business.

Neither do vocational courses necessarily lead to better pay, as many assume. According to PayScale, which rates subjects according to the earnings potential they offer, business comes in 56th place. Students who studied degrees such as philosophy, history and American studies make significantly more money than business graduates. It does not help that one out of every five graduates studied business, so there is even more competition between students of that field in an already competitive world.

What you study clearly affects your future, but other factors can have an equal or even more significant impact. Researcher Esther Cho found that students who took modules with lots of reading gained more from their courses than others. By contrast, those joining social societies make significant losses in knowledge. (Interestingly, students who engage in off-campus activities and volunteer opportunities make no notable gains or losses in learning.) Lastly, students who study alone tend to make better progress than those who study in groups. The key question is perhaps not what should students study, but how should they study.

5 Do the tasks in the *Strategy focus* box. Then answer Questions 1–7 based on the reading passage.

Strategy focus *Matching features*

1 Look at the task below. Are you going to scan for the names or for the opinions?
2 Do you need all the options A–H?
3 Before you scan, underline the key words in the statements 1–7.

Questions 1–7

Target time: 10 minutes
Target score: ____ / 7

Look at the following statements and the list of people/organisations, ***A–H****, below.*
Match each statement with the correct name.

1 Skills used while studying are key to academic progress.
2 Many business students make poor progress.
3 It isn't necessary to study some school subjects.
4 Business students don't make the most money.
5 Companies welcome non-business graduates.
6 Mental skills affect income significantly.
7 Some of what is taught has little connection with working lives.

A Roger C. Shank
B Esther Cho
C NACE
D Daniel Willingham
E PayScale
F John P. Smith III
G Richard Arum and Josipa Roksa
H Andrew Hacker

6 Answer Questions 8–14.

Questions 8–14

Target time: 10 minutes
Target score: ____ / 7

Complete each sentence with the correct ending, ***A–I****.*

8 Chemistry
9 Physics
10 Maths
11 Social science
12 Arts
13 Social societies
14 Volunteering

A contains some difficult topics.
B isn't easy to remember in the long term.
C can lead to a decline in academic performance.
D is based on real discoveries.
E degrees are wanted by most companies.
F is a relatively easy subject.
G will have no effect on academic study.
H often leads to major invention.
I students make better progress than others.

Vocabulary extra

Find:

1 the noun for *relevant*
2 two synonyms for *salary*
3 a word meaning 'course' that's used after *degree*
4 the noun for someone who has finished university
5 a noun meaning the grounds/buildings of a university.

Explore further

7 Ask and answer these questions with a partner.

1 The reading passage suggests that the main reason to go to university is to have a successful career. What do *you* think the main reason is?

- to gain more knowledge
- to have a good social life
- to contribute to knowledge
- to earn more for your family
- to make useful contacts
- other ____________

2 According to the reading passage, enthusiastic learners have more successful lives. What could your school have done to help you enjoy learning more?

➤ IELTS quiz
page 7, question 1

LISTENING

LESSON AIMS

- Section 1: Conversation between two speakers
- Form completion

1 **Imagine that you're starting university soon. Look at the photos and discuss the questions with a partner.**

1 Which of these places would you prefer to stay in, and why?
2 What would you like to know about your accommodation before moving in?

Prepare to listen

2 **Think of two ideas for each of the following:**

- a useful facility in a student residence (eg catering)
- a way of travelling in town
- a way to contact someone
- a normal price for a room
- a popular university subject
- a month when courses usually start

3 **Match each of the items in Exercise 2 with one of the gaps in Questions 1–10 (see below and page 14). What type of information are you listening for in the other four gaps, eg a name?**

4 1.2 **Listen and write the letters or numbers you hear.**

1 ______ 2 ______ 3 ______ 4 ______ 5 ______

5 1.3 **Listen to the first part of a conversation with a student organising his accommodation and answer Questions 1–3.**

Questions 1–3

Target score: ____ **/ 3**

Complete the form below.
*Write **NO MORE THAN TWO WORDS AND/OR A NUMBER** for each answer.*

The Accommodation Department: student booking

Course date:	*12th* **1** ....
Student:	**2** .... *Osman*
Nationality:	*Sudanese*
Status:	*Offer accepted*
Course:	**3** ....

6 🎧 **1.4 Listen to the rest of the conversation and answer Questions 4–10.**

Questions 4–10

Target score: ____ **/ 7**

Complete the information below.
Write ***NO MORE THAN TWO WORDS AND/OR A NUMBER*** *for each answer.*

Option 1	**Option 2**
Student village	Greenfield Lane (student house)
Location: **4** .... campus	£110 per week
Price of rooms: **5** £ .... per week	Sharing with **7** .... students
Includes: catering, laundrette,	Access to **8** .... from rooms.
6	Recommended transport: **9** ....

Details will be sent by **10** ....

Explore further **7 Do you think Mr Osman made the correct choice? Discuss with a partner.**

8 What are the positives and negatives of living with other people? Complete the table with your ideas. Compare your lists with a partner's.

Positives	Negatives
A good social life	Noisy housemates

➤ **IELTS quiz**
page 8, questions 1 and 2

SPEAKING

LESSON AIMS

- Extending Part 1 responses
- Using sentence stress
- Talking about clubs and societies

1 Imagine that you're going to live and study in another country. Rank these aspects from 1 (most challenging) to 5 (easiest to deal with). Then compare your ranking with a partner's.

money ☐ language ☐ accommodation ☐ culture ☐ making friends ☐

2 Which problems might be helped by joining a club or society?

Vocabulary focus **3 Match the clubs and societies (1–9) with the images (a–i).**

1 archery 2 ballroom dancing 3 chess 4 conservation 5 cooking
6 debating 7 mountaineering 8 role-playing games 9 rowing

a

b

c

d

e

f

g

h

i

4 Which of the clubs/societies in Exercise 3 would you be interested in joining? Which other ones would you prefer to join? Discuss with a partner.

Prepare to speak

5 Which of these questions require you to talk about a) the past, b) the present, c) the future?

1 What do you enjoy doing in your free time?
2 What sporting activities did you enjoy at your secondary school?
3 After class, do you prefer to spend time alone or with others?
4 Is there an interest or hobby you would like to try? Why?

6 1.5–1.6 Listen to two candidates answering the questions in Exercise 5 and complete these sentences.

1 I ______________________ outdoor activities.
2 I ______________________ caving.
3 I ______________________ athletics.
4 I ______________________ painting.

7 1.5–1.6 Listen again and answer the *You're the examiner* questions.

> **You're the examiner**
> Which candidate successfully …
> **1** extends their answers?
> **2** uses stress to emphasise words?
> **3** uses accurate grammar? (Can you find the other candidate's mistakes?)
> **4** uses some high-level words and phrases? (Which are they?)

8 Work with a partner. Extend Candidate 1's responses with two or three more sentences. Then listen to another pair and compare your ideas.

Pronunciation focus

9 1.7 Look at these questions and responses. Underline the word(s) that would be stressed the most in each response. Then listen and check.

1 A What interests or hobbies do you have?
B I enjoy films most of all.
2 A Where do you do these?
B I see films at my local cinema.
3 A When do you do these activities?
B I go to the cinema every Friday if I can.

10 Look at the stressed word in each of these responses. Write the question the person was asked.

1 I often watch movies online in the ***evening***.
2 I ***often*** watch movies online in the evening.
3 I often watch movies ***online*** in the evening.

11 Ask and answer the questions in Exercise 9 with a partner.

> **Boost your band score** *Sentence stress*
> Sentence stress is important for comprehensible speech. If the stress pattern is incorrect, the listener may not understand easily. You can practise this by stressing different words in a sentence and thinking about how it changes the meaning.

Over to you

12 Work with a partner.

Student A: Ask your partner the questions from Exercise 5.
Student B: Ask your partner these questions.

1 What's your favourite hobby or interest?
2 Did you do art or music in your primary school?
3 What team activity would you like to try?
4 Do you spend most of your free time outdoors or indoors? Why?

13 Feed back to your partner. Use the *You're the examiner* questions to help you think about their speaking skills.

WRITING

LESSON AIMS

- Task 1: Describing data trends
- Word formation in trend vocabulary

1 Draw a line graph and a pie chart to show the information in Tables A and B. Does the data surprise you? Which shows a trend, the line graph or the pie chart?

A

Total foreign students studying in OECD* countries	
1975	0.8m
2011	4.3m

B

% of all foreign students studying in OECD countries	77
% of all foreign students studying in non-OECD countries	23

**Organisation for Economic Cooperation and Development (a club of wealthy countries)*

2 Are you planning to work or study abroad? Why? / Why not?

Prepare to write

3 Check the meaning of the words in bold in these questions. Then look at the line graph below and answer the questions.

1 Does the data show a **rising** or **falling trend** in student numbers overall?
2 When did the number of foreign students in the country **peak**?
3 Which category saw the **steadiest** rise in student numbers?
4 Which category showed the most **fluctuation**?
5 Did the percentage of students who are from other countries rise or **drop** in 2011?

The number of foreign and domestic* students in a European country

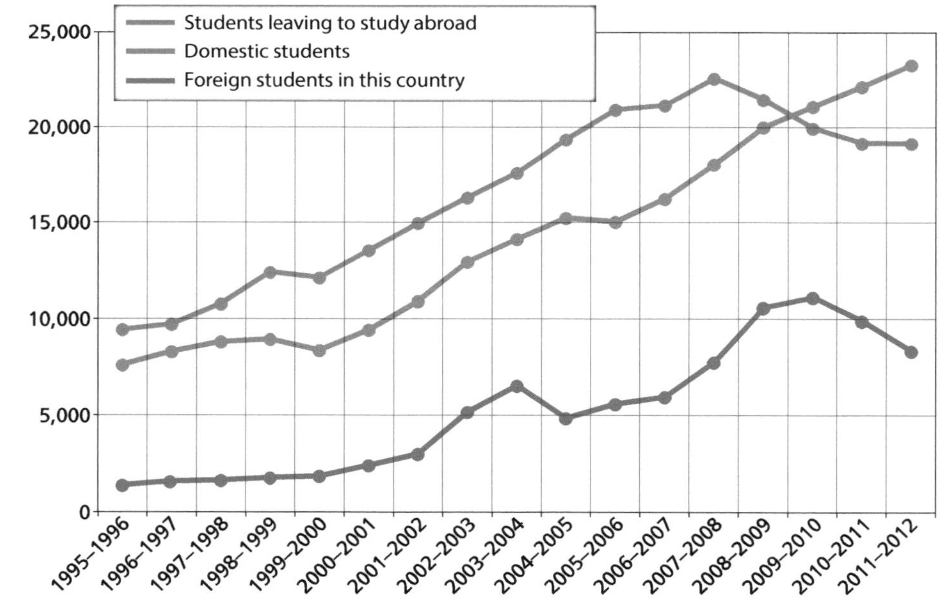

** Students studying in their own country*

4 Rewrite the questions and your answers from Exercise 3 as five statements.
Example: 1 Overall, the data shows a rising trend in student numbers.

5 Read this task relating to the graph on page 16 and the extracts from two sample answers below. Then answer the *You're the examiner* questions.

Summarise the information by selecting and reporting the main features, and make comparisons where relevant.

Candidate 1

The line graph reveals trends in student numbers for a European country from 1995 to 2012, including both students who have entered and those who have left. Growth in numbers was significant in all sectors, but was particularly notable for foreign students, given their low starting point. Their numbers grew five-fold over the period shown, despite a small decline at the end ...

Candidate 2

The line graph shows international and domestic students in a European country. The x-axis shows dates from 1995 to 2012; the y-axis shows student numbers. The green line is for international students. Their numbers increased dramatically from 1995 to 2009, from just over 1,000 to 8,000, despite considerable fluctuations. These were probably caused by global economic problems ...

You're the examiner

Which candidate has successfully ...

1 made comparisons?
2 selected important features?
3 included data?
4 done what the task requires (and no more)?

Language focus

6 Complete this continuation of Candidate 1's answer using the correct form of the words in brackets.

The number of [1]__________ (*student*) who [2]__________ (*leave*) the country for study purposes also [3]__________ (*grow*), doubling from a starting point of around 10,000. However, there was a [4]__________ (*note*) fall in numbers in both students entering and leaving the country towards the end of the period. They [5]__________ (*peak*) in 2007–2009 and [6]__________ (*fall*) back by around 2,000. The [7]__________ (*grow*) in 'home' students (those who didn't go abroad) was in fact much [8]__________ (*consist*). It continued [9]__________ (*grow/ steady*) from a starting point of 6,500 throughout the period, [10]__________ (*reach*) 24,000 by 2012. By the end of the period, it [11]__________ (*overtake*) the number of students leaving. Despite the changes, it is important to note that a far greater number of students [12]__________ (*go*) abroad to study than entered the country.

Boost your band score ***Information selection***

Don't try to describe every piece of information. Select important information to compare, and group the information logically.

Over to you

7 Turn to page 90 and complete Task 1.

8 Exchange your work with a partner. Use the *You're the examiner* and *Boost your band score* boxes to evaluate their writing. Underline any comparisons and circle the key information.

9 Turn to page 98 and compare your answer with sample answer 1.

UNIT 2 Society

TOPIC FOCUS

1 Look at some statistics and predictions about changes in modern society. Circle the one you find most worrying.

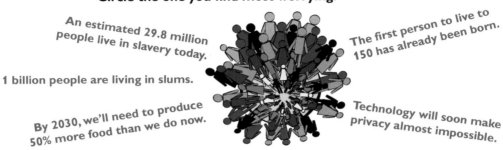

An estimated 29.8 million people live in slavery today.

1 billion people are living in slums.

By 2030, we'll need to produce 50% more food than we do now.

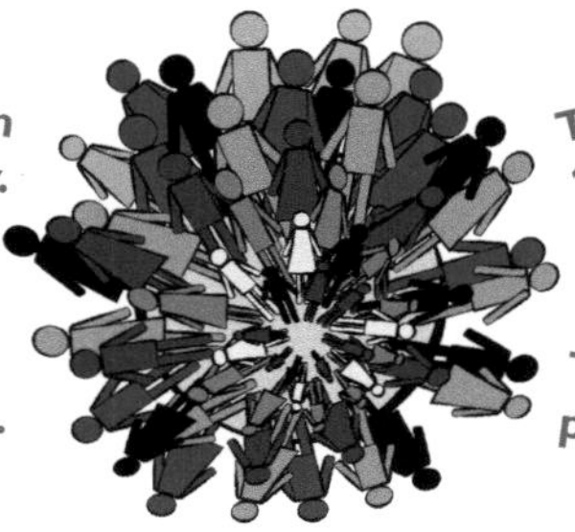

The first person to live to 150 has already been born.

Technology will soon make privacy almost impossible.

2 Compare with a partner and explain your choices.

➤ **IELTS quiz**
page 6, question 4

READING

LESSON AIMS

- Review: Matching features
- Identifying the writer's views/claims (Yes / No / Not Given)

1 Discuss these questions.

1 How many internet groups do you participate in regularly? Think about:
- social media groups
- social games
- virtual worlds
- discussion forums
- chats (eg #blogchat).

2 Do you spend more time with people on the internet or in person? Why?

3 Look at the title of the reading passage on page 19. What is the author worried about?

Skills focus **2 What can you remember about the 'matching features' questions in Unit 1? Discuss your task strategy with a partner, then attempt Questions 1–5 based on the reading passage.**

Questions 1–5

Target time: 8 minutes
Target score: ____ / 5

*Look at the following researchers and the list of opinions, **A–F**, below.*
Match each researcher with the opinion they express in the passage.

1 Putnam **2** Benkler **3** Katz et al. **4** Havas **5** Peck

List of Opinions

A Local communities take time to develop.
B Internet communities are less concerned about local issues.
C Offline communities can benefit from the internet.
D Internet users speak to each other more than other groups.
E Online groups can change politics and business practices.
F Users of technology participate less in local events.

The death of community?

The number of people who would be happy to visit their neighbours is decreasing, research studies have shown. For many, this shows that our sense of community is dying, and one of the key culprits is said to be the internet. Modern citizens spend increasing amounts of time logged on, interacting with screens, isolated from those around them. But of course the internet has created opportunities for new communities of web users to come together. Are these new communities equally strong, or are we losing connections that are fundamental to a healthy society?

We can define a 'community' as a collection of people who have developed a shared identity due to something they have in common. They may share an area of land, a religious belief, or membership of an institution. They normally have a common interest or purpose, too. A community can be strong or weak, depending on how much common ground and mutual support its members establish. Those with long shared histories, who have survived difficult circumstances together, form the closest bonds.

To this extent, internet communities may not be the strongest. Thanks to tools that allow us to follow other users, share information or join mailing lists, they are easy to enter and leave. Communities of users can be set up instantly around a new 'meme' or hashtag that may lose appeal as quickly as it gains it. Online communities are also vulnerable to division and break-up, particularly due to the online disinhibition effect, whereby community members feel they can act aggressively without consequence. The internet therefore hosts loose, limited-purpose and volatile communities.

It is also true that online groups can grow at the expense of traditional communities. For example, internet users are more likely to admit to weak ties with their neighbours than non-users. As well as isolating us from our immediate area, the internet permits us to avoid communities we choose not to be a part of. While in the street we remain aware of others around us, online we can be entirely selective about the people we interact with. Putnam argues that this 'technological individualising' has led to a decline in civic participation, for example in bowling leagues or local elections.

Yet many claim damage to offline communities is exaggerated. Benkler argues that pre-existing relations with friends and family can even grow online. Katz, Rice and Aspden (2001), for example, found that internet users interact through other media (especially telephone) too, even more than non-users do. As commuting, travel and migration force us apart, the internet has arguably allowed offline groupings to stay closer together. Online interactions may therefore support some offline groupings, and are certainly a more sociable alternative to television. But an offline community that has no online presence, or which fails to engage its members online, may become weaker.

What's more, online communities have something to offer that offline groupings can only dream of, namely scale. In normal circumstances we would not talk of a city as a community, yet online communities involve millions. This has lent them a degree of what we call 'social capital' or power. Through group action, online communities can influence events like political protests. They can even affect corporate policies by boycotting or endorsing products, behaviour that is often termed *co-creation*. And people can join multiple online communities anonymously, without the fear of embarrassment and without having to pay membership fees or travel expenses. Therefore, we are seeing powerful groupings forming rapidly around important global issues.

Academics also point out that although purely online communities may not always bond as effectively, they have what is known as 'bridging' social capital. In other words, they are able to develop across the racial, geographical and even temporal divides that normally separate traditional communities from each other. According to a report from Havas, internet users are therefore more likely to see themselves as 'global citizens' and to identify with others of a similar socio-economic background rather than race or nationality.

Internet communities therefore operate on two quite distinct levels. On the one hand, they can help to create democratic and powerful communities which can effect change. They can also promote bonding of pre-existing social groupings. But these strengths are also weaknesses. Because internet users select the communities they wish to join, members often meet groups with very similar pre-existing ideas. Members of local communities, by comparison, bond with people of different ages, cultural backgrounds, political views. Peck has argued that community development amongst such diverse groupings is like a kind of peace process. After initial politeness passes, members may show quite different behaviour and slowly learn to reconcile themselves to differences.

It is this kind of challenging community development that helps us question ourselves, work at relationships and overcome differences: skills which are essential to the formation of stable communities. It may be true that the internet permits us to learn and to adjust our viewpoints. However, it hardly forces us to negotiate and compromise with those who are different from us. Consequently, although our sense of community is not disappearing, offline communities are perhaps becoming more susceptible to intolerance and division.

3 **Do the tasks in the *Strategy focus* box. Then answer Questions 6–13 below.**

Strategy focus ***Yes / No / Not Given***

A Read the opinions below (1–3). Find words in the last paragraph of the reading passage that are similar to the words in bold. Underline the sentences they appear in.

1 The internet allows its users to **change** their **opinions**.
2 **Negotiation** has become easier because of the internet.
3 Online communities are more easily **divided** nowadays.

B Carefully read the sentences you underlined. For each of the opinions above (1–3), say whether:

- the author agrees (*Yes*)
- the author disagrees (*No*)
- there isn't enough information to say whether the author agrees or disagrees (*Not Given*).

Questions 6–13

Target time: 12 minutes
Target score: ____ / 8

Do the following statements reflect the claims of the writer in the reading passage?

Write

YES	*if the statement reflects the claims of the writer*
NO	*if the statement contradicts the claims of the writer*
NOT GIVEN	*if it is impossible to say what the writer thinks about this*

6 Communities with difficult pasts are often the strongest.
7 Online communities are generally quite stable.
8 Internet users are generally less confident at chatting with neighbours.
9 Many people are choosing to use the internet instead of watching TV.
10 People feel more confident within internet communities.
11 Low costs attract people to online communities.
12 Internet groups are often based on race or particular geographical areas.
13 Internet communities have more extreme views than local communities.

Vocabulary extra

1 Complete the phrases with the correct preposition.
1 to interact _______ sb (para. 4)
2 to be isolated _______ sb (para. 1)
3 to have membership _______ sth (para. 2)
4 to identify/bond _______ sb (paras 7+8)
5 to be vulnerable/susceptible _______ sth (paras 3+9)

2 Write a sentence with each phrase.

Explore further

4 **Discuss these questions with a partner.**

1 In your opinion, has the ability to socialise online improved our social lives?
2 Should children be allowed to use social media? If so, from what age?

5 **Work with a partner. Which of these statements do you agree with?**

1 Groups become stronger after an argument.

2 It's never good to lose social inhibitions.

3 Banning social networking would make us better citizens of our towns and cities.

4 The best social unit is the village.

LISTENING

LESSON AIMS

- Section 2: Monologue
- Labelling a map
- Short-answer questions

1 Work with a partner. Tell them the things you like and don't like about the area you live in.

2 Imagine you could create your perfect neighbourhood. Rate the list below in order of importance (1 = most important, 8 = least important). Then compare your ratings with a partner's and give reasons for your choices.

- ❑ good schools
- ❑ outdoor leisure facilities (eg tennis courts)
- ❑ nightlife and entertainment
- ❑ shopping outlets and restaurants
- ❑ wide footpaths and cycle ways
- ❑ access to medical care
- ❑ access to public transport
- ❑ green spaces

Prepare to listen

3 Look at the tasks in Exercises 4 and 5 and answer these questions.

1 Read Questions 1–5. What do you need to write, words or letters?
2 Look at locations A–J. Describe their location to a partner (eg *A is behind the cinema*).
3 Read Questions 6–10. Which of these options is true?
   A You must write exactly three words.
   B You can write one, two or three words.
   C More than three words is fine.

4 1.8 Listen to the first part of a presentation and answer Questions 1–5.

Questions 1–5

Target score: ____ / 5

Label the plan below.
*Write the correct letter, **A–J**, next to questions **1–5**.*

1 public gardens ....
2 street market ....
3 bus station ....
4 shopping centre ....
5 medical practice ....

Noughton: a 21st-century development

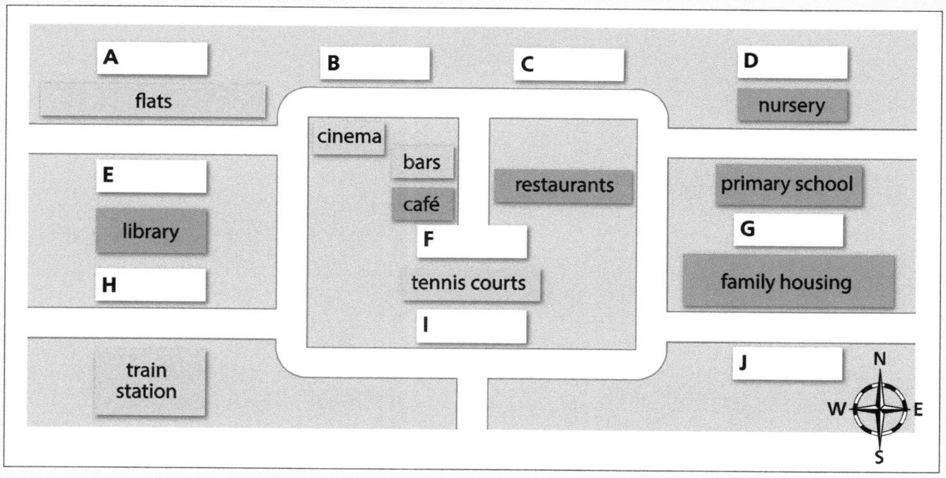

5 **1.9 Listen to the next part of the presentation and answer Questions 6–10.**

Questions 6–10

Target score: ____ / 5

Answer the questions below.
*Write **NO MORE THAN THREE WORDS AND/OR A NUMBER** for each answer.*

6 How many children can attend the school? ....
7 What else is provided for children in Noughton? ....
8 In which building will rain water be used? ....
9 What can people in Noughton produce? ....
10 What can residents use for free? ....

Explore further

6 **Look at audio transcript 1.9 on pages 104–105. What phrases did the speaker use to express location?**

7 **Would you like to live in Noughton? What would you change about it?**

IELTS quiz
page 8, question 3

SPEAKING

LESSON AIMS

- Part 2: Long turn
- Character adjectives

Prepare to speak

1 **Which of these people do you respect a) the most, b) the least? Why?**

- soldiers
- aid workers
- investigative journalists
- billionnaires
- MPs (members of parliament)
- parents

2 **Look at the Speaking Part 2 task below. Write the name of the person you would choose to speak about and tell a partner why.**

Describe a person you know well that you admire.
You should say:
what their relationship is to you
how they have spent their life
what they are like
and explain why you admire them.

3 **1.10–1.11 Listen to two candidates attempting the task. Who does each candidate choose to talk about?**

4 **1.10–1.11 Listen again and answer the *You're the examiner* questions.**

You're the examiner

Which candidate ...
1 relies on the task sheet too much?
2 uses the greater range of vocabulary?
3 is more likely to be able to speak for two minutes? Why?

Vocabulary focus

5 **Find the meanings of these adjectives, then use three of them to describe different people you know to a partner.**

courageous dedicated (to sb/sth) determined devoted (to sth/sb) energetic enterprising inspiring passionate (about sth) resourceful selfless

6 Replace the words in bold in the text below with phrases using the adjectives from Exercise 5.

I've always admired my grandmother, partly because she **has so little concern for herself**. When I was younger, she **spent all her time with** me and **cared for me constantly**. She **always found a clever way to help me** when I couldn't do a school project. However, as I've grown older, I realise that there are many other reasons I admire her. I think to survive her childhood, she must have been very **keen to succeed**, and her efforts to sell things prove she was quite **willing to try new ideas**. Also, when my grandfather went off to fight in the war, she **didn't let her worry affect her behaviour**. Now that I'm an adult, she **believes strongly in** helping people who are less fortunate. She **puts in a lot of physical effort** for someone who is 70. It **makes me think I can be like her too**.

Fluency focus

7 Look at the way three candidates have used their preparation time to help them speak fluently. Which was the best use of the time?

A

Describe a person you know well that you admire.
You should say:
what their relationship is to you – mother
how they have spent their life – in a poor family, then helping us
what they are like – selfless, determined
and explain why you admire them. – inspiring and energetic

B

Relationship
Grandmother
more like Mum?
Life
circumstances
business activities
Character
selfless
devoted, etc.
Why her?
inspiring
rare nowadays

C

She was just always there for me.
She was born into a poor family.
As I've grown older, many other reasons I admire her.

Boost your band score *Fluency*

You'll get a better mark for fluency if you can speak at length without needing to repeat yourself, hesitate or depend on the task sheet. While you're speaking, you should:

- avoid looking at the task sheet
- use short notes and maintain eye contact with the examiner
- aim to spend 30 seconds on each prompt, adding plenty of extra information.

Over to you

8 Prepare this task, then speak to a partner on the topic for two minutes.

Describe a person who is influential in your country.
You should say:
what they do
how they became well known
how they influence people
and explain why they have become so influential.

9 Feed back to your partner. Use the *You're the examiner* box to help you.

➤ IELTS quiz
page 9, question 3

WRITING

LESSON AIMS

- Task 2: Analysing essay questions
- Introducing essays
- Rephrasing the essay question

Prepare to write

1 Match the photos (a–c) with the essay questions (1–3).

a

b

c

1 ***People are living longer and there are more older people to look after. Some people believe the elderly should be cared for by family members, while others say governments should provide homes for old people. Discuss both views and give your opinion.***

2 ***In some countries, large numbers of people are moving from rural to urban areas. What problems can this cause? How can governments solve the problems?***

3 ***Old ways of life are slowly being lost. Some people believe we need to preserve traditional skills and customs. To what extent do you agree?***

2 Read the essay questions again. Which one requires you to:

a give your opinion and the reasons for it?
b present two sides of a debate?
c explain something with your own ideas?

3 Match these instruction words to the question types (a–c) in Exercise 2.

1 What problems are associated with ...?
2 Do you agree or disagree?
3 What are the advantages and disadvantages of ...?
4 Present a written argument or case for ...

4 **Look at the essay question below. Which part of the question (1–3):**

a presents the issue you must discuss?
b introduces the topic?
c tells us the type of essay you must write?

[1]Modern societies suffer from a range of social problems, from crime to loneliness. [2]The best way to improve society is to create more jobs. [3]Do you agree or disagree?

5 **Read two introductions to the task in Exercise 4. Then answer the *You're the examiner* questions.**

Candidate 1

Modern societies suffer from a range of social problems, from crime to loneliness. Would creating jobs solve these problems? If the government created jobs, people would feel better and have more money, so they wouldn't commit crime. They would also be able to make friends. Therefore, many of these problems could be avoided.

Candidate 2

There are a wide variety of issues that can affect societies these days. In cities especially, many experience a sense of isolation from others, and there is often a high level of crime. I therefore think the government should act now to improve parks and leisure opportunities for citizens. There are a variety of reasons for this.

You're the examiner

Which candidate has successfully …

1 stated an opinion that's relevant to the question?
2 used their own language?
3 avoided giving reasons for their opinion in the introduction?

Boost your band score *Task response*

Make sure you include all the elements of the question prompt in your introduction. Include a statement about the topic, outline the issue and state a position that's relevant to the question. Remember to use your own words.

Language focus

6 **Read the introduction below for essay 1 in Exercise 1. Replace each of the words in bold with a synonym from the box.**

accommodate address argue close relatives community members offer senior citizens supported surviving the State

Nowadays people are [1]**living** longer than they used to and consequently there are more older [2]**people** to look after. Some people [3]**believe** that [4]**the elderly** should be [5]**cared for** by their [6]**families**, while others say [7]**governments** should [8]**provide homes for** old people. This essay will [9]**discuss** both views and [10]**give** an opinion.

Over to you

7 **Write an introduction for the other two essay questions in Exercise 1.**

8 **Exchange your work with a partner. Use the *You're the examiner* and *Boost your band score* boxes to evaluate their writing, then compare your introductions to sample answer 2 on page 98.**

Reading

Answer Questions 1–14 based on the reading passage.

Questions 1–6

Complete each sentence with the correct ending, ***A–H****, below.*

1 Six-year-olds
2 Girls aged 11
3 People in their late 20s
4 Teens
5 Emerging adults
6 A third of young adults

A tend to do things that aren't stimulating.
B have brains that aren't flexible.
C have brains almost the size of an adult.
D claim they are depressed.
E become better at making the right choices.
F delay making decisions.
G have reached a peak in brain development.
H can't perform as well as expected.

Questions 7–14

Do the following statements reflect the claims of the writer in the reading passage?
Write

YES	*if the statement reflects the claims of the writer*
NO	*if the statement contradicts the claims of the writer*
NOT GIVEN	*if it is impossible to say what the writer thinks about this*

7 The brain doesn't change in important ways after childhood.
8 The hobbies that teenagers have affect their ability later in life.
9 Teens argue more frequently than other age groups.
10 Young people are making important decisions sooner nowadays.
11 Stress levels fall in the late 20s.
12 Our maths skills peak in our mid-20s.
13 Inability to make decisions isn't a big problem for young people.
14 Older people are no better at crosswords than younger people.

Journey of the mind

From birth through to adulthood, our brains go on an amazing journey, and scientists are discovering how much more of the key events in the brain are still happening through teenage years and into our early adult lives. So how does the journey start? After birth, the human brain grows rapidly, more than doubling to reach 60% of its adult size by a child's first birthday. By the age of six, the brain is already 95% of its adult size. Even then, the brain never stops changing, for better or worse.

The grey matter, or 'thinking' part of the brain, continues to develop as the brain cells get extra connections. This process of making stronger links peaks at about age 11 in girls and age 12 in boys, roughly about the same time as puberty. This developmental phase is interesting, because of the 'use it or lose it' principle. Research shows that those cells and connections that are used will survive and flourish. Those cells and connections that are not used will wither and die. So if a teen is doing music, sports or is busy studying, those are the cells and connections that will be hard-wired. If they're lying on the couch or playing video games or watching MTV, those are the cells and connections that are going to survive.

Right around the time of puberty and on into the adult years is a particularly critical time for development. So in some ways, it's unfair that many adults expect teens to have sophisticated organisational or decision-making skills before their brains are finished being built. It's perhaps no wonder that so many teens have arguments with their parents about focusing on a task, finishing things and making plans. Planning exactly what to do, where and when is important and obvious to an adult, but teenagers are perhaps more laid back about such things.

So when exactly do we become good decision-makers? Recent research into how the brain develops suggests that people are better equipped to make major choices in their late 20s than earlier in life. 'Until very recently, we had to make some pretty important life decisions about education and career paths, who to marry and whether to go into the military at a time when parts of our brains weren't optimal yet,' says neuroscientist Jay Giedd at the American National Institute of Mental Health. Postponing those decisions makes sense biologically, he says. However, most people still have to make many key decisions about what career to follow or degree to take in their late teens. It's little wonder that young people jump from career option to career option from one month to the next. 'It should be reassuring for parents to know that it's very typical in the 20s not to know what you're going to do and change your mind and seem very unstable in your life. It's the norm,' says Jeffrey J. Arnett, a professor of psychology at Clark University in Worcester, Massachussetts.

Such findings are part of a new wave of research into 'emerging adulthood', a term coined by Professor Arnett. These are the years roughly from 18 to 29, which psychologists, sociologists and neuroscientists increasingly see as a distinct life stage. The gap between adolescence and full adulthood is becoming ever wider as more young people willingly, or because of economic necessity, prolong their education and postpone traditional adult responsibilities. As recently as the 1960s, the average age for a first marriage in the US was 20 for women and 22 for men, whereas today, the average is 26 for women and 28 for men.

For young adults, this period can be a stressful time. High rates of anxiety, depression, motor-vehicle accidents and alcohol use are at their peak from 18 to 25, trends that tend to level out by age 28, studies show. And a recent survey by Clark University, which polled more than 1,000 young adults nationwide, found that 72% said this time of life was stressful and 33% said they were often depressed. Still, 89% believed they would eventually get what they wanted out of life.

This lack of development can actually be seen as a positive thing. The fact that the brain stays unfinished during early adulthood 'is the best thing that ever happened to humans' because it allows us to adapt to changing environments, says Dr Giedd. 'We can figure out what kind of world we live in and what we need to be really good at.' So how can emerging adults maximise their brain potential in this period? 'Things that are cognitively stimulating are important,' says Dr Laurence Steinberg of Temple University. 'Watching talking cats on YouTube isn't as good for cognitive development as reading or taking classes.'

So when does the brain's power peak and then decline? According to recent tests, the top performance is achieved at around the age of 22. From then on, reasoning, spatial visualisation and speed of thought all start to go downhill when someone reaches their late 20s. The first age at which there is any marked decline in these factors is at 27. Memory stays stronger for much longer and doesn't decline until 37, while abilities that are based on accumulated knowledge, such as general knowledge and crosswords, actually increase until the age of 60.

It's perhaps not surprising then that there can be so much conflict and judgement between different age groups. Whether it's an adult frustrated at their teenager's lack of knowledge or the teenager annoyed by the adult's lack of speed, both are probably equally irritating. Understanding each other's strengths and weaknesses, though, could make some moments much smoother.

Listening

Section 1 1.12

Questions 1–5

Complete the notes below.
*Write **NO MORE THAN TWO WORDS AND/OR A NUMBER** for each answer.*

New youth club member
Age: nearly **1** ....
Planning to come on **2** .... at **3** ....
Name: **4** ....
Contact number: **5** ....

Questions 6–10

Complete the table below.
*Write **NO MORE THAN TWO WORDS AND/OR A NUMBER** for each answer.*

Hunton community youth clubs

	Ages 10–14	Age 15+
Cost	**6**	£1.50 (Money is for **7** .... , such as noodles)
Activities	Sports, films	Making **8** .... , street dance
Equipment	Sports equipment, **9**	Sports equipment Wear **10** ....

Section 2 1.13

Questions 11–15

Label the plan below.
*Write the correct letter, **A–H**, next to questions **11–15**.*

A computing department
B cafeteria
C exhibition
D dentistry
E main university library
F IT suite
G talks
H faculty library

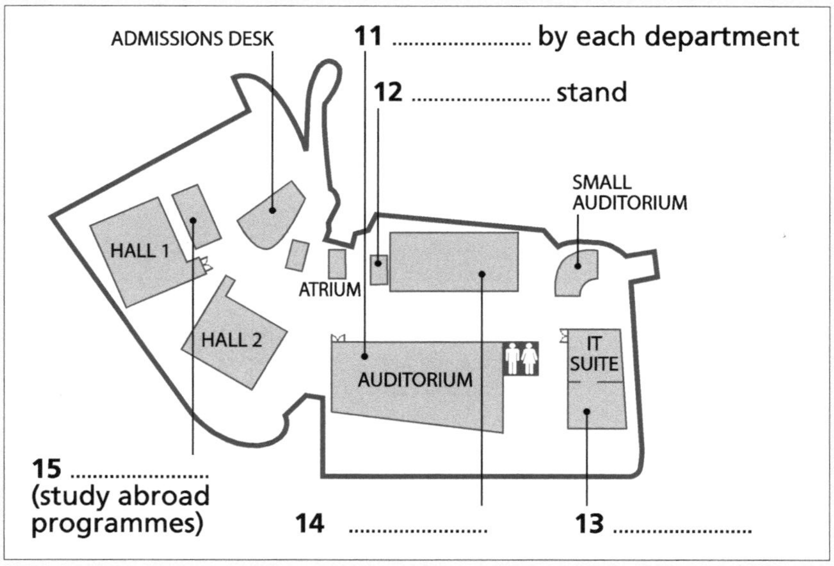

Questions 16–20

Answer the questions.
Write ***NO MORE THAN THREE WORDS AND/OR A NUMBER*** *for each answer.*

16 Who goes on 'study abroad' programmes? ....
17 What percentage of students study abroad? ....
18 Which employers may be interested in 'study abroad' students? ....
19 What will students have to improve in the first year? ....
20 Where can the shuttle bus take you? ....

Speaking

Part 1 **EITHER**

a 1.14 **Listen and answer eight questions on two topics. After each question, you will have 15 seconds to respond.**

OR

b **Turn to audio transcript 1.14 on page 106. Ask and answer the questions with a partner.**

Part 2 **Prepare to speak about the topic on the card below. Think or make notes for one minute. Speak for between one and two minutes about the topic on the card. Record yourself or ask a partner to listen to you.**

Describe a person in your local area (eg a neighbour) that you respect.
You should say:
where the person lives
what the person does
how well you know the person
and explain why you respect this person.

Writing

Task 1
You should spend about 20 minutes on this task. Turn to Task 2 on page 90.

Task 2
You should spend about 40 minutes on this task.
Write about the following topic:

Students nowadays can get large quantities of information from mobile phones. Despite this, many people think that they should not be allowed to use them in the classroom.

To what extent do you agree or disagree?

Give reasons for your answer and include any relevant examples from your knowledge or experience.
Write at least 250 words.

UNIT 3 Communication

TOPIC FOCUS

Woo Hoo!

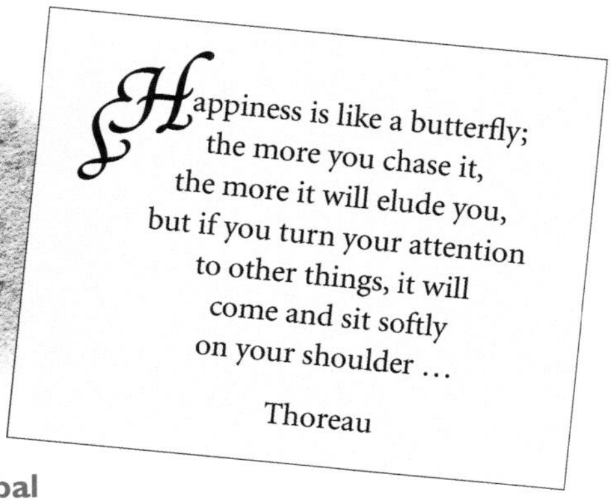
Happiness is like a butterfly;
the more you chase it,
the more it will elude you,
but if you turn your attention
to other things, it will
come and sit softly
on your shoulder …
Thoreau

verbal

non-verbal

1 **Look at the images. What's the difference between verbal and non-verbal communication?**

2 **Which pair of images communicates the idea of happiness most effectively?**

3 **Put these forms of communication into two categories: *verbal* or *non-verbal*.**
phone calls clapping photo messaging online chat hugs presentations emoji

4 **When do you use each of the communication methods in Exercise 3? Who do you use each one with?**

➤ **IELTS quiz** page 6, question 5

READING

LESSON AIMS

- Sentence completion
- Review: Yes / No / Not Given

1 **When did you last have a good laugh? Share your memories in groups.**

2 **Read the first and last paragraphs of the article on page 31 about laughter. Is it about:**
A the purpose of laughter? B the dangers of laughter? C the benefits of laughter?

• Laughter is no joke •

There is one international language that we all know. We use it all the time, often without thinking. It helps us communicate across different cultures and it is fun to use, too. It is the language of laughter. We would probably not think of our giggles as anything more than a sign that we find something funny, but evidence shows that laughter communicates far more than we may think.

Laughter is rarely something we decide to do. Like crying, it is a natural instinct and one that is very difficult to control. While we can all sing or speak at will, it is almost impossible to laugh on command, and the impulse to laugh may strike during even the most serious of meetings. Indeed, our laughter 'triggers' lie in our subconscious mind and are activated spontaneously, suggesting that it fulfils quite a basic role in our lives.

The nature of this role seems to be largely social. True, there are certain things we might laugh at by ourselves, especially those that release tension. For example, we often smile after feelings of fear or confusion pass, or when people we perceive as more powerful than ourselves suffer a misfortune. Yet such moments often provoke a simple smile rather than a laugh. According to Robert R. Provine, a neuroscientist and Professor of Psychology at the University of Maryland, real laughter is 30 times more common when we are with other people and it almost disappears when we do not have an audience.

What is more, the things we consider humorous when alone tend to be very different from those we normally laugh at with others. For example, in company we often laugh at things we say ourselves. Speakers apparently laugh over 50% more than their audiences, suggesting that laughter is more often a signal than simply a response. In particular, it can be used to show when we are playfully manipulating social roles. For instance, we may laugh when we ask 'And where have you been?' to indicate we are playing an authority role, like that of a parent.

But we do not always need a reason to laugh together, and it can be contagious, like a yawn. One well-known example is the 1962 outbreak of laughter in a girls' boarding school in Tanzania. On 30 January, three girls started giggling. Before long, 95 students were laughing uncontrollably, and on 18 March the school was forced to close. Soon other schools became involved, and eventually nearly 1,000 people were in fits of laughter. Reasons for the outbreak remain a mystery, but perhaps such cases indicate how laughter promotes social bonding.

The causes become even more complex when we consider gender. Further research from Provine has revealed that when men and women speak, females laughed 126% more frequently. One might think this is because men suppress laughter, but it is more likely to be because they are expected to initiate humour more often. In personal ads, women more frequently state interest in a 'sense of humour', while men more frequently claim to possess it. Provine also claims that in many societies across the world, from the Tamil of Southern India to the Tzeltal of Mexico, laughter among women is an unconscious way of suggesting solidarity or the passing of control to a more socially dominant male in a family or social group.

However, we should also note that effects of gender tend to evaporate in relationships of authority. In an office environment, it is more often the case that a senior manager will cause junior members of staff to laugh rather than vice versa, quite irrespective of gender. Leaders rarely laugh, at least while they are leading.

In conclusion, laughter may often be seen as a way of surrendering control to others. This might explain why it bonds people socially since it would therefore signal mutual respect and humility. It is, in short, an important communication tool.

Skills focus 3 **What can you remember about 'Yes / No / Not Given' tasks? Discuss your task strategy with a partner.**

4 **Answer Questions 1–6 based on the reading passage on page 31.**

Questions 1–6

Target time: 9 minutes
Target score: ____ / 6

Do the following statements reflect the claims of the writer in the reading passage?

Write

YES	*if the statement agrees with the author*
NO	*if the statement contradicts the author*
NOT GIVEN	*if there is no information on this*

1 Laughter is often intentional.
2 Serious situations cause most people to laugh.
3 We laugh and smile for different reasons.
4 We rarely laugh on our own.
5 We laugh at different things with different people.
6 Listeners laugh more than speakers.

5 **Do the task in the *Strategy focus* box. Then answer Questions 7–14.**

Strategy focus *Sentence completion*

1 Look at this sentence. What kind of word goes in the gap: a verb or a noun?
If people look too hard for happiness, it will often ____________ them.
2 Are you looking for a word with a positive or negative meaning?
3 Read the quote in the Topic focus section on page 30. Which word from the quote completes the gap in the sentence above?

Questions 7–14

Target time: 12 minutes
Target score: ____ / 8

Complete the sentences below.
*Choose **NO MORE THAN THREE WORDS** from the passage for each answer.*

7 Laughter in groups can happen without ....
8 School girls in Tanzania once laughed .... for months.
9 The Tanzania case may suggest laughter improves .... relationships.
10 People expect men to .... conversations that cause laughter.
11 Men often claim they have a good ....
12 In some societies, women laugh to indicate men are ....
13 In offices, gender does not affect how much we laugh as much as ....
14 Laughter is a valuable method of ....

Vocabulary extra

Find in the reading passage:
a a noun form of *laugh*
b four phrases with *role* (one with a verb, three with an adjective)
c the opposite of *junior*
d the collective noun for people who listen
e a synonym for *laughter*

Explore further 6 **What questions are these people answering?**

1 I think face-to-face communication is more important because ...

2 By laughing, I think. We wouldn't argue at all if we laughed more because ...

3 Parents and children should talk seriously and laugh a lot too, because ...

7 **Ask and answer the questions from Exercise 6 in pairs. Extend the answers using ideas from the article.**

➤ **IELTS quiz**
page 7, question 4

LISTENING

LESSON AIMS

- Section 3: Three-way dialogues
- Choosing from a list
- Note completion

1 Read these three statements about communication. Tick the one(s) you agree with.

'Effective communication is 20% what you know and 80% how you feel about what you know.' Jim Rohn

'It takes one hour of preparation for each minute of presentation time.' Wayne Burgraff

'The audience is likely to remember only three things from your presentation or speech.' Stephen Keague

2 Compare your opinions with a partner's and discuss the reasons for your choice.

Prepare to listen

3 Read Questions 1–6 below and answer these questions.

1. How many options must you choose in Questions 1–3?
2. Should you write letters or words?
3. Look at the options in Questions 1–3. Think of different ways of expressing the same idea, eg B online resources → *useful websites, online information.*
4. Why are these answers not possible in Questions 4–6?
   4 *listeners*
   5 *put some punctuation*
   6 *to print*

4 🎧 **1.15 Listen to two students discussing a presentation and answer Questions 1–6.**

Questions 1–6

Target score: ____ / 6

Questions 1–3

*Choose **THREE** letters, **A–G**.*
*Which **THREE** things are mentioned by the speakers?*

A text messaging
B online resources
C newspapers
D advertisements
E tutor's requirements
F effective speaking
G story books

Questions 4–6

*Complete the notes below. Write **NO MORE THAN TWO WORDS** for each answer.*

Effective communication means explaining yourself clearly:

- You need to think about who **4** .... is.
- You need to use stress and **5** .... in the right place.
- It's best not to **6** .... a presentation.

5 1.16 **Listen to the rest of the conversation and answer Questions 7–10.**

Questions 7–10

Target score: ____ / 4

How important to the students are these presentation features?
Write the correct letter: L, M or H.

L = low importance
M = medium importance
H = high importance

7 Moving images
8 Text
9 Quotations
10 Design

Explore further 6 **Look at audio transcript 1.16 on page 106. What phrases did the three speakers use to express agreement and disagreement?**

7 **What makes someone good at a) presenting and b) working in teams? Discuss in groups. Use the language of agreement and disagreement.**

➤ **IELTS quiz** page 8, question 4

SPEAKING

LESSON AIMS

- Part 3: Evaluating responses
- Practising connected speech

1 **Read the text and look at the graph below. Discuss these questions with a partner.**

1 Are you surprised that data companies know where you are?
2 Do you often see adverts based on your internet searches?
3 Do you worry about who buys and sells information about you online?

Meet Acxiom, sometimes described as 'the biggest company you've never heard of'. But they've heard a lot about you. Acxiom is one of the largest data firms in the world. It is one of hundreds of companies who are looking into your personal life by collecting data from everything you do online, and much of what you do in the real world. Data is now a $300-billion-a-year industry. Those who trade in it collect contact details, your age, your gender, the things you like to do – when, where and with who.

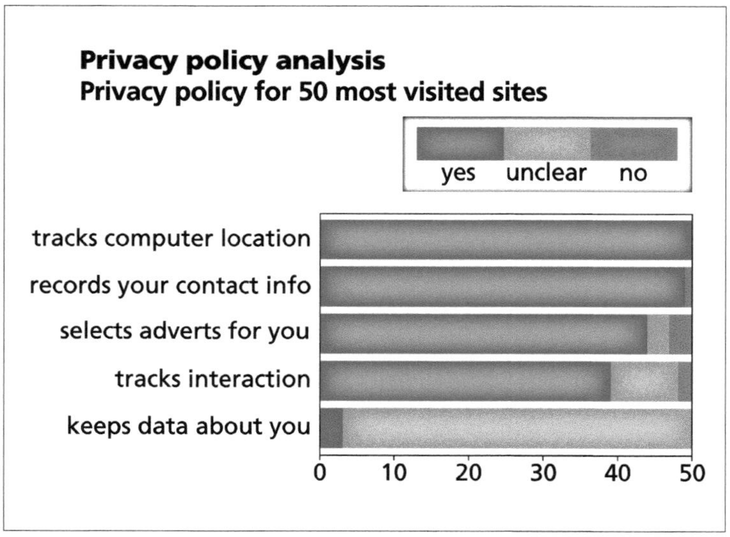

Vocabulary focus **2 Complete the statements below with expressions from the box.**

bookmark	cyber crime	digital footprint	internet security	log off/out
protect your privacy	public network	share your passwords		

1 It's vital to __________ every time you leave your computer.
2 __________ by not using apps that track the things you do.
3 __________ is a bigger problem than crime in the physical world.
4 Never log onto your bank account on a __________ .
5 Be cautious about everything you write online. It is your __________ .
6 Never __________ . You need to be careful about internet security.
7 Use software for __________ . It's easy to get a virus.
8 Do not __________ pages. Companies use this information to advertise things to you.

3 Discuss your opinions on the statements in Exercise 2 with a partner.

Prepare to speak **4 Read questions 1–4 and make notes on how you might answer them.**

1 What information do people usually put online?
2 Is it a good idea to share photographs on the internet? Why? / Why not?
3 What crimes do people commit on the internet?
4 Why do some people change their passwords regularly?
5 Is the internet a good place to meet people?
6 Is it useful to receive advertisements that are chosen for you?
7 Should governments be allowed to find out who we send emails to?
8 Will the internet be a safer or a more dangerous place in the future?

5 1.17 **Listen to answers to the first four questions in Exercise 4 and look at your notes. Do the candidates mention any of the things you wrote down?**

6 1.17 **Listen again and answer the *You're the examiner* questions.**

You're the examiner

Which candidate …
1 needs to use more precise vocabulary?
2 makes several grammar mistakes? (Can you identify them?)
3 hesitates while they search for words?
Look at audio transcript 1.17 on page 106. Can you improve Candidate 2 and Candidate 3's responses?

Pronunciation focus **7 Look at how Candidate 4 connects his speech in this sentence.**

There are a wide range of reasons to change your password, but the main reason is that people are concerned about internet security.

Read the *Boost your band score* box below, then mark the connected speech in this sentence.

If people can access your password, they might attempt to access your bank account or buy things from any of your online shopping accounts.

8 1.18 **Listen to Candidate 4 again and check your ideas.**

Boost your band score *Connecting words*

Connecting words may improve your pronunciation score. We usually connect:
1 a consonant at the end of a word to a vowel at the beginning of the next word:
photos and /fəʊtəʊzənd/
2 two vowel sounds. These are connected with a /j/, /w/ or /r/ sound:
I am /aɪjæm/ you are /juːwɑː/ tutor is* /tjuːtərɪz/

* Classified as two vowel sounds because the 'r' is usually silent.

Over to you 9 **Work with a partner.**

Student A: Ask your partner questions 2, 4, 6 and 8 from Exercise 4.

Student B: Ask your partner questions 1, 3, 5 and 7 from Exercise 4.

10 **Listen to another pair. Use the *You're the examiner* box to help you give feedback.**

➤ **IELTS quiz**
page 9, question 4

WRITING

LESSON AIMS

- Task 1: Comparing data sets
- Vocabulary for comparative tasks

1 **How long ago did you check the following?**

1 Your email account	<5m	30m	1hr	2–5hrs	>6hrs
2 Your texts	<5m	30m	1hr	2–5hrs	>6hrs
3 A news / social media feed	<5m	30m	1hr	2–5hrs	>6hrs

2 **Compare your answers to Exercise 1 in groups. Which group member uses their mobile device the most?**

3 **Look at this definition of *addicted*. Is anyone in your group addicted to their mobile device?**

addicted /ə'dɪktɪd/ *adjective*
1 physically and mentally dependent on a particular substance
*She became **addicted** to alcohol and diet pills.*
2 (informal) enthusiastically devoted to a particular thing or activity
*He's **addicted** to computers.*

Prepare to write 4 **Look at the bar chart below. Decide if these statements are True, False or Not Given.**

1 Younger adults don't use mobiles as frequently as older adults.
2 Smartphone addiction is falling.
3 Usage of mobile devices is on the rise.
4 The majority of adults check mobiles more than once an hour.
5 Smartphone addiction has reached dangerous levels.

Smartphone usage amongst US adults
% of American smartphone owners who check their phones at least several times an hour by age group

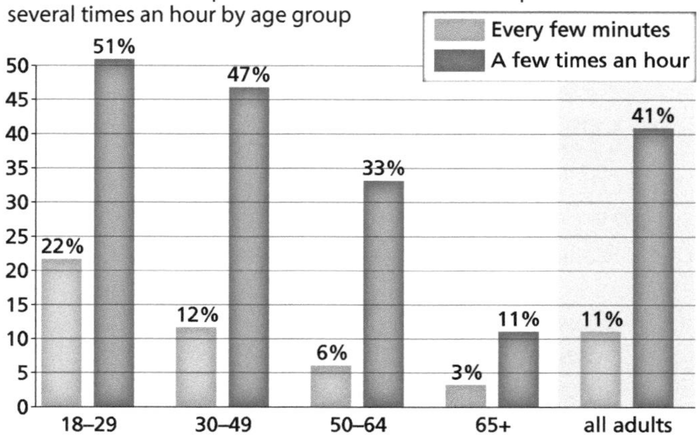

5 Read the two sample answers below, then answer the *You're the examiner* questions.

Candidate 1

The chart shows typical smartphone usage amongst US citizens. We can see that the percentage of all American smartphone owners who use their phones several times an hour is 41%.

Candidate 2

The chart reveals how often American smartphone owners over the age of 18 checked their devices in 2015. In general, we can see that over 50% of adults claimed to make use of their mobiles at least a few times every hour.

You're the examiner

Which candidate has successfully …

1 used their own vocabulary?
2 provided an overview of the data?
3 given accurate information/language?

Language focus

6 Complete Candidate 2's response with words from the box.

accounts contrast minority particularly pattern suggests

The chart reveals how often American smartphone owners over the age of 18 checked their devices in 2015. In general, we can see that over 50% of adults claimed to make use of their mobiles at least a few times every hour. The frequency of use is [1]__________ high among the youngest age group. More than half of the adults surveyed under the age of 30 check their phone a few times every hour. By [2]__________, users in that age group who check their devices every few minutes were a small [3]__________, and [4]__________ for only 27% of the total. The frequency with which phones are used declines steadily with age so that the [5]__________ becomes quite different for the oldest age group. Only 11% of people at retirement age use their phones a few or more times an hour. This [6]__________ that high-frequency phone usage is a phenomenon that affects younger phone users more than older ones.

Boost your band score ***Vocabulary***

It isn't always necessary to use new words to increase your vocabulary score. You can also use different parts of speech.

a Find the four members of the word family *use* that appear in the sample answer in Exercise 6 (there are two examples of one form).
b Write four true sentences about mobile devices in your country, using all four forms.

Over to you

7 Turn to page 91 and complete Task 3.

8 Exchange your work with a partner. Use the *You're the examiner* and *Boost your band score* boxes to evaluate their writing.

9 Turn to page 99 and compare your answer with sample answer 5.

UNIT 4 Travel

TOPIC FOCUS

1 Look at the photos. Discuss the questions below with a partner.

backpacking

volunteering

adventure holidays

ecotourism

1 Are any of these types of travelling popular in your country?
2 Which one would you be most interested in, and why?
3 How would you describe a typical holiday someone might take in your country?
4 How have holidays changed since your grandparents' generation?

2 What do you think are the main reasons people visit your country? Tell a partner.

➤ **IELTS quiz**
page 6, question 6

READING

LESSON AIMS

- Review: Sentence completion
- Multiple choice

1 Discuss these questions with a partner.

1 When did you last travel? Where did you go, and what did you do?
2 What do you think are the benefits of travel?
3 Which kind of holiday (1–5) do you think would suit each personality type (A–E)?

1 jungle tour	A open to experience
2 backpacking	B conscientious
3 resort holiday	C extrovert
4 relaxing at home	D agreeable (= nice)
5 conservation holiday	E emotionally unstable

Skills focus **2 What can you remember about 'sentence completion' tasks from Unit 3? Discuss your task strategy with a partner, then attempt Questions 1–7 based on the reading passage on page 39.**

Questions 1–7

Target time: 10 minutes
Target score: ____ / 7

Complete the sentences below.
Choose ***NO MORE THAN TWO WORDS*** *from the passage for each answer.*

1 Our personalities remain quite stable because of ....
2 We can affect our personalities by creating .... for ourselves.
3 Researchers study personality change .... to see how experience affects it.
4 The Zimmerman and Neyer study investigated the personality development of ....
5 Some of the research subjects went abroad for up to ....
6 Participants did a .... before going away.
7 Researchers wanted to know if alterations to .... helped change personality.

Is travel good for you?

When we return from a foreign holiday, our minds are often filled with the memories of new places and people. We may also feel we understand a foreign culture better and appreciate our own culture more. Travel seems to make us different, better people, and researchers have now found evidence to prove it.

Psychologists will often try to measure how people change by observing personality dimensions. These are commonly put into five broad categories, referred to as the 'Big Five' by Lewis Goldberg: openness to experience, conscientiousness, extroversion, agreeableness, and neuroticism (emotional stability). To some extent, our personalities remain constant, since they are influenced by our genes. Openness to experience, for example, has been linked to the 'seretonin transporter' gene. But psychologists believe that by setting goals in life, we can also strengthen aspects of our personality.

However, studying the experiences that influence personality is difficult because researchers have to study change in individuals over time to explore how those experiences lead to changes in personality. One such study was conducted by Julia Zimmermann and Franz Neyer and published in the *Journal of Personality and Social Psychology*. It examined how extended travel influenced personality development in a large sample of German college students. Some of the students in their sample studied in another country for an extended period of time (one or two semesters), while the control group was in college, but did not study abroad.

Prior to the travel period, all participants were given a personality test to measure the 'Big Five' personality dimensions. Participants also gave an extended list of their social networks so that
...s in
...ersonality
...fter an
...nts who
...taken

...llowed
...d of
...fore
...them.
...ality
...antly, as
...se to study
...ersion. On
...e-semester
...isness,
...rules and to
...t abroad for

both semesters were generally higher in openness to experience than those who did not travel.

After returning from their trip, those who travelled tended to show an increase in openness to experience, agreeableness and emotional stability relative to those who did not travel. The effects were not huge, but they were reliable. These changes in personality were related to changes in people's social networks as a result of travel. As you might expect, those people who did not travel maintained a similar social network over the study period. In contrast, those people who travelled tended to meet a lot of new people from the host country of their travel and to lose touch with people from their home country. These changes in social network were particularly strongly related to the observed changes in openness to experience and emotional stability.

How can we explain these results? One idea is that extended foreign travel takes people outside their comfort zone. Travellers have to adapt to new people and new cultural practices. Even students going from Germany to another EU country had to adjust to differences in language, food and outlook. This may have made travellers more confident in seeking new experiences and contacts in the future. As regards emotional stability, the experience of dealing with change may help make travellers less emotionally reactive to day-to-day situations, increasing their emotional stability.

It is not clear whether travel affects adults' personalities to the same degree. College years are an intense period of transition for people, so they may be more susceptible to personality change. However, research by Adam Galinsky of Columbia University has shown that spending a period of time living in a foreign country can make adults think more creatively. In foreign cultures, people often learn ways of interacting with others in order to achieve social goals or carry out successful transactions, which may explain how people living abroad become more creative in problem solving, for example. As creativity is related to openness, it seems likely that adult personalities can be affected, if not by changes in social networks then at least by thought processes.

It is therefore not simply personality that can be changed by travel; our mental processes evolve too. A further study by the US Travel Association even claims that travel helps our brains grow. As we travel, we have to make sense of a range of new stimuli, not least language, and this encourages the brain to make new connections, keeping it constantly active. It seems that travel makes us not only better people but cleverer people, too.

3 Do the tasks in the *Strategy focus* box. Then answer Questions 8–13 based on the same reading passage.

Strategy focus *Multiple choice*

1 Multiple-choice questions usually involve finding a sentence with a similar meaning. Read sentences 1 and 2. In each case, which sentence has a similar meaning, a or b?

1 Travelling abroad for an extended period of time develops people's minds.
a Long periods in another country have a positive effect on brain development.
b Foreign travel causes our minds to work more quickly.

2 People who are not open to new experiences do not like change in their environment.
a Those that dislike doing new things often want a stable daily life.
b People with open minds worry about changes to their environment.

2 Underline the words in sentences 1 and 2 and the matching sentences that have a similar meaning.

Questions 8–13

Target time: 9 minutes
Target score: ____ / 6

*Choose the correct letter, **A**, **B**, **C** or **D**.*

8 The research was interesting because
A more than one thing was studied.
B it hadn't been done before.
C it revealed which holidays were most popular.
D it explained why people go abroad.

9 The most conscientious students
A went abroad for the longest period.
B preferred not to travel abroad.
C chose shorter foreign-study programmes.
D didn't want to leave their studies for long.

10 After the trip, students who had been abroad
A had changed their personalities a lot.
B couldn't relate to people who hadn't travelled.
C had more friends than those who hadn't travelled.
D lost some old friends.

11 Students who travelled short distances
A saw least change in their personalities.
B changed the most in some cases.
C experienced similar changes to others.
D travelled more confidently.

12 The impact of travel on personality
A probably affects students and adults equally.
B only affects college students.
C doesn't affect adults.
D may not affect adults and students for the same reasons.

13 People who travel
A can become more intelligent.
B are more active.
C sometimes become less creative.
D usually learn languages.

Vocabulary extra

Answer the questions about these verbs from the reading passage.

adapt adjust affect evolve influence maintain remain

1 Which of these verbs are linked to the idea of a) change and b) no change?
2 Which verbs can't be followed by an object?
3 Which verb is also a noun?

Explore further **4 Work with a partner. Would you like to spend an extended period in another country? Why? / Why not?**

➤ **IELTS quiz**
page 7, questions 5 and 6

LISTENING

LESSON AIMS

- Section 4: Monologue on an academic subject
- Multiple choice
- Labelling a diagram

1 Look at this advertisement. Would you like to go on this holiday? Tell a partner why / why not.

Prepare to listen

2 Ask and answer these questions with a partner

1 Look at Questions 1–6 below. How are Questions 4–6 different from Questions 1–3? How are they similar?
2 Can you predict any of the answers?

3 1.19 Listen to the first part of a lecture on ecotourism and answer Questions 1–6.

Questions 1–6

Target score: ____ / 6

Questions 1–3

Choose the correct letter, ***A****,* ***B*** *or* ***C****.*

1 The ecotourism movement started in the
A 1960s.
B 1970s.
C 1980s.

2 Bigodi is the name of a
A new school.
B community.
C craft project.

3 In ecotourism projects, tourists always
A spend time in the countryside.
B take part in exciting activities.
C educate local people.

Questions 4–6

Choose ***THREE*** *letters,* ***A–G****.*
Which ***THREE*** *problems of ecotourism projects are mentioned by the speaker?*

A The money from them doesn't help everyone.
B Farm animals might be destroyed.
C They are too small.
D They have few facilities.
E Local culture is slowly lost.
F Tourists damage wildlife.
G Environment is not a priority.

4 1.20 **Listen to the second part of the lecture and answer Questions 7–10.**

Questions 7–10

Target score: ____ / 4

Label the diagram using words from the box.
*Write the correct letter, **A–I**.*

A	lake water
B	hot water
C	fresh water
D	sea water
E	heated water
F	cold water
G	frozen water
H	waste water
I	air conditioning

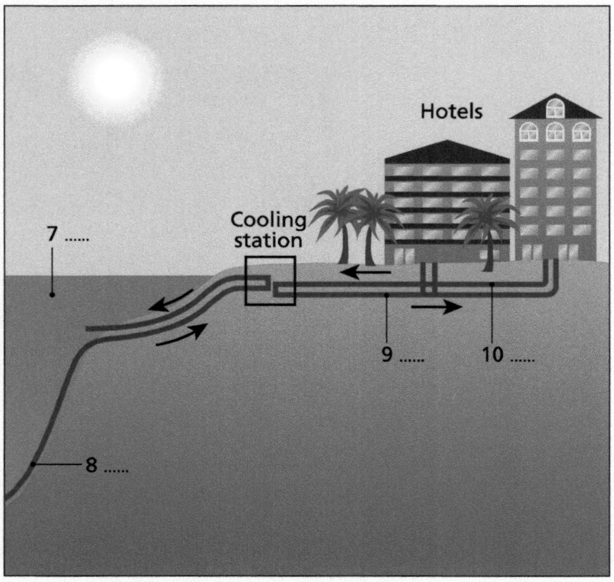

Explore further 5 **Find out about the popular ecotourism destinations of Costa Rica, Kenya, Norway and Palau. Which would you like to visit? Which place would you associate each of the following with?**

1 elephants 2 rainforests 3 scuba diving 4 snowy mountains

➤ **IELTS quiz** page 8, question 5

SPEAKING

LESSON AIMS

- Part 1: Giving personal information
- Speaking for between one and two minutes on a topic
- Discussing a topic

1 **Look at the photos. Tick the activities you like to do on holiday.**

sunbathing ❑

shopping ❑

sightseeing ❑

visiting museums ❑

eating out ❑

2 **Compare your activities with a partner's. Tell them about your ideal holiday.**

Vocabulary focus 3 **Put these places in the correct column of the table.**

a the main square **b** public gardens **c** the old town **d** statues
e cathedrals and mosques **f** markets and bazaars **g** museums and galleries
h historic monuments **i** fountains **j** the harbour **k** a mall

Objects you look at	Outdoor spaces	Buildings you enter

4 Make questions by re-ordering these words, putting the verb in brackets in the correct form.

1 around / do / gardens / like / public / (walk) / you / ?
2 a / (go) / gallery / have / recently / to / you / ?
3 at / can / famous / in / (look) / statues / town / what / you / your / ?
4 around / malls / markets or / prefer / (walk) / would / you / ?
5 at / do / enjoy / historic / (look) / monuments / you / ?

5 Ask and answer the questions in Exercise 4 with a partner.

Prepare to speak

6 1.21–1.22 Listen to two candidates answering Part 1 questions. Which candidate answers each question? Number them 1 or 2.

a What do you like to do on holiday? ❑
b Do you prefer travelling alone or with friends? ❑
c Where in the world would you like to visit if you had the chance? ❑
d What's your favourite way to travel? ❑
e Do you often travel abroad? ❑
f Have you travelled to other places? Where are they? ❑

7 1.21–1.22 Listen again and answer the *You're the examiner* questions. Compare your answers with a partner's.

> ### You're the examiner
> Which candidate successfully …
> **1** varies their language? (How?)
> **2** avoids grammar mistakes? (Can you find three mistakes made by the other candidate?)
> **3** uses some high-level phrases. (Which are they?)

Fluency focus

8 Match each pair of adverbs with its function.

1 occasionally, rarely	a Used to talk about frequency
2 actually, strangely	b Used to make a guess
3 basically, generally	c Used to say something surprising
4 possibly, perhaps	d Used to say something is fundamentally true

9 Add an adverb from Exercise 8 to each response below. Then extend the responses using another adverb.

Example: I'll go abroad this year … ➔ I'll *probably* go abroad this year. *It's basically too expensive in this country.*

1 I've never travelled abroad … 2 I go for a walk … 3 I like travelling …

> **Boost your band score** *Fluency*
> In Part 1, you should aim to speak for about 12 seconds on each question. This means you need three or four sentences in response to each question. You can extend your responses by using:
> - adverbs of frequency to talk about how often you do things
> - adverbs such as *generally, actually, maybe* to talk about preferences.

Over to you

10 Work with a partner.

Student A: Ask your partner four questions from Exercise 6.
Student B: Ask your partner the four questions below.

1 Do you have many tourists in your country?
2 Is there a popular tourist destination in your country?
3 When is the best season to travel in your country?
4 What recommendations would you make for a tourist in your country?

11 Feed back to your partner. Use the *You're the examiner* box to help.

➤ **IELTS quiz**
page 9, question 5

WRITING

LESSON AIMS

- Task 2: Opinion essays
- Making your opinion clear

1 Look at these forms of transport. Which would you prefer to use to travel to a foreign country, and why?

2 Make notes on these questions. Then discuss them in groups.

A In what ways can newer forms of transport be better?
B Are there any ways in which more traditional types of transport are better?
C Should governments take action to reduce air travel? Why? / Why not?

Prepare to write

3 Read this task and decide which of the questions in Exercise 2 (A–C) is closest to it.

Write about the following topic:

> *People who travel by air often see very little of the countries they visit.*
> *It's better for tourists and local communities when people use traditional forms of travel, like ferries and trains.*
> *To what extent do you agree or disagree?*

Give reasons for your answer and include any relevant examples from your knowledge or experience.
Write at least 250 words.

4 Read these two extracts from sample answers, then answer the *You're the examiner* questions.

Candidate 1

Air travellers land in international airports, arrive in international hotels and visit the most famous sites. Some see this as a way of making international travel more convenient. Others believe it stops people interacting with local populations. I will discuss both views.

Those who believe air travel has improved tourism argue that air travellers get to destinations quickly and have access to the facilities of international airports and hotels, which are similar in all countries. There they can interact with people who speak English, so it's more convenient for them.

Candidate 2

Nowadays it is possible to travel to a foreign country by air using only the services of international companies and tour operators. As a result, we are losing the benefits of travel.

The first reason for this view is that modern tourists and local people don't have the opportunity to mix and learn about each other. Air travellers may meet some local taxi drivers, but when a tourist travels by train, for example, they can travel through a range of landscapes and remote locations, meeting people from rural areas.

You're the examiner

Which candidate has successfully …
1 responded clearly to the instructions?
2 stated a reason in the second paragraph (rather than a viewpoint)?
3 avoided using key words and phrases more than once?

Language focus

5 The words below can be used to admit or concede information. Answer these questions about them.

1 Which ones can link two clauses together?
2 Which ones are often followed immediately by a comma?

admittedly although even if maybe true

6 Complete this continuation of Candidate 2's answer using the adverbs from Exercise 5.

Secondly, by using trains and ferries, tourists can support the local economy. Air passengers paying high fares are [1] __________ useful for the economy. However, [2] __________ they generate income and create jobs, many of the profits of airlines or hotels go to large corporations that are owned by wealthy nations. People travelling by slower, less direct, forms of transport can buy local products and services.

Trains and ferries also allow tourists the time to reflect on their lives. [3] __________, with air travel you can achieve a lot quickly and [4] __________ air travellers do have time to themselves. But in-flight entertainment rarely gives you time to think or gain new experiences. Train or ferry travel gives you time for contemplation, [5] __________ you're travelling relatively short distances.

7 Look again at the sample answer in Exercise 6 and answer these questions.

1 Does Candidate 2 think air travel is good or bad?
2 Underline the ideas that *don't* support Candidate 2's opinion.
3 Why does Candidate 2 use the five adverbs in the box?
  a To tell us an idea supports their argument.
  b To tell us an idea *doesn't* supports their argument.

> **Boost your band score** *Using adverbs*
> Making your views clear throughout the response will help you gain a higher score for task response. Using adverbs to do this will also give you an opportunity to use a wider range of grammar.

Over to you

8 Write about this topic.

> ***Modern media, like documentaries and virtual reality, let us experience other countries without travelling to them. Long-distance travel has therefore become unnecessary.***
> ***To what extent do you agree with this?***

Give reasons for your answer and include any relevant examples from your knowledge or experience.
Write at least 250 words.

9 Exchange your work with a partner. Use the *You're the examiner* and the *Boost your band score* boxes to evaluate their writing.

- Underline any part that doesn't respond to the instructions.
- Highlight words that are repeated too often.
- Circle words used to show agreement/disagreement.

10 Turn to page 99 and compare your answer with sample answer 6.

Reading

Answer Questions 1–13 based on the reading passage.

Questions 1–8

Complete the sentences below.
Choose ***NO MORE THAN TWO WORDS*** *from the passage for each answer.*

1 Bird calls are usually given in a specific ....
2 Birds with the longest calls are generally ....
3 Birds sing to attract partners and to protect their ....
4 Researchers have learnt about birdsong by studying birds' reactions to ....
5 Researchers found that female birds chose .... near to the loudspeakers.
6 Singing is a more .... strategy for birds than fighting.
7 It's difficult for less .... birds to produce powerful songs.
8 Species communicate their .... in different ways.

Questions 9–13

Choose the correct letter, ***A, B, C*** *or* ***D.***

9 Weaker cockerels generally produce
A louder sounds than competitors.
B calls that suggest they are stronger than they are.
C less energetic calls.
D high-energy elements in their songs.

10 Birds show they can survive for a long time by
A learning new songs regularly.
B using only older bird calls.
C sounding more relaxed than younger birds.
D having more skilful songs.

11 Birds who live near to each other
A repeat each other's songs.
B don't need to sing to each other as frequently.
C often grow tired of competition.
D usually fight less regularly.

12 New arrivals in a territory
A take turns with local birds to sing.
B will sing the same songs as existing residents.
C often cannot copy the songs of local birds.
D usually sing more intensely than others.

13 Birds resemble humans because
A they learn less as they get older.
B young members of the species have fewer language abilities than older members.
C elements of their language are shared by all members of the species.
D they communicate in a similar way to humans.

The secrets of birdsong

For centuries, birdsong has been a source of great pleasure for humans, celebrated in music and poetry and enjoyed in gardens and parks the world over. But scientists have long suspected that their 'singing' has a much more serious purpose. Indeed, thanks to the efforts of researchers, we have come to a detailed understanding of how birdsong serves bird populations.

Birds are able to communicate messages with their song. There may be specific calls for 'come here', 'go away' or 'scan for danger', often given in sequences. In fact, successful communication requires the calls to be given in a certain order, suggesting that these messages have a structure similar to human grammar.

But birdsong is more than just a means of communication. Birds use song as a way of competing with other rivals. While all birds may have short 'calls', it is the male birds who have the most extensive songs, and this has been shown to assist them in their efforts to mate and defend territory. Researchers can easily demonstrate this. First, they record the birdsongs before removing all the birds from an area of woodland. They then play the song recordings back through loudspeakers. When birdsong is being played, male birds stop entering the area, suggesting that competing males recognise the sounds as a claim to territory. Also, female birds are attracted to the sound and inhabit nesting sites close by.

The use of song to compete with rivals may seem strange at first. Many animal species would use aggression or physical displays to compete with other members of their species. Clearly, though, in the dense forest foliage, sound is more useful than visual display, and competing through song is certainly more effective than attempting to resolve conflict through fighting, since for two males, a bloody confrontation is in neither's interests.

However, if songs are to be used in place of aggression, then it is necessary for a song to give real information about the strength of each bird. If there were no direct relationship between fighting skills and singing, then it might be possible for a bird to fake a threatening song and pretend to be dominant. This, in turn, would allow weaker birds to win contests and the population would go into decline. Besides, as with humans, if you go around threatening people, sooner or later you may have to back up the claim to dominance. How, then, can singing give real information about strength? There are a number of ways that this is possible, depending on species.

The particular language that many birds use to signal strength is very difficult to fake for a weaker bird and has a high cost in terms of energy expenditure. By producing song that requires a greater degree of effort, birds can therefore reveal how strong they are. Dominant cockerels, for example, produce higher-pitched sounds, which require more energy to create and sustain. Other species include 'expensive' elements in their songs, like trills, and others will increase the volume and intensity of their singing.

However, cost may not be the only strength signal. While some may attempt to use high-pitched notes, other species compete by using lower-pitched sounds. It is believed that, as with humans, these low notes can signal relaxation and confidence. Still others achieve success by having a repertoire of different tunes and indeed learn new songs each year to add to their collection. It seems this musical knowledge indicates an ability to survive for a long time, since time is required to learn songs.

However, it would be exhausting to compete all the time, and male birds also use their voices to avoid unnecessary conflict with neighbours. Generally, birds who have been neighbours for a long time are not as dangerous as new arrivals and they use certain patterns of singing to indicate neighbourly status. Interactions therefore follow one of two patterns, depending on the origin of the bird. Neighbouring birds will often reply to each other using a different song, but a version of a song that they both know, like a track from the same album. This behaviour, known as 'repertoire matching', contrasts markedly to the response to a new arrival. In the latter scenario, the bird will match the tune of the new arrival as closely as possible in a process called 'song matching'. As the intensity of the confrontation builds, the songs may even be sung at the same time in an overlapping sequence.

It is therefore important that birds not only learn to sing but also learn specific versions of songs that can be selected to indicate origin. In short, an element of cultural learning has to take place. Researchers have found that this learning is very close to human learning in many respects. Young birds learn from other birds around them, mimicking parents, and despite some birds' habit of learning throughout their life, most species do their learning during a small period of time in their younger years. Such similarities have encouraged researchers to use birds as a model for understanding human speech development.

Listening

Section 3 1.23

Questions 1–3

*Choose **THREE** letters, **A–G**.*
*Which **THREE** things do the students ask about?*

A Answering the essay question
B Writing a simple essay
C Using books and articles
D Organising ideas in essays
E The location of useful books
F Giving the essay to the tutor
G Checking results online

Questions 4–6

*Who will do the following tasks? Choose the correct letter, **R**, **T** or **D**.*

R = Rehab
T = Tutor
D = Dev

4 Printing a document
5 Finding some books
6 Getting information about books

Questions 7–10

*Choose the correct letter, **A**, **B** or **C**.*

7 The sample essay got a bad mark because
A it didn't answer the question.
B it used poor-quality information.
C it didn't include a list of articles.

8 The main weakness with students' essays is usually
A poor essay structure.
B lack of thought.
C quality of information.

9 Students will get feedback
A in 15 days.
B in tutorials.
C online.

10 The tutor's comments will help students in the
A test.
B presentation.
C next assignment.

Section 4 1.24

Questions 11–16

Complete the notes below.
*Write **NO MORE THAN TWO WORDS AND/OR A NUMBER** for each answer.*

11 People in Egypt used both .... and images to communicate.
12 The first writing system had .... letters.
13 Most early documents were written on ....
14 The first machine for printing was as big as ....
15 Printing introduced a period of ....
16 The first attempt at making a .... was over 100 years ago.

Questions 17–20

Complete the diagrams.
*Write **NO MORE THAN TWO WORDS** for each answer.*

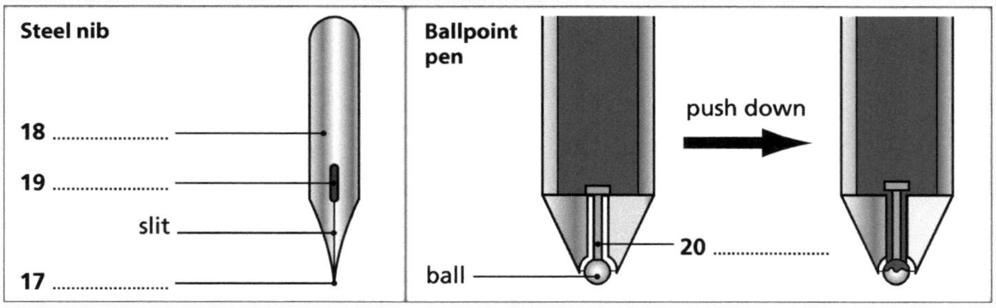

Speaking

Part 1 **EITHER**

a 🎧 1.25 **Listen and answer eight questions on two topics. After each question, you will have 15 seconds to respond.**

OR

b **Turn to audio transcript 1.25 on page 108. Ask and answer the questions with a partner.**

Part 2 **Prepare to speak about the topic on the card below. Think or make notes for one minute. Speak for between one and two minutes about the topic on the card. Record yourself or ask a partner to listen to you.**

> **Describe a long journey that you've enjoyed.**
> **You should say:**
> **how you bought the ticket for the journey**
> **what kinds of transport you used**
> **what the destination was like**
> **and explain why you enjoyed the journey.**

Part 3 **EITHER**

a 🎧 1.26 **Listen and answer nine questions on three topics. After each question, you will have 25 seconds to respond.**

OR

b **Turn to audio transcript 1.26 on page 108. Ask and answer the questions with a partner.**

Writing

Task 1

You should spend about 20 minutes on this task. Turn to Task 4 on page 91.

Task 2

You should spend about 40 minutes on this task.
Write about the following topic:

> ***Many modern families are choosing to take children to school by car rather than allow them to walk or cycle. School authorities should discourage this trend.***
>
> ***To what extent do you agree or disagree?***

Give reasons for your answer and include any relevant examples from your knowledge or experience.
Write at least 250 words.

UNIT **5** Health

TOPIC FOCUS

1 Work with a partner. What's the best way to have a long and happy life?

2 Here are the most popular answers in a survey of 68 American people aged over 100. Do any of your ideas from Exercise 1 appear?

Spend time with your family.

Slow down and focus on your partner.

Spend less and save more.

Stay active.

➤ **IELTS quiz** page 6, question 7

READING

LESSON AIMS

- Review: Multiple choice
- Matching paragraph headings

1 Decide whether these adjectives express positive or negative emotions.
anxious calm irritated joyful relaxed stressed thankful upset

2 Skim the reading passage on page 51. Why does the author think these emotions are important?

Skills focus **3 What can you remember about 'multiple-choice' tasks from Unit 4? Discuss your task strategy with a partner, then attempt Questions 1–6 based on the reading passage.**

Questions 1–6

Target time: 9 minutes
Target score: ___ / 6

Choose the correct letter, ***A, B, C*** *or* ***D.***

1 Feelings of anger
A don't increase our blood pressure.
B affect us negatively for a long period.
C should be hidden.
D are sometimes good for our health.

2 Crying when we feel emotional
A increases negative feelings.
B is generally unnecessary.
C can improve your digestion.
D is linked to higher stress.

3 Researchers have found that romantic experiences
A lead to a permanent state of calm.
B aren't forgotten easily.
C reduce physical and mental stress.
D usually end after about 12 months.

Health is all in the mind

A We are constantly given advice on what is or is not good for our health – from the amount of exercise we should do through to what diet we should be following. But what effect can our emotions have on us physically? Is being angry actually physically bad for us as well as emotionally draining?

B As you become more irritated, you feel like your blood pressure is increasing, which is exactly what is happening. But that is just one of several negative effects of anger. Researchers at Ohio State University found that a disagreement can also cause a surge in cytokines (immune molecules), which are connected to arthritis, diabetes, heart-disease and cancer. In people over 50, outbursts of only a few minutes can increase the risk of a heart attack or stroke by up to five times. According to research published in the *International Journal of Psychophysiology*, the results can be long lasting, too. Even a week after the event made us tense, we can still see increases in blood pressure when we think about what happened.

C Having said that, hiding your anger is perhaps no better. A long-term study in Michigan found that the risk of dying from conditions such as heart attack, stroke or cancer doubled in women who hid their anger during arguments. It therefore seems that both hiding anger and letting it out are bad for our health, though hiding it may prevent you angering others.

D One reaction to an argument that is often seen as weak – crying – may actually be good for our health. When you cry, you really do cry out negative emotion. Dr William Frey, a US biochemist, compared the tears of women who cried for emotional reasons with those who cried on exposure to onions. Emotional tears were found to contain high levels of hormones and neurotransmitters associated with stress. They also led to lower blood pressure and pulse rate. Dr Frey concluded that the purpose of emotional crying is to remove stress chemicals. He says the continued presence of these substances when you hold tears in would keep you in a needless state of tension. Your body would then be prone to the negative effects of anxiety, including weakened immunity, impaired memory and poor digestion.

E If negative emotions are so bad for us physically, what physical benefits can we gain from positive emotions? We may think of romance as a stressful business, but researchers at the University of Pavia, Italy, would disagree. They found that a new relationship raises levels of Nerve Growth Factor for about a year. This hormone-like substance helps to restore the nervous system and improves memory by causing new brain cells to grow. It also starts a calming effect on the body and mind. Unfortunately, researchers found levels dropped after about a year from the point at which feelings of romance fall away.

F Not only can love help restore your nervous system but – according to Dr Hyla Cass, Professor of Psychiatry at the University of California, Los Angeles – the oxytocin that cuddles and physical touch make our body release can help in a number of other ways. It can initiate the release of DHEA, an anti-ageing, anti-stress hormone that triggers cellular restoration in the body. Other forms of touch, such as massage, have also been found to help the body heal from major illness.

G It is often said that 'laughter is the world's best medicine', and it seems there may actually be some truth in this. Scientists at the University of California have discovered that laughter relaxes tense muscles, reduces production of stress-causing hormones, lowers blood pressure, and helps increase oxygen absorption in the blood. Not only does it depress stress levels and reduce the risk of a heart attack, but laughing also burns calories, since it is possible to move 400 muscles of the body when laughing. Some researchers estimate that laughing even briefly 100 times is the same as ten minutes on a rowing machine or 15 minutes on an exercise bike.

H Feeling grateful for what you have got, whether it be a partner, an achievement or simply being alive, is all it takes to boost immunity, lower blood pressure, and speed healing throughout the body. Dr Rollin McCraty of the Institute of HeartMath in the US is studying the link between emotions and physical health. He has found that, like love, gratitude and contentment both trigger oxytocin. It switches off stress by causing the nervous system to relax. It can even help the heart and brain to operate more effectively.

I Perhaps the most important lesson we can learn from this research is that it is important to stop negative emotions whenever possible or you will suffer, psychologically and physically. If you are in an argument or feel stressed, try to remove yourself from the situation and take deep breaths. This can lower your heart rate and blood pressure almost immediately. If you are having an argument, try to return to the room and discuss things calmly instead. If that is not possible, leave.

J We can also trick our body into feeling positive. Visualising positive emotional states can start them in the body, with beneficial effects on health. The mind cannot differentiate between an imagined state and an actual 'external' state. So, if you vividly imagine a positive state, you may experience the benefits as if they are real. Visualise yourself laughing, joyful and full of energy – the more vivid you make it, the more effective it will be.

4 The chemical oxytocin
- **A** causes us to feel love.
- **B** reduces the effects of getting old.
- **C** can weaken cells in the body.
- **D** is released when we have a massage.

5 We should laugh more because it
- **A** increases oxygen that enters the body.
- **B** is often better for us than taking medicine.
- **C** reduces depression.
- **D** is better for us than other forms of exercise.

6 Being thankful towards someone
- **A** releases a chemical called oxytocin.
- **B** switches off parts of the nervous system.
- **C** makes your heart beat faster.
- **D** helps the brain to grow.

4 Do the task in the *Strategy focus* box. Then answer Questions 7–14 based on the same reading passage.

Strategy focus *Matching paragraph headings*

1 A topic sentence is the sentence of a paragraph that gives the main idea. This is usually the first or second sentence. Underline the topic sentence in paragraph B.

2 Key ideas in the topic sentence are often repeated later in the paragraph. Read the rest of paragraph B and find words or phrases that express the idea of a) anger or b) effect.

3 In 'matching paragraph headings' tasks, you choose a heading that's similar to the topic sentence. Choose the best heading for paragraph B:
A The consequences of irritation
B The chemistry of emotion
C The causes of anger

Questions 7–14

Target time: 12 minutes
Target score: ___ / 8

The reading passage has ten paragraphs, **A–J**.
*Choose the correct heading for paragraphs **C–J** from the list of headings below.*
*Write the correct number **i–x** next to Questions 7–14.*

Example: Paragraph **B** **x**

List of Headings

- **i** Reality isn't important
- **ii** Consequences of anger management
- **iii** The best method of exercise?
- **iv** Lovers stay younger
- **v** Many reasons to be thankful
- **vi** Problems linked to crying
- **vii** Avoiding negative emotions
- **viii** Let your sadness show
- **ix** Surprising impact of love
- ~~**x** The consequences of irritation~~

7 Paragraph **C**
8 Paragraph **D**
9 Paragraph **E**
10 Paragraph **F**
11 Paragraph **G**
12 Paragraph **H**
13 Paragraph **I**
14 Paragraph **J**

Vocabulary extra

1 Find words in the text that mean the following.
- a exhausting (paragraph A)
- b showing or feeling slight anger (paragraph B)
- c sudden shows of emotion (paragraph B)
- d worry (paragraph D)
- e relaxing (paragraph E)
- f feeling thankful (paragraph H)

2 Write true sentences for you using the words you found.

Explore further

5 In which part of the IELTS test might you have to describe your feelings?

6 Visualise yourself doing something you love. Tell a partner about it and describe your feelings when you do the activity.

➤ **IELTS quiz**
page 7, question 7

LISTENING

LESSON AIMS

- Section 1: Conversation between two speakers
- Notes and flow-chart completion

1 In which place would you do these things?

report to reception   sit in the waiting room   have a consultation
pick up a prescription   lie down   register with the practice   make an appointment

2 What order would you do them in?

Prepare to listen

3 Look at Questions 1–5 below and answer these questions (a–c).

a Which question asks you to give a time?
b Say the time 15:15 in three different ways.
c Look at Question 4. Why is the answer *3.15pm* not possible?

4 Think about how you register at a health centre in your country. Try and predict the answers in the flow chart (Questions 6–10).

5 1.27 **You're going to hear someone registering at a medical practice. Listen to the first part of the conversation and answer Questions 1–5.**

Questions 1–5

Complete the notes below. Write ***NO MORE THAN THREE WORDS AND/OR A NUMBER*** *for each answer.*

Notes about UMP (medical centre)
Five **1** .... doctors.
Iranian doctor: Dr **2** ....
His clinics are on **3** ....
Urgent appointments – call early morning or at **4** .... in the afternoon.
After hours, contact (01345) **5** ....

6 1.28 **Listen to the second part of the conversation and answer Questions 6–10.**

Questions 6–10

Complete the flow chart below.
Write ***NO MORE THAN THREE WORDS AND/OR A NUMBER*** *for each answer.*

Registration process

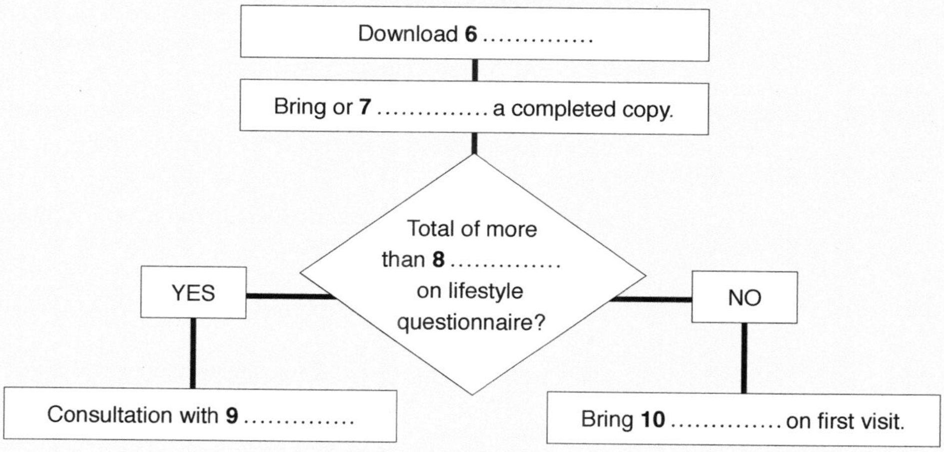
Download **6** ....
Bring or **7** .... a completed copy.
Total of more than **8** .... on lifestyle questionnaire?
YES
NO
Consultation with **9** ....
Bring **10** .... on first visit.

Explore further **7 The speakers mentioned a lifestyle questionnaire. What topics do you think might be included?**

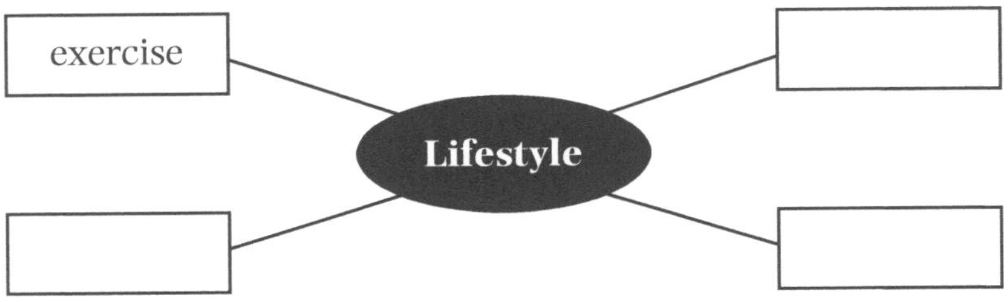

8 Add questions to this lifestyle questionnaire, then ask a partner the questions.

1 How often do you exercise?
2 How many portions of fruit and vegetables do you eat every day?
3 ____________________
4 ____________________
5 ____________________
6 ____________________

➤ **IELTS quiz**
page 8, question 7

SPEAKING

LESSON AIMS

- Part 2: Long turn
- Grouping words
- Talking about physical activities

1 Discuss these questions with a partner.

1 Do you do many physical activities? Why? / Why not?
2 What physical activities do you most enjoy doing?

Vocabulary focus **2 Write these activities in the correct category (A–E), then add one more activity to each category.**

aerobics ☐ baseball ☐ judo ☐ karate ☐ kite surfing ☐ long jump ☐
rugby ☐ scuba diving ☐ sprinting ☐ yoga ☐

A Gym classes: ____________________
B Track and field: ____________________
C Water sports: ____________________
D Martial arts: ____________________
E Ball games: ____________________

3 1.29 **Listen to five people each describing an activity from Exercise 2. Write the number of the speaker next to the correct sport.**

Prepare to speak **4 Look at this Speaking Part 2 task. Write the name of the sport you would choose to speak about, and tell a partner why.**

> Describe a physical activity that is popular in your country.
> You should say:
> what the activity is
> who does it and where
> how you do the activity
> and explain why you think the activity is popular.

5 🎧 **1.30–1.31 Listen to two candidates attempting the task and answer the *You're the examiner* questions.**

> **You're the examiner**
> Which candidate:
> **1** gives information in a logical order?
> **2** uses precise vocabulary?
> **3** gives lots of extra details?

Pronunciation focus

6 🎧 **1.32 Look at these sentences and put a forward slash (/) where you would pause slightly. Then listen and repeat the sentences.**

1 Some people just do it to get fit but others do it to protect themselves.
2 You need regular classes and it takes a long time to prepare for the assessments.
3 Martial arts such as karate, judo and taekwondo are popular in my country.
4 Anyone can do karate but it's not popular with older people because you get lots of injuries.
5 Lessons often happen in gyms or sports halls which have the special equipment we need.

> **Boost your band score** *Grouping words (chunking)*
> As you speak, pause between groups of words. This will also help your speech sound more controlled and easier to understand.

Over to you

7 Prepare this Speaking Part 2 task. Speak to a partner on the topic for two minutes.

> **Describe a dangerous sport that is popular in your country.**
> **You should say:**
> **what it is**
> **where people do it**
> **why it might be dangerous**
> **and explain why it is so popular.**

8 Feed back to your partner. Use the *You're the examiner* box to help you.

WRITING

LESSON AIMS

- Task 1: Describing processes
- Using passives and linkers

1 **Life expectancy has doubled in the past 150 years. Rank these factors in order of importance (1 = most important, 6 = least important).**

Vaccines have been invented. ❑
Clean running water has become more widely available. ❑
Diets have improved. ❑
Sewers and drains have been put in. ❑
Soap has become more widely used. ❑
The standard of housing has improved. ❑

2 **Compare your rankings with a partner's.**

Prepare to write

3 **Look at the diagram below. Find two similarities and two differences between the past and the present.**

The diagram below illustrates the main stages of soap production in the past and present. Summarise the information by selecting and reporting the main features, and make comparisons where relevant.

Soap production past and present

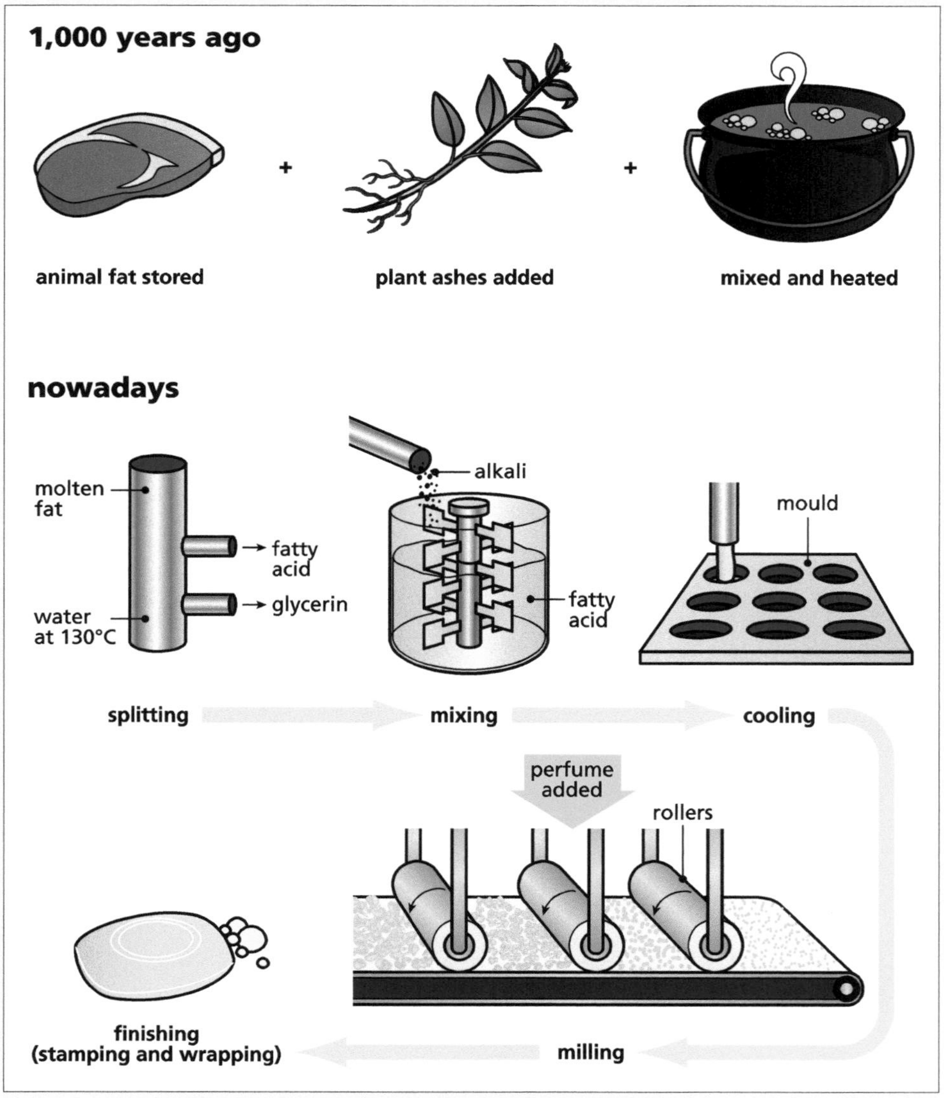

4 Read these two extracts from sample answers, then answer the *You're the examiner* questions.

Candidate 1

> The flow charts reveal how soap production has changed. In general, the modern process would still be recognisable to a manufacturer from the past, but it has become much more industrialised. 1,000 years ago, people mixed fat from animals and plant ashes together and they then heated them …

Candidate 2

> *The diagram shows the main stages of soap production. In the past, there were two basic ingredients to soap: animal fat and plant ashes. After these had been mixed together, they were then heated …*

You're the examiner

Which candidate has successfully …

1 included an overview of the diagram?
2 avoided using words from the question?
3 used the passive?

Language focus

5 Use the diagram in Exercise 3 to complete this description. Write each verb in brackets in the correct form of the passive.

The modern process involves five basic stages. First, animal fat in a molten state 1 ________ (*add*) to a large, vertical container and mixed with water which 2 ________ (*fed*) into it from the other end at 130 degrees Celcius. This produces glycerine and fatty acid. Then, these products 3 ________ (*mix*) together again in a new container, together with an alkali substance. Once this new mixture 4 ________ (*cool*) in a mould, the hardened forms 5 ________ (*mill*) under large rollers. It is at this stage that perfume 6 ________ (*often / add*). After the milling 7 ________ (*complete*), the pieces 8 ________ (*press*) together into a bar shape, which 9 ________ (*then / stamp*) and wrapped, ready for distribution to shops.

6 Underline the linking words in the paragraph above.

Boost your band score *Linking words*

Flow charts and pictures that show processes usually require you to describe the stages in which something happens. Using linking words to move between stages and the passive to highlight the process rather than who is involved can help boost your score.

Over to you

7 Turn to page 92 and complete Task 5.

8 Exchange your work with a partner. Use the *You're the examiner* and *Boost your band score* boxes to evaluate their writing.

- Underline the overview of the diagram.
- Circle synonyms of the words and phrases used in the question.
- Highlight any use of the passive.

9 Turn to page 100 and compare your answer with sample answer 9.

UNIT 6 The environment

TOPIC FOCUS

1 Match the photos with the environmental problem.

air pollution   deforestation   extreme weather events   resource depletion
soil degradation   species loss   waste   water pollution

1 

2 

3 

4 

5 

6 

7 

8 

2 Discuss these questions with a partner.

1 Which problems are most serious where you live?
2 Do you worry about any of the problems? Why? / Why not?

➤ **IELTS quiz**
page 6, question 8

READING

LESSON AIMS

- Review: Matching paragraph headings
- Summary completion (with word pool)

1 The table below shows the percentage of people from 12 countries who think certain environmental problems are very serious. Answer these questions.

1 Which problem caused people to worry most?
2 Did people worry more in 2012 than in 1992?

	1992	**2012**
Air quality	62%	51%
Water pollution	64%	58%
Loss of natural resources	42%	38%

(source: Globescan)

2 Look at the title of the reading passage on page 59 and skim-read the text. Would the author like to:

a explain the trend in the table?
b reverse the trend in the table?
c both of the above?

Skills focus **3 What can you remember about 'matching paragraph headings' tasks from Unit 5? Discuss your task strategy with a partner, then attempt Questions 1–7 on page 60 based on the reading passage.**

Nature calls: why aren't we answering?

A Air pollution has created health emergencies in many cities; extreme weather events are occurring four to five times more often than they used to; and at present rates of decline, rainforests may disappear within a hundred years ... the world is facing major environmental threats. Not surprisingly, then, media stories on environmental topics have become increasingly common over the past 30 years, and this has no doubt increased our awareness of the issues. But do we, the world's citizens, actually care? We might expect to have seen an increase in protests and calls for government action. But a recent Globescan poll showed that levels of concern over the environment across 12 countries recently reached their lowest point in 20 years. Why has interest in environmental issues not risen in line with the problems, and what can we do about it?

B Lack of concern tends to be greatest among poorer populations, suggesting that one cause may be economic. This pattern is certainly ironic. After all, the greatest environmental threats, like extreme weather events or deforestation, are experienced in poorer countries, and it is the poor who are most likely to be affected by environmental damage, since they are often forced to live in areas where pollution or flood risk is particularly high. But it is also not surprising. Put simply, when people face financial difficulties, they tend not to focus on complex issues like the environment. Rising global inequality and the failure of governments to improve the plight of the poor may have made the environment a lower political priority in precisely the areas where it should be high. Incidentally, the pattern can be seen in richer countries too, where children from less affluent backgrounds express less interest in nature than better-off children.

C A further reason for this lack of interest among poorer communities in developed countries may be that they tend to reside in inner-city areas. Living away from nature is said to reduce 'nature connectedness', which includes a desire to protect nature. Given that urban population levels have in fact now overtaken those of rural areas, an increase in city living generally may be undermining interest in environmentalism. This does not mean that people have no *knowledge* of nature. Awareness of 'rural' environmental issues, like water pollution, soil degradation or deforestation, is actually higher among educated city dwellers. But it does mean urban inhabitants may be less concerned about protecting the environment.

D Urbanisation aside, there has perhaps been a more general tendency in the modern world to engage less with nature. One recent study from the UK claims that three-quarters of children spend less time outside than prison inmates, and that one in nine has not visited a park, beach, forest or any other natural environment during the preceding year. Fear of strangers, traffic or accidents is deterring parents and teachers from allowing children to go outside. What's more, the quality of modern digital entertainment has left many youngsters happily 'cocooned' in their bedrooms, weakening still further their engagement with the natural world.

E We should also note that there is a great deal of competition for our attention in modern times. Some argue that the long-term, persistent nature of environmental threats means that media stories about them make less impact and go out of fashion more quickly than new issues, like terrorism. There are also greater demands on our time these days. Many managers claim they are working longer hours, and most full-time workers claim that it is becoming increasingly difficult to find work–life balance. This is partly because wages are failing to keep up with living expenses but also because fewer workers have partners at home who can help with childcare, and many are taking work home. We may simply be too preoccupied with other issues to worry about the great threat that looms over us.

F An interesting solution may therefore be to help people make a connection between their lifestyles and the environment. If protecting nature can also improve people's standard of living, they may support green causes. This idea lies behind many tourism initiatives in developing countries that ask locals to protect the environment in exchange for a share of the proceeds of eco-tourism. In wealthier nations, the principle has been used to persuade people to embrace solar energy or electrical vehicle technology in return for a promise of lower living costs. Similarly, efforts have been made to link the organic agriculture movement to improvements in public health. But such targeted steps are unlikely to increase levels of environmental concern more generally.

G For many, the solution is simply to put people back in touch with nature, and since 30% of the world's population is under 18, the obvious place to start is with the young. Some governments are planning to increase the number of educational trips to national parks that are available to young people, and others are attempting to introduce gardening and conservation trips into the science curriculum. Local governments, for their part, are bringing nature into the cities through the creation of more green spaces and 'urban forest' initiatives. While many of these steps may have the primary aim of increasing public health, it is hoped that they may also reawaken interest in nature and conservation. Will they be successful? According to some research, one day spent in a national park was sufficient to make young people more connected with nature. Besides, the alternative, to take action only when natural disasters have already unfolded, is clearly unsustainable.

Questions 1–7

Target time: 11 minutes
Target score: ____ / 7

The reading passage has seven paragraphs, **A–G**.
*Choose the correct heading for paragraphs **A–G** from the list of headings below.*
*Write the correct number **i–ix** next to Questions **1–7**.*

List of Headings

i	Giving people reasons to care
ii	How poverty affects opinion
iii	Technology replacing nature
iv	Renewed contact with the natural world
v	Attitudes in urban areas
vi	A lack of environmental concern
vii	Environmental problems in rural areas
viii	The effects of indoors living
ix	A range of competing priorities

1 Paragraph **A**
2 Paragraph **B**
3 Paragraph **C**
4 Paragraph **D**
5 Paragraph **E**
6 Paragraph **F**
7 Paragraph **G**

4 Do the tasks in the *Strategy focus* box. Then answer Questions 8–12 based on the same reading passage.

Strategy focus *Summary completion*

1 Read the sentence below. What part of speech is required in the gap: an uncountable noun or a plural noun? How do you know?
We worry less about nature now, despite the growing number of ____________ concerning the environment over the past few decades.

2 Look at these options. Which three words could fit the gap above?
articles disasters emergency media problems serious

3 Read the first paragraph of the passage again. Underline the sentence that refers to a growing number of something.

4 Which of the three options you chose in step 2 matches the meaning in the text that you underlined in step 3?

Questions 8–12

Target time: 8 minutes
Target score: ____ / 5

*Complete the summary using the list of words, **A–K**, below. Write the correct letter **A–K** in the gaps.*

There are a variety of reasons why interest in environmental issues has not grown. People with little **8** .... don't focus on complex issues, and we are increasingly living in urban areas, where people **9** .... less about the environment. In both urban and rural areas, the perception that local areas are **10** .... and the popularity of new types of **11** .... mean that many young people are spending less time outdoors. What's more, there are so many other things to worry about in today's world, like the cost of living and **12** .... news stories.

A serious	**E** money	**I** technology	**M** boring
B education	**F** understanding	**J** current	**N** polluted
C worry	**G** transport	**K** dangerous	
D know	**H** time	**L** crime	

Vocabulary extra

1 Look at the reading passage again and find words from the same word families as these.
connect engage environment urban

2 Decide what type of word each one is: adjective, countable noun or abstract noun.

3 How many more words can you find in the same word families? Use your dictionary. Find an example sentence for each.

Explore further **5 In pairs, discuss how these activities might harm the environment. Which of them would you be prepared to give up?**

- using your car
- flying
- showering daily
- buying imported food
- using plastic bags
- drinking bottled water

LISTENING

LESSON AIMS

- Section 2: Monologue
- Sentence and summary completion

1 Which of these natural areas do you have in your country?

deserts

forests

nature reserves

mountains

glaciers

jungles

rivers

coastline

2 Tell your partner:

1 which natural areas in your country are the most famous.
2 where they're located.
3 if these areas are protected.

Prepare to listen

3 Look at Questions 1–10 below and answer these questions (a–c).

a What topic is being discussed in Questions 1–5?
b How are Questions 6–10 connected to Questions 1–5?
c Underline the key ideas in each sentence of Questions 6–10. (The first one has been done for you.) What synonyms or similar expressions can you think of?

4 2.2 You're going to hear a presentation by a school headteacher. Listen and answer Questions 1–10.

Questions 1–5

*Complete the summary. Write **NO MORE THAN TWO WORDS** for each answer.*

Summary of council plans

There are plans to create some new **1** .... , which means that the school would lose the **2** .... at the back of the art block, which is used for **3** .... about nature and some lessons too. The council would also need to put an **4** .... through one of the school fields. In return, the school will gain football pitches and a **5** ....

Questions 6–10

*Complete the sentences. Write **NO MORE THAN TWO WORDS AND/OR A NUMBER** for each answer.*

6 People at the meeting are asked to .... for a different plan.
7 The school plans to .... the people who use the nature area.
8 Plants and animals in the nature area aren't very ....
9 People are needed to help produce a .... and develop a social media profile.
10 Information about the campaign will be posted to ....

Explore further

5 How much do you agree or disagree with each of these statements? (1 = strongly disagree, 6 = strongly agree)

1 New buildings and roads should not be built if they damage the local area.	1	2	3	4	5	6
2 All cities should provide more green spaces.	1	2	3	4	5	6
3 Economic development is more important than protecting the environment.	1	2	3	4	5	6
4 Animals should not be protected. Extinction is a normal part of change in the world.	1	2	3	4	5	6
5 Many cities are 'unliveable' because of the damage caused by people.	1	2	3	4	5	6

6 Compare your opinions with a partner's. Give reasons for your choices.

➤ **IELTS quiz**
page 8, question 6

SPEAKING

LESSON AIMS

- Part 3: Evaluating
- Adding expressions to fill and structure speech

1 How do you think the water on Earth is distributed? Label the pie charts with the words and phrases from the boxes.

sea water water with no salt
H_2O in atmosphere

ice under the ground rivers and lakes

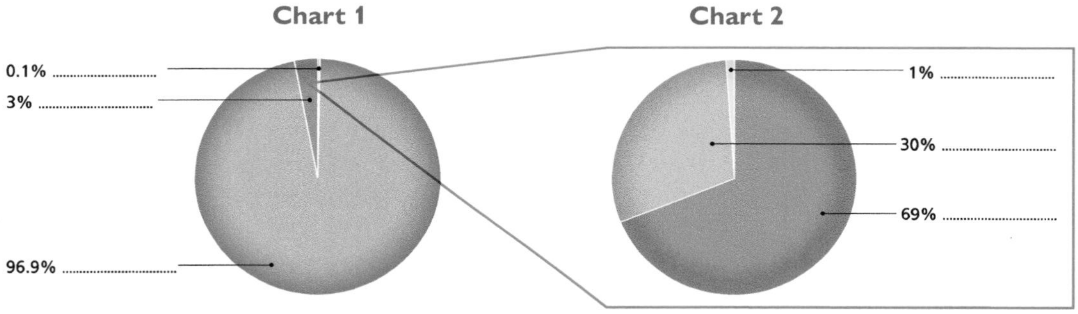

The relative quantities of various types of water on Earth

2 Does the information in the pie charts surprise you?

Vocabulary focus

3 Match the labels in the pie charts with these synonyms.

a surface water **d** saltwater
b glaciers **e** groundwater
c freshwater **f** vapour

4 Complete the diagram with the words and phrases from the box.

canals coasts
harbours ports
potable water
reservoirs
running water
sewerage waterfalls
white water

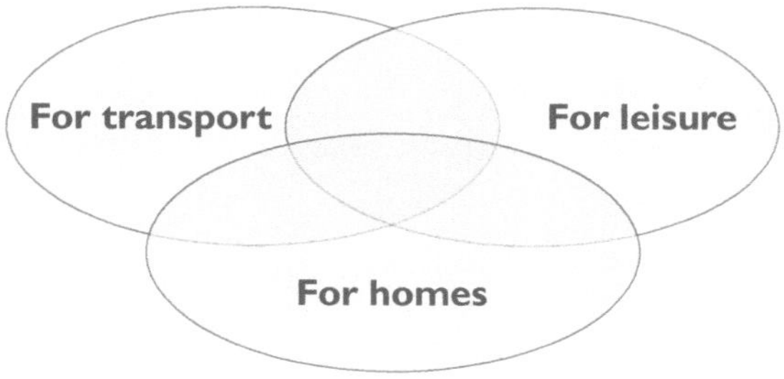

5 Look again at the words and phrases in Exercise 4. Which are commonly found in your country?

Prepare to speak

6 These Part 3 questions are about two topics: a) being near water and b) using water at home. Decide which topic each question relates to and write (a) or (b) beside each one.

1 What are the advantages and disadvantages of living near water? ____
2 Why do some people like walking by rivers or along coasts? ____
3 Did people in the past consume more or less water than people now? Why? ____
4 How do industrial cities benefit from being close to rivers or seas? ____
5 Some people use more water in homes and gardens than others. Is this fair? ____
6 What can governments do to stop us wasting so much water? ____

7 2.3–2.5 Listen to three candidates responding to one of the questions in Exercise 6. Which question is each speaker answering?

8 2.3–2.5 Listen again and answer the *You're the examiner* questions.

> **You're the examiner**
> Which candidate:
> **1** structures their answer most clearly?
> **2** uses 'filler' expressions to help continue speaking?
> **3** demonstrates the greatest range of grammar and vocabulary?

Fluency focus

9 Look at audio transcripts 2.3–2.5 on page 109. Underline the expressions or other words that Candidates 2 and 3 use to a) fill gaps and b) structure language.

10 Find expressions in the transcripts that are used to:

1 give your main idea.
2 introduce an explanation (*two expressions*).
3 make a new, less important point.
4 show you're still thinking.
5 suggest that information is unusual/surprising.
6 explain the question is difficult for you.

11 Complete the extract below with the expressions from the box.

> Actually for example Generally speaking I mean most importantly um Well What else Without doubt

[1]__________, trade is the biggest advantage. [2]__________, the closer a city is to water, the more it can import raw materials – coal and timber, [3]__________ – and, [4]__________, sell products. [5]__________? [6]__________, it's useful for travellers too, I suppose. [7]__________, it provides a way for them to ... [8]__________ ... access cities. [9]__________, many come by plane and car nowadays, but water transport is still popular for tourists.

> **Boost your band score** *Filling and structuring speech*
> Adding expressions into your speech to fill gaps and structure language will help a listener to understand you. Most importantly, it will help you improve your fluency score.

Over to you

12 2.6 Listen to the questions. In pairs, take turns to answer. You will have 25 seconds after each question to respond.

13 Feed back to your partner. Use the *You're the examiner* box to help you.

➤ **IELTS quiz**
page 9, question 7

WRITING

LESSON AIMS

- Task 2: Answering explanation questions
- Connecting ideas with pronouns

1 Look at these statistics about waste. Which one do you find most shocking?

- Each year, 35 million mobile phones are disposed of.
- Every year, consumers in industrialised countries waste almost as much food as the entire net food production of sub-Saharan Africa (222 million vs 230 million tons).
- In Europe, more than 60% of functioning flat-screen TVs were replaced for an upgrade in 2012, but only a quarter of purchases were made to replace a faulty product.
- The Whitegoods Trade Association estimate that the life expectancy of a washing machine has decreased by three years in the past decade.

2 How do high levels of waste affect the environment? Discuss your answers with a partner.

3

> France has become so worried about the trend towards throwing things away that a law has recently been introduced to force manufacturers to say how long a product is expected to last.

Work with a partner. What other laws would you introduce to deal with excessive waste?

Prepare to write

4 Read this task. How many questions are there?

> You should spend about 40 minutes on this task.
> Write about the following topic:
>
> ***Modern consumers buy new products instead of mending old possessions. Why does this happen, and what are the consequences?***
>
> Give reasons for your answer and include any relevant examples from your knowledge or experience.
> Write at least 250 words.

5 Look at the 'brainstorm' on the left for the first part of the essay. Put ideas A–F under the correct topics (1–3).

A poor design
B frequent product launches
C cheap materials
D increase in advertising
E people are wealthier
F no time to mend things

6 Read this paragraph about the first topic, marketing. Has the writer told us the topic first or the two ideas from the brainstorm?

> One reason for this trend is the way companies market products. For example, they use aggressive advertising to sell their stock and they frequently launch new products. This encourages people to buy more goods.

7 Read the next paragraph and a) circle the ways the writer avoids repeating *products*, and b) underline the pronouns that refer to earlier ideas in the paragraph.

> Another reason is the way that products are made. Today, consumer goods are produced with poor-quality parts, and these are designed to fail within a few years. The companies do this intentionally and make each individual item expensive to buy when replacing it. As a result, it is usually cheaper and quicker to simply order a complete new item than to attempt to repair the old one.

8 Read these two extracts from the second part of the essay, then answer the *You're the examiner* questions.

Candidate 1

Several problems have emerged from this constant cycle of purchasing. Examples include the difficulty of dealing with increasingly high levels of consumer waste. Many of the items we throw away end up in landfill, but a great deal is shipped to the waste dumps of other countries. Furthermore, there simply aren't the resources to maintain a high level of production ...

Candidate 2

There is a lot of waste created by society. Some of the rubbish created by society is necessary but much of it originates from society not repairing old products and simply throwing them away. The new products that replace them are made using valuable raw materials. Shipping them uses up valuable energy resources too.

You're the examiner

Which candidate has successfully:

1 included a clear topic sentence?
2 used synonyms to repeat ideas?
3 used pronouns to refer back to earlier ideas?

Language focus

9 Complete the sentences with the pronouns from the box on the left.

it	one	their
they	these	this

1 Students may find it is essential to purchase a new edition. __________ might not be able to use the older __________ .
2 Every company can influence how long a product lasts. __________ aim for higher profits often means __________ has a shorter life.
3 Individuals do not always demand the latest product. __________ misconception is created by companies who want to create a throw-away culture.
4 Many factors impact on people's attitude to consumption. __________ range from low prices to fashion trends.

10 Write the third paragraph of the essay on the topic of 'consumers'. Use synonyms and pronouns to connect your ideas.

Boost your band score *Using pronouns and synonyms*

Candidates often over-use connecting words such as *however, furthermore* and *whereas* to organise their work. While these are useful, don't use them again and again. Using pronouns and synonyms also helps to create well-organised and less repetitive work.

Over to you

11 Complete the task.

You should spend about 40 minutes on this task.
Write about the following topic:

Many people choose to shop at large supermarkets rather than at local shops. What effects does this have on our lives and on the environment?

Give reasons for your answer and include any relevant examples from your knowledge or experience.
Write at least 250 words.

12 Exchange your work with a partner. Use the *You're the examiner* and *Boost your band score* boxes to evaluate their writing.

- Circle any pronouns used. Which earlier idea do they refer to?
- Underline the main ideas. What synonyms do they use to refer back to them?

Then turn to page 101 and compare your answer with sample answer 10.

Reading

Answer Questions 1–14 based on the reading passage.

Questions 1–8

The reading passage has eight paragraphs, **A–H**.
*Choose the correct heading for paragraphs **A–H** from the list of headings below.*
*Write the correct number **i–x** next to Questions **1–8**.*

List of Headings

i	Medicine in the Muslim world
ii	Rising status of medical knowledge
iii	Ending the ageing process
iv	Improving standards of care
v	Early operations
vi	Evidence of early medical practice
vii	Defeating the world's killers
viii	The hope of medical advancement
ix	A set of ideas still relevant today
x	A new approach to medicine

1 Paragraph **A**
2 Paragraph **B**
3 Paragraph **C**
4 Paragraph **D**
5 Paragraph **E**
6 Paragraph **F**
7 Paragraph **G**
8 Paragraph **H**

Questions 9–14

*Complete the summary using the list of words, **A–L**, below. Write the correct letter **A–L** in the gaps.*

There is a long history of the study of medicine. The first **9** .... were simple, and medical knowledge often depended on key individuals. In fact, many of the **10** .... used in medicine were first conceived by one man, Hippocrates. It is only in the last 800 years that medical **11** .... began. But individuals continued to play a key role. Florence Nightingale, in particular, helped to improve the **12** .... in hospitals. In the 20th century, the medical world was transformed by the development of **13** ...., and some scientists are currently studying how to stop organisms becoming **14** ....

A treatments	**E** research	**I** science
B operations	**F** education	**J** old
C rules	**G** ill	**K** vaccinations
D equipment	**H** words	**L** conditions

A brief history of medicine

A From eradicating diseases to transferring organs, medicine has come a long way over the centuries. However, many of the basic procedures that people think of as modern are actually thousands of years old. The oldest medical books date back to around 1000BC. Many of these early books introduced the practices of diagnosis, prognosis, physical examination and remedies. These texts contain lists of medical symptoms and often detailed empirical observations. In most cultures at this time, the remedies were quite basic, and the symptoms and diseases of a patient were treated through therapeutic means such as bandages, herbs and creams. However, in many countries, even some basic surgery was being practised at this time.

B One such form of medicine known for describing a range of these early surgical procedures is Ayurveda. Ayurveda is a medical system developed in India. The word can be translated literally as 'complete knowledge for long life'. Its basic principles are that health and disease are not predetermined and life may be prolonged by human effort. One of the early books in this field is notable for describing rhinoplasty, the repair of torn ear lobes, perineal lithotomy, eye surgery and several other procedures. In total, it describes over 125 surgical instruments and 300 surgical interventions.

C As each culture developed its own insights, many prominent figures rose up in particular fields. In Europe, one such figure was the physician Hippocrates of Kos (Greece), who is considered the 'father of Western medicine'. He is given credit for the description of many medical conditions from lung cancer to heart disease, categorising them as 'acute', 'chronic', 'endemic' and 'epidemic', and using terms such as *exacerbation, relapse, resolution, crisis, paroxysm, peak* and *convalescence*. His teachings remain relevant to present-day students of pulmonary medicine and surgery, and even today the 'Hippocratic oath', which states the obligations and proper conduct of doctors, is still used in some medical schools. Unfortunately, after 400AD, much of his work was lost to Europe, as the Roman Empire went into decline. His works were largely kept alive in the Muslim world, and only in the 12th century did translations come back from Muslim and Jewish sources in Spain.

D Until the 13th century, much medical knowledge had come through talented individuals or groups of scientists working together. There was no opportunity for the formal study of medicine. In 1220, the University of Padua was founded, and it began teaching medicine in 1222. The university played a leading role in the identification and treatment of diseases and ailments. By the 18th century, science was held in high regard, and doctors could improve their social status by proving their knowledge through using scientific practices. Unfortunately, the health field was crowded with self-trained surgeons, nurses and many other frauds. Medical education largely relied on lectures and readings, and students had very little opportunity to practise surgery. But the professionalisation of medicine was by now well under way.

E Although having a professional status was widely regarded as positive, it did have the downside of pushing women to one side. Most women at the time did not have access to formal education, and so the profession became closed to them or they were pushed to the side in minor roles. However, one nurse active in the 19th century, Florence Nightingale, resolved to professionalise the role. The model she developed was widely copied around the world in countries such as Russia, America and Japan. Not only did she manage to achieve this, but she also pioneered the analysis of large amounts of statistical data, using graphs and tables, to evaluate the performance of hospital services. Her analytical methods also played a huge role in raising people's awareness of the importance of hygiene in hospitals.

F Medicine was revolutionised in the 19th century and beyond by advances in chemistry and laboratory techniques and equipment. Both bacteriology and virology rose to prominence under the research of Pasteur, Koch and Cohen. To the general public, Louis Pasteur was perhaps most famous for the development of pasteurisation – a process that made milk safe to drink. However, it was his research into the vaccination of animals against different diseases that helped develop the field so much. In fact, it is often said that English surgeon Edward Jenner discovered the concept of vaccination and that Pasteur invented vaccines that could actually be used. This ushered in the era of preventative medicine such as antibiotics – no longer were we limited to treating illnesses, but science was enabling us to prevent them.

G In 1948, the World Health Organization was founded as a United Nations agency to improve global health. Vaccines have allowed humans to contemplate the elimination of many potentially fatal diseases. The long-known vaccine against smallpox finally eradicated the disease in the 1970s, and Rinderpest was cleared in 2011. To combat infectious diseases, it takes an international effort. Many new vaccines have been developed against infections such as measles, mumps, several strains of influenza and human papilloma virus. It is likely in the near future that polio will also be eradicated. The World Health Organization has also enabled people to develop a response system against epidemics such as SARS in 2003, Influenza A virus subtype H5N1 ('bird flu') in 2004, and Ebola virus in West Africa in 2015.

H The rise of vaccination and improved hygiene standards around the world have led to an increase in life expectancy, as infectious diseases are now less frequently lethal. However, modern lifestyles have seen an increase in other common causes of death. In the developed world, the most common causes of death today are tumours and heart disease. Can the medical world rise to the challenge of these new threats? Cancer treatment has certainly improved dramatically over the last few decades. In some cases, science fiction may be about to become science fact. A group of scientists in California are studying the Laron Syndrome condition, a rare condition that makes people age more slowly. Perhaps we are even in the early stages of developing drugs that make humans live for ever.

Listening

Section 1 2.7

Questions 1–5

Complete the notes.
Write ***NO MORE THAN TWO WORDS AND/OR A NUMBER*** *for each answer.*

Jungle Jim – tree-top adventure course!

Available days:	**1** .... morning
Time needed to complete the tree-top adventure:	**2** ....
Difficulty:	Three levels of difficulty; the **3** .... is the easiest!
Preparation:	Bring **4** .... with you and coats in case it rains.
	Wear **5** ....

Questions 6–10

Complete the flowchart.
Write ***NO MORE THAN TWO WORDS OR A NUMBER*** *for each answer.*

Course introduction process

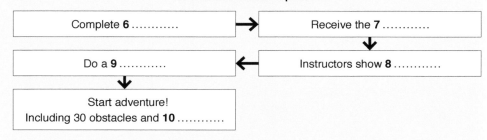

Complete **6** .... → Receive the **7** .... → Instructors show **8** .... → Do a **9** .... → Start adventure! Including 30 obstacles and **10** ....

Section 2 2.8

Questions 11–13

Choose the correct letter, ***A***, ***B*** *or* ***C***.

11 Which people are most at risk from water?
- **A** Walkers
- **B** Runners and cyclists
- **C** Young people

12 What problem with picnics is discussed?
- **A** Lack of water
- **B** Leaving bottles
- **C** Carrying too much

13 What advice is given about walking through fields with animals?
- **A** Walk quickly through a field.
- **B** Keep dogs close to you.
- **C** Keep to the edge of the field.

Questions 14 and 15

Choose ***TWO*** *letters,* ***A–F***.
Which ***TWO*** *items does the speaker suggest taking on longer walks?*

- **A** A medical kit
- **B** A warm hat
- **C** Money for shops
- **D** Snacks
- **E** A blanket
- **F** A working mobile

Questions 16–20

Complete the summary. Write ***NO MORE THAN TWO WORDS*** *for each answer.*

Two keen walkers had come to Grimswick on their **16** .... Despite being well-prepared with boots and **17** .... for walking, one of them hurt her **18** .... This slowed them down and before long, they found themselves stuck in the mountains because they didn't have a **19** .... that worked. They had to spend a night out in the cold, and one of them began to suffer from hypothermia. Luckily, the **20** .... called the emergency services, who took them to hospital.

Speaking

Part 1 **EITHER**

a 2.9 **Listen and answer eight questions on two topics. After each question, you will have 15 seconds to respond.**

OR

b **Turn to audio transcript 2.9 on page 110. Ask and answer the questions with a partner.**

Part 2 **Prepare to speak about the topic on the card below. Think or make notes for one minute. Speak for between one and two minutes about the topic on the card. Record yourself or ask a partner to listen to you.**

Describe a sporting event that made you feel disappointed.
You should say:
what the event was
who was participating in the event
what happened during the event
and explain why you felt disappointed.

Part 3 **EITHER**

a 2.10 **Listen and answer nine questions on three topics. After each question, you will have 25 seconds to respond.**

OR

b **Turn to audio transcript 2.10 on page 110. Ask and answer the questions with a partner**

Writing

Task 1
You should spend about 20 minutes on this task. Turn to Task 6 on page 92.

Task 2
You should spend about 40 minutes on this task.
Write about the following topic:

In modern life, there is an increasing range of health risks, from poor air quality to traffic accidents and fatty foods. Which risks are the most difficult to protect people against, and what steps can individuals take to protect themselves?

Give reasons for your answer and include any relevant examples from your knowledge or experience.
Write at least 250 words.

UNIT 7 Work

TOPIC FOCUS

1 Match the brands (1–6) with the types of business (a–f).

1

2

3

4

5

6

a technology company
b car manufacturer
c fast-food chain
d online retailer
e financial services provider
f energy company

2 Which of the companies in Exercise 1 would you most like to work for? Why?

➤ **IELTS quiz**
page 6, question 9

READING

LESSON AIMS

- Summary completion (without word pool)
- Matching information

1 Complete the sectors with the words *manufacturing*, *medicine* and *mining*.

1 Primary sector: fishing, farming, ___________
2 Secondary sector: construction, carpentry, ___________
3 Tertiary sector: teaching, accountancy, ___________

2 Discuss these questions with a partner.

1 In which sector have machines taken over the most human jobs?
2 Could machines do all the jobs in Exercise 1?
3 Skim the reading passage on page 71. Does the author think machines will take over all jobs?

Skills focus

3 Look at Questions 1–7 on page 72. How is this task different from the summary completion task on page 60?

4 Questions 1–7 require a similar strategy to sentence-completion tasks. What can you remember about these tasks from Unit 3? Discuss your task strategy with a partner.

A world without work?

A Ever since societies began to industrialise, people have been asking whether machines will one day take over all our jobs, leaving humans to lead a life of leisure. Many of the posts in factories and farms, which used to provide employment for countless labourers, have long since become mechanised. Now, as computers become more powerful, service jobs in retail, accountancy and medicine are also said to be under threat. And as the age of humanoid robotics dawns, the prospect of mass unemployment for all of us seems closer than ever. Androids are being developed to fulfill a variety of roles, from prison guards and bartenders to receptionists and care workers.

B The prospect of a machine-led workforce raises serious questions for both politicians and economists. For example, if the profits from business go to a narrow class of machine owners, what impact will this have on inequality? Can we really rely on governments to distribute wealth evenly? And if the number of wage-earners declines in the future, who will there be to purchase all the future fruits of industry? In short, falling employment could cost society dearly. It is therefore important that we ask how close we are to a work-free world.

C One way to approach this question is to ask how likely it is that machines will be able to replicate human qualities. Certainly our ability to work with information, diagnosing problems, analysing trends or quantifying risks and so on are all skills that machines can almost certainly do better. Machines also operate without the weaknesses that human employees suffer from, working accurately and tirelessly without allowing self-interest or emotion to affect judgement. However, there are a variety of qualities that machines are less able to replicate, not least empathy and friendship. It is likely that customers in service transactions will always be happy to pay a premium for real human contact.

D A second approach is to focus on some of the most developed societies to look for signs that employment opportunities are declining. In fact, to date the world's job market has remained fairly robust. Unemployment rates hover at just under 6% and are predicted to fall slightly. This is despite a rapidly growing population worldwide and the absorption of a growing percentage of women into the workforce. Admittedly, manufacturing industries employ fewer in advanced economies, and an increasing proportion of employment may be in low-paid service-sector positions. But so far, there has been little evidence of an impending employment crisis.

E To understand why, it is important to note that although there are fewer jobs in factories these days, industrial productivity has continued to increase, as machines turn out ever larger quantities of goods. All of these need transporting, selling and delivering, and the machines that make them need servicing and inspecting. The increasing success of industry has supported a variety of ancilliary services. Some of these, like logistics, may become increasingly automated, but others, like customer management and advertising, are likely to require a human touch.

F The total volume of economic activity has also increased, thanks to the world wide web, resulting in more employment. The 'internet economy' is larger in value terms than the agricultural sector, accounting for over 5% of the economy in richer countries, and will continue to help establish a greater number of economic connections between producers and buyers. The internet is also facilitating offline economic development, helping put investors in touch with budding entrepreneurs through crowd-funding websites. And it has also created whole new markets for trade. If economic activity continues to grow at this pace, we can afford to lose a few jobs to machines.

G In advanced economies, we have also seen new sectors of the economy opening up, largely thanks to the internet. Growth has been particularly strong in what is known as the quaternary sector: jobs in science, media and design. Scientific and IT hubs like Silicon Valley in California and Silicon Fen near Cambridge are providing jobs for an increasing proportion of their nation's citizens. The Osaka Innovation Hub accounts for a full 40% of new jobs in Japan. Here, the very human skills of networking and creativity help the world's innovators to dream up new ideas, and to research and design revolutionary digital products. In this field, a human workforce is essential.

H We have also seen a growing 'armchair army' of professional internet users, led by the self-publishers. Any blog or e-book that becomes popular can generate income for the author if they agree to publish their content with advertisements, and many have grasped this opportunity. Hundreds of millionaires have been created among those who post videos to YouTube, for example. In addition to self-publishers, there are those who make money in virtual worlds like Second Life, whose users have traded over half a billion dollars in digital goods with each other. And there are those who get paid to watch adverts and fill out surveys too.

I The kind of 'professional consumerism' seen in paying survey respondents seems to represent a broader trend. Companies have long paid 'mystery shoppers' and reviewers to report back on their experiences of service encounters or products, but there seems to be greater willingness to make such payments. A closer look at the Osaka Innovation Hub reveals something about the more active role that consumers might soon play in the world economy. Here, businesses are arranged in a kind of shopping mall that is often teeming with consumers. But rather than taking their money, companies invite them to come in and try out their products so that they can gain feedback. In effect, it is the consumers that provide the service to the businesses.

J In conclusion, as robots begin to take a greater role in our world, we may well be squeezed out of some jobs. But it is probably not the case that we will find ourselves sitting on a deckchair with little to do. Our 'free time' will become time when we generate income, and activities like socialising, writing diaries or taking photos, once amateur pastimes, will become money-making activities. Those able to create ideas, generate content and connect with others will remain in high demand.

5 The summary below describes how the internet is creating new jobs. Find the three paragraphs of the reading passage on page 71 that discuss the internet. Then attempt Questions 1–7 based on the reading passage.

Questions 1–7

Target time: 11 minutes
Target score: ____ / 7

Complete the summary below.
*Choose **NO MORE THAN TWO WORDS** from the passage for each answer.*

The world's jobs market has remained strong, mostly because of the role of the internet. The digital economy has increased **1** .... in the wider economy. For example, it has helped entrepreneurs find **2** .... It has also supported a large expansion of the **3** .... sector in developed countries, and many are finding new jobs in technology **4** .... like Silicon Valley, where human skills, especially creativity and **5** ...., are in great demand. Finally, the internet has given a source of income to many people, from **6** .... to professional consumers. They have been able to earn money either through advertising, trading **7** .... directly, or giving their time.

6 Do the tasks in the *Strategy focus* box. Then answer Questions 8–14 based on the same reading passage.

Strategy focus *Information matching*

1 Look at this question. Why has the student underlined two of the phrases?

> Which paragraph contains this information:
> *Some hobbies you can make money from.*

2 Think of:
   1 words that have the same meaning as *hobby* and *make money*
   2 examples of hobbies.

3 Paragraphs H–J all contain ideas connected to 'hobbies' and 'making money'. Underline the text that matches the sentence above most closely. Which paragraph is it in?

Questions 8–14

Target time: 11 minutes
Target score: ____ / 7

The reading passage has ten paragraphs, **A–J**.
Which paragraph contains the following information?

8 Roles that machines can do better than humans
9 A way of trying products before they enter the shops
10 An expected change in levels of unemployment
11 How much is bought and sold online
12 A comparison between trends in different industries
13 Places where there are many jobs in technology
14 Some new ways people are currently earning money

Vocabulary extra

1 The author of the reading passage on page 71 has tried to avoid using the words *worker* and *job* repeatedly. Read the first four paragraphs again and underline all the words or phrases with a similar meaning. There are four that mean 'workers' and five that mean 'jobs'.

2 Which two of the words you found are from the same word family? Do you know any other words in the same word family? Find some in your dictionaries.

Explore further

7 Which three skills in this table do you think are most important for a) professional YouTubers, b) computer programmers, c) managers?

Learning skills	Literacy skills	Life skills
critical thinking, creative thinking, collaborating, communicating	understanding and using information / media / technology	flexibility, initiative, social skills, productivity, leadership

8 How could a school help students develop skills like those in the table above?

➤ **IELTS quiz**
page 7, question 9

LISTENING

LESSON AIMS

- Section 2: Monologue
- Table completion and multiple choice (images)

1 What are the advantages and disadvantages of doing these jobs? Discuss your ideas with a partner.

accountant

hairdresser

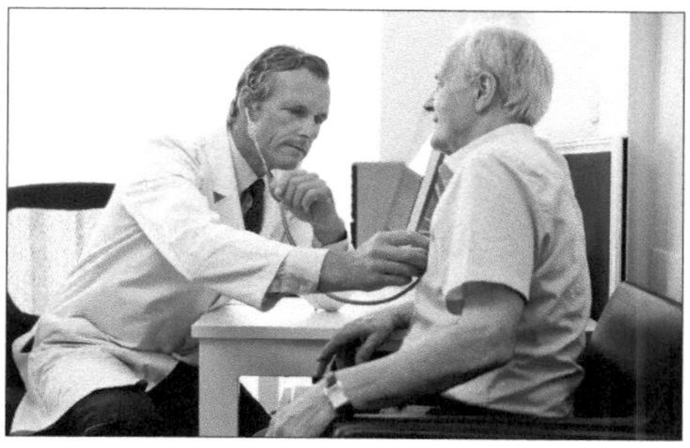

doctor

police officer

Prepare to listen

2 Look at Questions 1–7 below and answer these questions.

1 What might be a suitable heading for each column of the table?
2 What type of information is required in each gap?

3 Look at Questions 8–10 on page 74. Work with a partner and take it in turns to describe the differences between each graph.

4 🎧 2.11 You're going to hear the first part of a conversation about career options. Listen and answer Questions 1–7.

Questions 1–7

Complete the table. Write ***NO MORE THAN THREE WORDS*** *for each answer.*

....	....	....
Marketing	• It's a very creative profession	• Jobs are **1** ....
Accounting	• Safe career • Salaries are **2**	• Challenging exams • **3** .... takes a long time
Human Resources	• Lots of different **4** .... • Wide range of companies	• Difficult **5** .... to make
6	• Courses available to help retrain • A **7** .... profession	• Many apply for each position

5 2.12 **Listen to the rest of the conversation and answer Questions 8–10.**

Questions 8–10

*Choose the correct letter, **A**, **B** or **C**.*

8 Percentage of graduates now finding work within six months, one year and two years

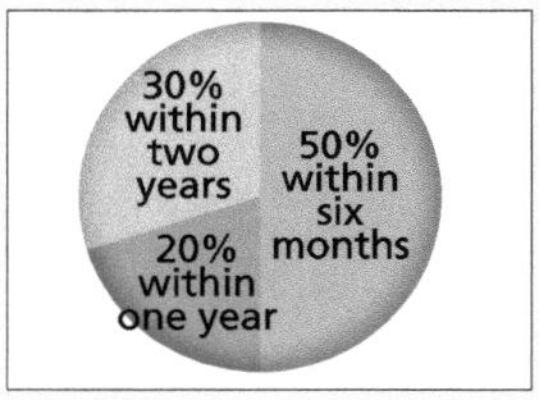

A

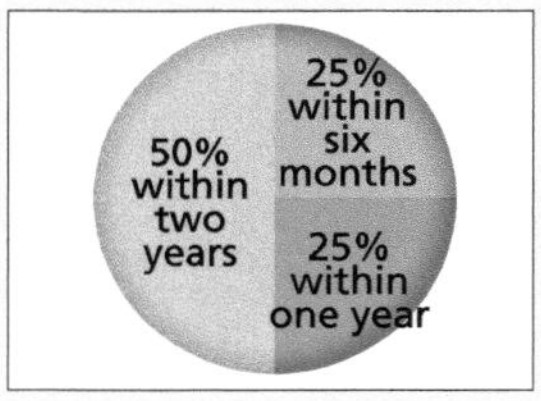

B

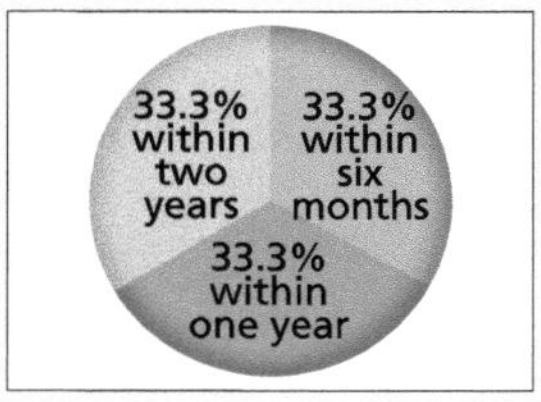

C

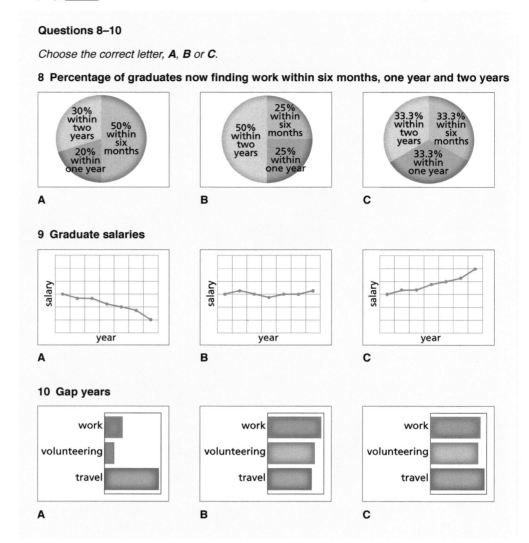

9 Graduate salaries

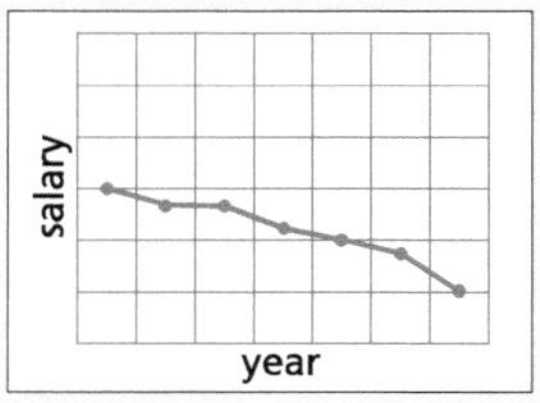

A

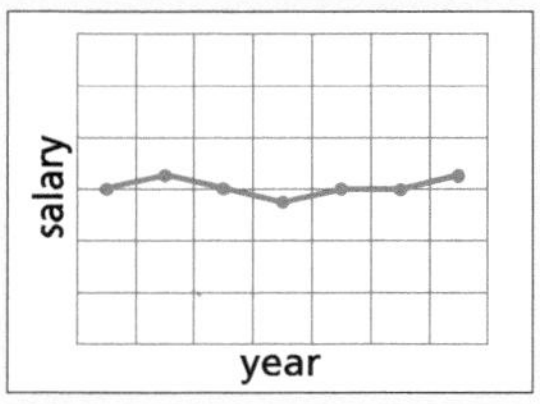

B

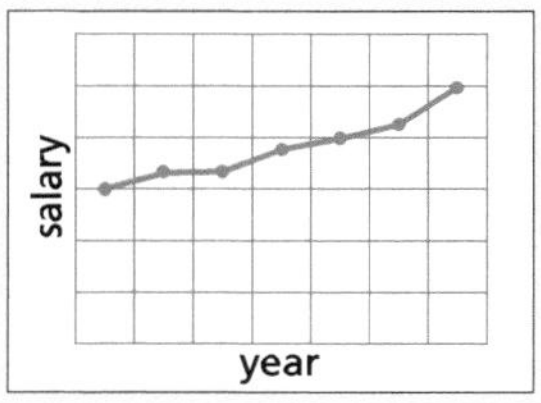

C

10 Gap years

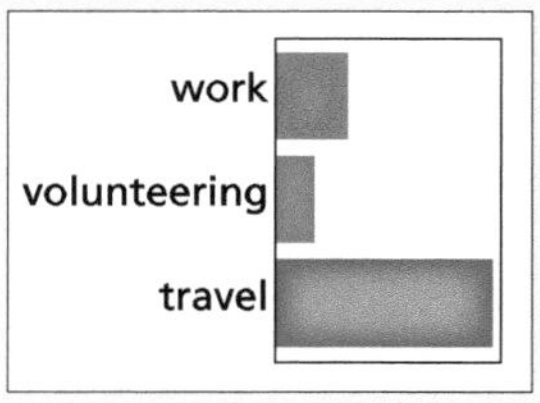

A

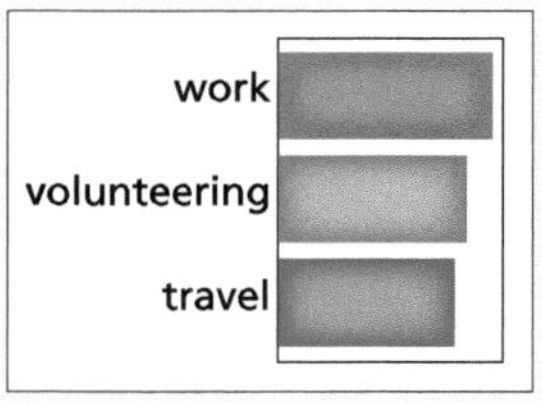

B

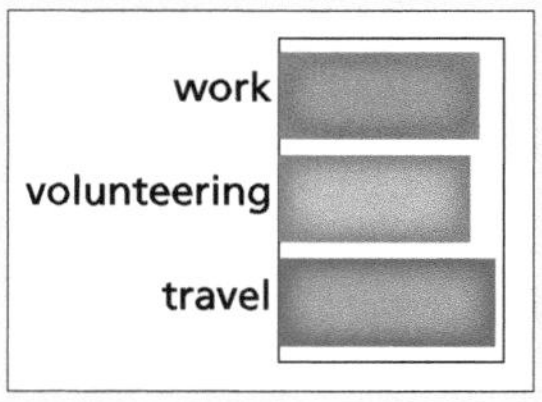

C

Explore further 6 **Discuss these questions with a partner.**

1 Is it easy to find graduate jobs in your country?
2 Do people take gap years in your country? Why? / Why not?
3 Who would you go to for careers advice? What's the best careers advice you've ever been given?

➤ **IELTS quiz**
page 8, question 8

SPEAKING

LESSON AIMS

- Part 2: Long turn
- Describing job benefits
- Using intonation

1 **Discuss these questions with a partner.**

1 What jobs do people in your family do?
2 Do your family members enjoy their work? Why? / Why not?

Vocabulary focus 2 **Susan has just had a job interview. Complete her notes about the job on page 75 with words from the box.**

account bonus boss clients/customers company
conferences home office pension team

Responsibilities

- Deal with [1]__________
- Attend international [2]__________

Working conditions

- Work from [3]__________ or have my own [4]__________
- Work in a supportive [5]__________ (and I'd be my own [6]__________ too!)

Benefits

- a large [7]__________ if you reach targets
- an expense [8]__________
- a [9]__________ car
- a generous [10]__________ scheme
- salary – to be confirmed

3 Discuss these questions with a partner.

1 Should Susan take the job? Why? / Why not?

2 Which features of the job would be most attractive to you?

Prepare to speak

4 Look at this task. What job would you choose to speak about, and why?

> **Describe a job that you would enjoy doing.**
> **You should say:**
> **where you would work**
> **what responsibilities you would have**
> **what skills you would need**
> **and explain why you would enjoy it.**

5 2.13–2.14 Listen to extracts from two responses to the task. What job has each candidate chosen?

6 2.13–2.14 Listen again and answer the *You're the examiner* questions.

You're the examiner

Which candidate:

1 sounded more confident?

2 paraphrased when they didn't know words?

3 used more appropriate grammar choices?

Pronunciation focus

7 Look at audio transcript 2.14 on page 111 and answer these questions. (Note that underlining indicates higher pitch and arrows indicate rising and falling intonation.)

1 Does the intonation rise or fall at the end of sentences and important ideas?

2 Which types of word are spoken at a higher pitch?

8 2.15 Mark these sentences in a similar way and read them aloud. Then listen and copy the intonation.

1 I'd absolutely love to have my own office. I'd have plants, photos of my family and a huge desk.

2 The other day, I was in the supermarket when I met my old boss. It was awkward.

3 The best thing about my current job is ... No, I can't think of anything.

Boost your band score *Pronunciation*

Using varied intonation makes you sound more friendly, more interesting and will communicate your ideas more clearly. It will improve your pronunciation score and help put you and the examiner at ease.

Over to you **9 Prepare this Speaking Part 2 task. Speak to your partner on the topic for two minutes.**

Describe someone you know who does interesting work.
You should say:
what kind of work they do
who they work with
where they go to work
and explain why you think it's interesting work.

10 Feed back to your partner. Use the *You're the examiner* box on page 75 to help.

➤ **IELTS quiz**
page 9, question 8

WRITING

LESSON AIMS

- Task 1: Summarising an illustration or diagram
- Describing change

1 Discuss these questions with a partner.

1 What kind of work did your grandparents do?
2 In your country, are there more or fewer jobs in the following industries now than there were in the past?
● agriculture ● leisure ● retail ● tourism
3 How have the changes you discussed in question 2 affected your city or village?

Prepare to write **2 Read this task and work with a partner.**

Student A: Cover Map B. Describe Map A to your partner. Then listen and try to draw Map B on a piece of paper.

Student B: Cover Map A. Listen and try to draw Map A on a piece of paper. Then describe Map B to your partner.

You should spend about 20 minutes on this task.

The two maps show a town in 1970 and in the present.
Summarise the information by selecting and reporting the main features, and make comparisons where relevant.

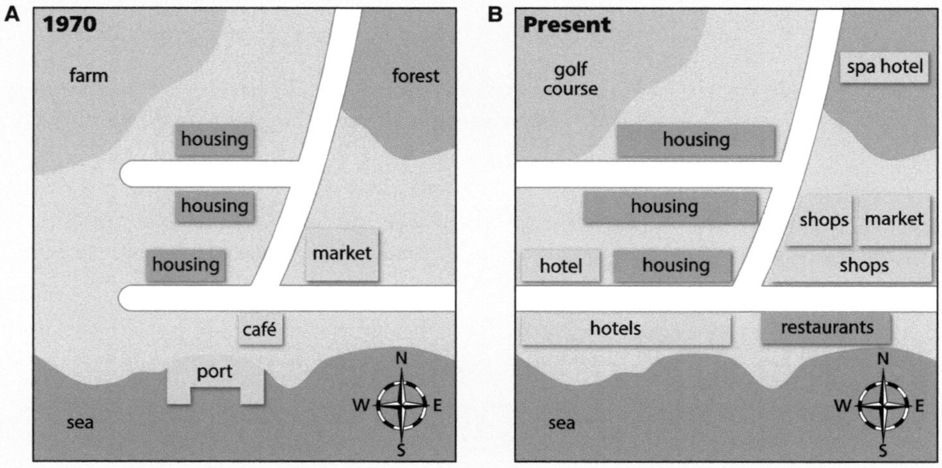

3 Read the extracts by two candidates on page 77 and answer these questions.

1 Circle the things that Candidate 1 describes on the maps.
2 Draw a box around the things Candidate 2 describes on the maps.
3 What difference do you notice about the location of the things they describe?

Candidate 1

The maps show the dramatic changes in the town between 1970 and today. The land to the north of the town was occupied by farmland and forest, while today its use is commercial. The forest that used to lie to the north-east of the town was cut down and replaced with a spa hotel. The area that used to be farmland, in the top left-hand corner, has been replaced with a golf course.

Candidate 2

The two maps show the town in the 1970s and today. There was a port, a farm and an area of forest too in the 1970s. However, there weren't many houses - in fact, there was quite a lot of space. Now, there are new shops, hotels, restaurants and a golf course. Today, it is clearly a tourist town, while in the past it was a small fishing village.

4 Read the extracts again, then answer the *You're the examiner* questions.

> **You're the examiner**
> Which candidate has:
> **1** used prepositions to describe specific locations?
> **2** used a wider variety of past structures?
> **3** included an overview statement?
> **4** used a greater range of linking words?

Language focus

5 Complete the continuation of Candidate 1's answer using the prepositions from the box.

along   between   by   in   opposite

[1]__________ the south of the town [2]__________ the sea, the area has been transformed from a fishing village to a commercial seaside town. The old port has been demolished. The road [3]__________ the seafront has been extended, and numerous hotels have been built [4]__________ this and the sea. [5]__________ the hotels, some of the old houses have also been converted into tourist accommodation. The market was originally near the seafront, but this has been relocated further away from the sea.

6 Find words in Candidate 1's answer (Exercise 3) and its continuation (Exercise 5) to match these definitions.

1 Made something longer
2 Knocked down or destroyed
3 Changed the use of something
4 Moved the location of something
5 Put one thing in place of another
6 Made a plant or tree fall to the ground

> **Boost your band score** *Grouping information*
> Before writing, ask yourself questions about the maps, for example *Is it more or less residential? Is there more or less countryside? How have the buildings changed?* Group these changes together either thematically or geographically in your response.

Over to you

7 Turn to page 93 and complete Task 7.

8 Exchange your work with a partner. Use the *You're the examiner* and *Boost your band score* boxes to evaluate their writing.

- Are the changes grouped together logically?
- Have they described the location accurately?
- Have they described all the changes?

9 Turn to page 102 and compare your answer with sample answer 13.

UNIT 8 Behaviour

TOPIC FOCUS

1 Decide if each of these words/phrases describes positive or negative behaviour.

anti-social apathetic community-minded empathetic energetic
engaged enthusiastic lacking respect lacking direction lazy

2 Which words from Exercise 1 would you use to describe teenagers and their behaviour? Compare your choices with a partner's.

3 Read these statistics about teenagers and the media. Do you find them surprising?

80% of American teenagers feel unfairly represented in the media.

Over 50% of stories in the UK media about teenage boys are connected to crime.

According to teachers surveyed in a Youth Media Agency report, the terms most frequently used by the media to describe teenagers were: 'lacking respect', 'lazy', 'anti-social', 'lacking direction' and 'apathetic'. Only 3% of teachers thought the media portrayed young people as empathetic, engaged, community-minded or enthusiastic.

4 Discuss these questions with a partner.

1 Were your words to describe teenagers in Exercise 2 largely positive or negative?
2 Why do you think the media portray teenagers so negatively?
3 Do the media in your country portray teenagers negatively?

➤ **IELTS quiz**
page 6, questions 2 and 10

READING

LESSON AIMS

- Review: Matching information
- True / False / Not Given

1 Use these numbers to complete the statistics below about lying.

3 6 31 60

1 Percentage of people who admit to lying on their CVs: ______%
2 Percentage of people who lie at least once during a ten-minute conversation: ______%
3 Average number of lies per day by men to their partner, boss or colleagues: ______
4 Average number of lies per day by women to their partner, boss or colleagues: ______

Source: www.dailymail.co.uk

2 Which of these common lies do you think are usually said by men and which by women? Explain your choices to a partner.

a Oh, this isn't new, I've had it for ages.
b It was in a sale.
c I had no signal.
d No, I didn't throw it away.
e My battery died.
f I'm stuck in traffic.

3 Skim the reading passage on page 79. It discusses lies told by which group of people?

Lie detection on trial

A In 1935, Judge Clayton F. Van Pelt was struggling to determine the guilt of two men. The only evidence available to him was the accusation of attempted murder by the sheriff and the counter claims of the two defendants. However, Judge Van Pelt had recently heard of a new device that was being developed by Professor Leonard Keeler at Northwestern University's School of Law, a device he believed could help him decide the case.

B At the Scientific Crime Detection Laboratory, Keeler and his team had developed a machine called the polygraph. It worked by measuring blood pressure and responses in the skin while the person was being questioned. Keeler argued that, in the hands of an expert questioner, the machine was able to identify if someone was telling the truth. Keeler was brought into the case and asked to use his device on the two defendants. As a result of the test, the two men were found guilty of attempted murder.

C The polygraph soon became one of the main investigative tools in legal cases. Keeler himself was using lie detectors in some of the country's best-known trials. Yet even at the time, Professor Keeler was worried about the accuracy of his device. When Judge Van Pelt asked if Keeler believed the device could 'decide the most important affairs of your life,' he refused to back his device. 'I wouldn't want to convict a man on the grounds of the records alone,' he said.

D Today, scientists are still far from convinced by the accuracy of lie-detecting machines. In courts around the world, the polygraph is now banned due to its inaccuracy. The main issue is that the test results are analysed by an examiner, and the interpretation is open to human error. Consequently, the accuracy largely depends on who the examiner is. While this can mean the tests are up to 95% accurate, it can also mean they are no more accurate than someone simply guessing.

E Yet researchers have not given up in their pursuit of reliable lie-detection technology. The P300, also called the EEG, and the functional Magnetic Resonance Imaging (fMRI) are two machines that have become particularly well-known. They work in different ways, but both analyse changes in the brain. The P300 focuses on brainwaves which are triggered when a person sees a familiar object. If a person is shown a murder weapon without activating the machine, then the item is considered unknown to them and they may be innocent. However, if they react, then they are potentially guilty, as the object is familiar to them. The fMRI works by monitoring blood flow to different areas of the brain. Blood flows faster when someone is lying simply because it is much harder to tell a lie than the truth. Unfortunately, the varied nature of lying has affected the accuracy of these machines. People's brains often react quite differently according to the size of the lie or how far the subject believes their own lie. As a result, they have yet to be used in criminal trials.

F Physiological changes in the body are not the only way to tell if a person is lying or not. Researchers at the University of Michigan have been working on lie-detection software which has been proven to be 75% accurate. The software, which analyses the physical reactions of liars, has made some interesting findings. Previously, it was thought that liars simply gave hesitant responses and tried to avoid eye contact. However, the software also showed that people usually look angry or pained, look the questioner directly in the eye, move both hands excessively and talk in the third person rather than the first person 'I' and 'we'. They now hope to get even closer to 100% by adding in observations of similar physical reactions to traditional lie detectors.

G Researchers from Cambridge, Lancaster and Utrecht Universities have also been working on a lie-detection suit that has been shown to be 70 to 80% accurate. The suit, which works using sensors to detect the wearer's movements, is based on the principle that people constantly move or fidget when they are telling lies. It can monitor up to 120 movements per second in 23 joints of the body. Even though good progress is being made, Bruce Burgess, one of the researchers in the team, is still surprised by some people's ability to lie. And apparently, he reveals, women are much better liars than men.

H Lie-detection research is not just limited to the study of physical reactions. Scientists are even developing software that can spot written lies. Even in just the limited 140 characters of a Tweet, the software will be able to spot a lie. The system used by the software works by looking at the quality of information and sources, the history and background of users, and how the conversation evolved on social media. Creators believe the system could prove useful to emergency services deciding which information to act upon. During recent riots in London, for example, some citizens made false claims on Twitter that animals were escaping from London Zoo, meaning that police resources could not be used effectively. With the advances being made in lie detection, it seems it may become increasingly difficult to lie and get away with it.

Skills focus

4 What can you remember about 'matching information' tasks from Unit 7? Discuss your task strategy with a partner, then attempt Questions 1–7 based on the reading passage on page 79.

Questions 1–7

Target time: 10 minutes
Target score: ____ / 7

The reading passage has eight paragraphs, **A–H**.
Which paragraph contains the following information? NB You may use any letter more than once.

1 An important decision made by polygraph
2 Untrue reports in the media
3 A reason for making something illegal
4 A comparison between two groups of people
5 The relative difficulty of telling a lie and telling the truth
6 New information about the appearance of liars
7 A reaction that depends on the degree of lying

5 Do the tasks in the *Strategy focus* box. Then answer Questions 8–14 based on the same reading passage.

Strategy focus *True / False / Not Given*

1 Look at the instructions for Questions 8–14 below and for Questions 6–13 on page 20. How and why are the instructions different?

2 Underline important words in sentences 1–3 (the first one has been done for you).
 1 *The defendants were arrested for the murder of a sheriff.*
 2 *Judge Van Pelt believed the two men were guilty.*
 3 *Judge Van Pelt had used a polygraph in court before.*

3 Read paragraph A. Do statements 1–3 above contradict the information in the text (False), or is there no information in the text about it (Not Given)? Which words help you decide?

Questions 8–14

Target time: 11 minutes
Target score: ____ / 7

Do the following statements agree with the information in the reading passage?
Write

TRUE	*if the statement agrees with the information*
FALSE	*if the statement contradicts the information*
NOT GIVEN	*if there is no information on this*

8 A polygraph measures two changes in the body.
9 The polygraph was banned very recently.
10 Keeler's polygraph was 95% accurate on average.
11 The P300 and fMRI focus on the brain.
12 The latest lie detectors are now used in courts.
13 Liars usually sit very still.
14 Lying in social media is very common.

Vocabulary extra

1 Complete each sentence with a verb from the reading passage on page 79.
 1 Machines can ______ a person's guilt. (para. A)
 2 The jury ______ the case on weak evidence. (para. A)
 3 The defendant was ______ guilty. (para. B)
 4 I couldn't ______ if he was being honest. (para. F)
 5 Police ______ an important decision. (para. F)

2 How are the verb meanings in each sentence related?

Explore further

6 How could we use lie-detection technology in these areas? Discuss in groups.
- exams
- politics
- sport

7 Discuss these questions with a partner.
1 It it ever acceptable to tell a lie? If so, when?
2 Would you always like people to be truthful to you?

➤ **IELTS quiz** page 7, question 2

LISTENING

LESSON AIMS

- Section 4: Monologue on an academic subject
- Note completion and matching

1 Say whether each of these statements is true or false for you.

1 I usually express my opinion freely, without choosing words carefully. **True** **False**
2 I get upset about small things. **True** **False**
3 I often buy things that I didn't plan to buy. **True** **False**
4 I often say things I regret later. **True** **False**

2 If you answered 'true' to most of the statements, you may have an impulsive character. If you answered 'false', then you're probably more cautious. Find out if there are more impulsive or cautious people in the class. Who is the most impulsive person you know?

Prepare to listen

3 Look at Questions 1–4 below and choose the correct option in each of these sentences.

1 Questions 1–4 all require *adjectives / nouns*.
2 Questions 1, 3 and 4 *will / won't* need an article.

4 These words and phrases appear in Questions 5–10. Predict similar words or phrases you might hear in the recording.

1 taking property
2 trying hard
3 control (behaviour)
4 behaving violently
5 responses
6 arguing
7 social activities

5 2.16 You're going to hear part of a lecture about the link between impulsivity and crime. Listen and answer Questions 1–4.

Questions 1–4

Complete the notes. Write ***NO MORE THAN TWO WORDS*** *for each answer.*

What is impulsivity?
Doing things with no **1** .... or thought, eg **2** .... or violence.
Causes of impulsivity:
1 Low activity in the brain's **3** ....
2 Forgetting about your **4** ....

6 2.17 Listen to the next part of the lecture and answer Questions 5–10.

Questions 5–10

Which group does the speaker link to these behaviours? Write the correct letter, ***C***, ***T*** *or* ***A***.

5 Taking others' property
6 Trying hard to control behaviour
7 Behaving violently
8 Having unusual responses for their age
9 Arguing with people in the family
10 Not doing social activities

C Impulsive children
T Impulsive teenagers
A Impulsive adults

Explore further **7 Match these sentence halves describing factors related to behaviour.**

1 Unemployment	a may not understand consequences of crime.
2 People who lack empathy	b may make people desperate for money.
3 Traumatic experiences	c may give people low self-esteem.
4 Inequality	d may make people emotional.
5 Addiction	e may make you worried about status.

8 Which of the factors in Exercise 7 do you think is the most important in affecting people's behaviour?

➤ **IELTS quiz**
page 8, questions 9 and 10

SPEAKING

LESSON AIMS

- Practising the whole Speaking test
- Organising ideas in responses
- Discussing student behaviour and rules

1 Look at these rules. Are they for school, home or both?

1 Be in the right place at the right time.
2 Respect other people's property.
3 Be helpful and cooperative towards others.
4 Take responsibility for your actions.

2 Do you have these rules in your school/home? Do you think more rules are needed where *you* live or study?

Vocabulary focus **3 Divide these words and phrases into problems, solutions or both.**

being spoiled clear rules harsh punishments lack of discipline large classes
large rewards poor behaviour relaxed parenting strict teaching

Problems: ______________________________

Solutions: ______________________________

Both: ______________________________

4 Complete these questions with words or phrases from Exercise 3.

1 Why do you think there is a __________ in some schools? ❑
2 Is __________ in schools a bigger problem now than it used to be? ❑
3 How can __________ by mums and dads create problems in schools? ❑
4 Do you think giving __________ to follow improves behaviour? ❑
5 Do you think children nowadays are __________ by their parents? ❑
6 Is __________ in schools necessary or unfair? ❑
7 Do you think __________ or __________ change children's behaviour more? ❑
8 Will behaviour improve if students don't have to study in __________? ❑

Prepare to speak **5 Think of four different questions you could be asked in Part 1 of the Speaking test on the topic of 'school'. Ask and answer your questions with a partner.**

1 A question about school now ______________________________
2 A question about school in the past ______________________________
3 A question comparing two things ______________________________
4 A question about the future ______________________________

6 Create a topic card for Part 2 of the Speaking test using ideas in the table.

Describe a school rule that you	thought was think is / would be	fair / unfair. important / silly.

Give your card to a partner. They speak for two minutes on your topic.

7 2.18 **Listen to a candidate answering three of the questions in Exercise 4. Tick the questions they answer.**

8 2.19 **Listen to a second candidate answering the same questions and answer the *You're the examiner* questions.**

You're the examiner

Which candidate:

1 organises their answers effectively?
2 answers the questions directly?
3 hesitates less?

Fluency focus

9 **Complete the sentences with the words and phrases from the box.**

consequently	for instance	however	leads to	what's more

1 I don't agree that parents are the main reason for poor behaviour. ________, many could probably do more to improve it.
2 Class sizes have grown dramatically over recent years. ________, maintaining discipline has become harder for teachers.
3 Young children's behaviour can usually be easily improved, ________ by using reward charts to highlight good behaviour.
4 I do think clearer rules would help to improve behaviour. Setting these ________ a situation where people clearly understand right from wrong.
5 Many parents are probably too lenient. ________, many are inconsistent, and as a result children do not learn how to behave.

10 **Ask and answer the questions in Exercise 4 with a partner. Use linking expressions from Exercise 9.**

Boost your band score *Organization*

It's important to organize your answers logically. Try to show when you're giving contrasting ideas, additional ideas, examples, cause and effect, or results by using the correct linking words. Start with a main point that responds directly to the question and support it with examples and reasons.

Over to you
Part 1

11 **EITHER**

a 2.20 **Listen and answer eight questions on two topics. After each question, you will have 15 seconds to respond.**

OR

b **Turn to audio transcript 2.20 on page 112. Ask and answer the questions with a partner.**

Part 2

12 **Prepare the task below (see page 29 for method). Speak to your partner on the topic for two minutes.**

Describe a reward for good behaviour you liked receiving as a child.
You should say:
what the reward was
why you received it
what you did with it
and explain why you liked it.

Part 3 **13 EITHER**

a 2.21 Listen and answer nine questions on three topics. After each question, you will have 25 seconds to respond.

OR

b Turn to audio transcript 2.21 on page 112. Ask and answer the questions with a partner.

14 Feed back to your partner. Use the *You're the examiner* box on page 83 to help.

➤ **IELTS quiz**
page 9, question 9

WRITING

LESSON AIMS

- Task 2: Discussion essays
- Maintaining a neutral style

1 The World Health Organization recommends no more than six teaspoons of sugar a day. How many teaspoons of sugar do you think are in each of these foods?

a yoghurt with fruit
b 100 grams of chocolate
c 4 grams of ketchup
d strawberry and banana smoothie (500ml)
e 50 grams of granola

2 How much sugar do you think you've eaten today?

3 Which is more likely to make you eat less sugar: a) information about sugar content or b) a higher price for sugary food?

Prepare to write

4 Read this task and the introduction below written by a test candidate. Has the candidate given their opinion? Why? / Why not?

High sugar content in food is contributing to a rise in obesity. Some people think the government should respond by raising tax on sugary food and drink. Others think there are far more effective solutions. Discuss both views and give your opinion.

Obesity is one of the major public health challenges of our time, but the correct response to it is a matter of debate. The idea of a tax on sugary food is a particularly controversial solution. While few deny that it would have some effect, many query whether it would be the most effective policy measure.

5 Read the two extracts from sample answers. Which is from the same essay as the introduction in Exercise 4? How do you know?

Candidate 1

A tax on soft drinks is a bad solution because it would have relatively little effect. We usually buy soft drinks because we feel a strong desire for them. A few pence on the price isn't going to stop our bodies wanting the sugar. If the government really wanted to help us, they should make supermarkets hide soft drinks from us. A sugar tax is clearly just a way of making money from our human weaknesses and won't solve the problem.

Candidate 2

There are several arguments against the tax. It may be unfair to poorer families, people often claim. Their argument is simple. Parents don't generally have much choice at the shops. They have to buy sugary food. Their children won't eat anything else! A sugar tax therefore impacts on poor families considerably. Arguably, richer families would pay the higher prices with no problem. As result, they'd be relatively unaffected by the move.

6 **Does the argument in Candidate 1 or Candidate 2's response convince you more? Discuss with a partner.**

7 **Read the extracts again, then answer the *You're the examiner* questions.**

You're the examiner

Which candidate has successfully used:

1 long, complex sentences?
2 structures to report others' views (to avoid giving their own opinion)?
3 modal verbs to seem cautious?

Language focus

8 **Rewrite these sentences in a neutral style using the words in brackets.**

1 A tax on sugary food and drink is a sensible solution. (*others believe*)
2 It's easier to tax products than force supermarkets to hide food. (*arguably*)
3 Also, the money raised can be used for education campaigns. (*could perhaps*)
4 The campaigns teach people about the dangers of eating too much sugar. (*might try*)

Boost your band score *Discussion questions*

In questions that ask you to discuss a topic, it's important to give a balanced view and to use cautious language such as modal verbs. In the conclusion, this is less important, as you should state your opinion clearly.

9 **Delete words in the conclusion so that the author's opinion is clear.**

In conclusion, it could be argued that the objections to a tax on sugary food are misplaced. While other measures may be more effective in the short term, one could say a tax is a realistic solution that would provide a foundation for other measures.

Over to you

10 **Do this Writing Task 2.**

Write about the following topic.

> ***Governments and business leaders in all countries are trying to improve levels of production in the workplace. Some believe the best way to do this is to increase pay. Others believe that pay is less important than other factors, like the working environment.***
> ***Discuss both views and give your opinion.***

Give reasons for your answer and include any relevant examples from your knowledge or experience.
Write at least 250 words.

11 **Exchange your work with a partner. Use the *You're the examiner* and the *Boost your band score* boxes to evaluate their writing.**

12 **Turn to page 102 and compare your answer with sample answer 14.**

Reading

Answer Questions 1–14 based on the reading passage.

Questions 1–5

The reading passage has eight paragraphs, **A–H**.
Which paragraph contains the following information?

1 A rising trend in crime rates
2 A substance people are choosing not to use
3 A change in the law
4 The impact of certain professions on crime
5 A change in the number of older people

Questions 6–11

Do the following statements agree with the information in the reading passage?
Write

TRUE *if the statement agrees with the information*
FALSE *if the statement disagrees with the information*
NOT GIVEN *if there is no information on this*

6 Economic depressions have been linked to a rise in crime.
7 Fewer people are suffering from depression.
8 There were fewer young males in the 1980s than in previous years.
9 Some people believe migration may be reducing crime rates.
10 A small increase in inflation results in a larger increase in crime.
11 People are buying more goods.

Questions 12–14

*Choose the correct letter, **A**, **B**, **C** or **D**.*

12 Technology has led to
A increased levels of personal security.
B a small change in levels of car theft.
C increases in theft of credit cards.
D more opportunities for theft.

13 People may be staying at home more because
A the streets are becoming more dangerous.
B the idea of spending time at home is becoming more attractive.
C video games have created a fear of street violence.
D homes provide more comfort than outdoor areas.

14 New explanations regarding the causes of crime
A have replaced older ideas.
B have brought researchers closer to a clear answer.
C are not particularly satisfactory.
D have made a simple conclusion less likely.

The great crime decline

A Many countries have been experiencing a long-term decline in serious crime over the last few decades. Homicide rates have been at a four-decade low in the United States, for example, and rates of serious crimes have been falling across Europe since the turn of the millennium, despite some quite severe economic shocks and depressions. Yet notwithstanding the obvious importance of understanding this trend, academics have been unable to explain it satisfactorily. The issue has, in fact, given rise to what is undoubtedly one of the most interesting academic debates of recent times.

B Medical experts have often pointed to the availability of certain medications as a likely cause. According to the Prison Reform Trust, 70% of prisoners have two or more mental health conditions, and researchers believe that the availability of medicine for treating depression and hyperactivity disorders, like Prozac and Ritalin, has enabled many potential criminals to treat these underlying conditions successfully and lift their moods. At the same time, the epidemics of illegal drug use associated with the 1980s have ended, meaning addiction has become less of a problem. Yet though both these changes to the availability of drugs might explain short-term trends, they are unlikely to explain long-term decline.

C Another health-related theory concerns the decision of many of the world's countries to stop putting the metal lead into petrol and paints. Lead in the blood stream is known to cause aggressive behaviour and slow cognitive development, and measures like the 1970 Clean Air Act in the USA, which removed lead from fuels, have been shown to coincide neatly with various crime trends in the 20th century. A study in Cincinnati showed that young people arrested for bad behaviour are four times more likely to have high levels of lead in their bones. Economist Jessica Reyes believes the removal of lead from products can explain up to 56% of the drop in crime. However, once again, it has been a long while since we stopped putting lead in petrol, and this seems less able to explain recent trends.

D Geographers have also weighed into the debate, pointing to some interesting population trends which they believe may have contributed to the trend. Basically, since it is young adult males who commit the majority of crimes, it follows that a decline in this demographic bracket should result in a decline in crime. And in fact it was during the 1980s that a particularly large cohort of young males started moving into middle age, removing them from the high-risk bracket. The percentage of young males in the population has been stable since then, but geographers continue to make their case. Ageing populations, they argue, have increased the presence of calmer moderating influences in families, who are able to offer guidance and mentoring to younger people.

E Another argument related to demography focuses on the changes that have been occurring to inner-city areas, once breeding grounds for serious crime. As migration has accelerated in this epoch of globalisation, many of these areas have been taken over by ambitious, hard-working migrant families. At the same time, efforts to replace old, derelict housing stock in these areas with new housing has encouraged middle-class families to return to city centres, bringing back more wealth and resources into areas once stricken by poverty.

F Economists, meanwhile, have connected the fall in crime to another trend related to globalisation, namely price inflation. Stiff international competition among producers of manufactured goods and in labour markets has generally kept prices low. A 10% increase in prices is said to result in a 3.5% increase in crime as the value of stolen goods rises, so an era of low inflation is likely to deter property theft. Certainly, the forms of crime that are still generating money have not become less popular. Cyber crime and online fraud in particular have witnessed steady growth. It may simply be that new forms of crime are replacing traditional varieties in the digital age, and as these new crimes become included in crime statistics, we may see total crime levels falling far less sharply.

G But arguments for the role of technology do not end there. The drop in prices of consumer goods has been matched by increases in our means of securing them. Anti-theft devices in cars have no doubt contributed to substantial falls in car theft; debit cards have meant that people carry less money with them these days, meaning there is generally less cash around to steal; and security cameras are deterring mugging and physical assault. What is more, entertainment systems at home, far from inspiring violence, may be encouraging people to stay in safer indoor environments more regularly instead of roaming the streets, as may the comforts of modern heating and air-conditioning systems.

H Still others have suggested that rising levels of incarceration in prison, better policing, even inspiring political leadership have contributed to increasing levels of safety on our streets. And so the ideas keep coming. The more that plausible answers are put forward, the less it seems likely that we will ever arrive at a neat, satisfactory explanation. Instead we may have to accept that causation is a messy business and that in all likelihood, a combination of a range of factors have contributed to the great crime decline.

Listening

Section 3 2.22

Questions 1–7

Complete the table. Write ***NO MORE THAN THREE WORDS*** *for each gap.*

	Theory X	**Theory Y**
Main idea	• Employees must be controlled	• Work is natural, like **1** ....
Managing people	• Employees respond when threatened with **2**	• **3** .... is normal
Attitude to leading	• Avoid being in charge	• The average worker looks for **4** ....
Views on achievement	• Lacks **5** .... • Workers like to have **6** .... in their lives	• Rewards and achievement are connected.
Professions	• Suitable for factory work	• Useful where you depend on the **7** .... of employees

Questions 8–10

Choose the correct letter, ***A, B*** *or* ***C***.

8 Satisfied in work

A

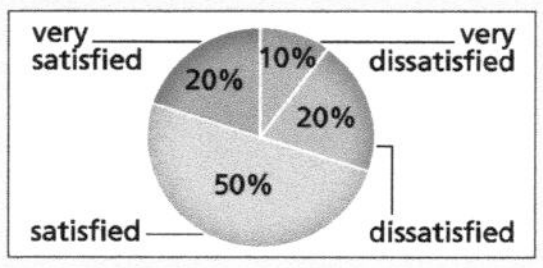

B

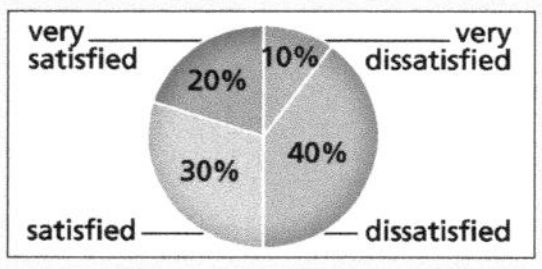

C

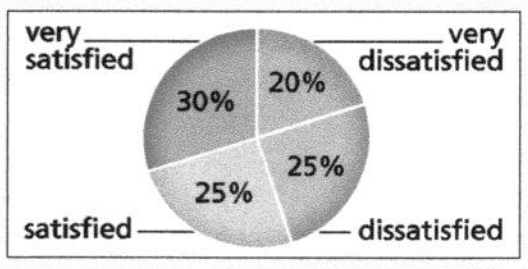

9 Factors affecting satisfaction

A

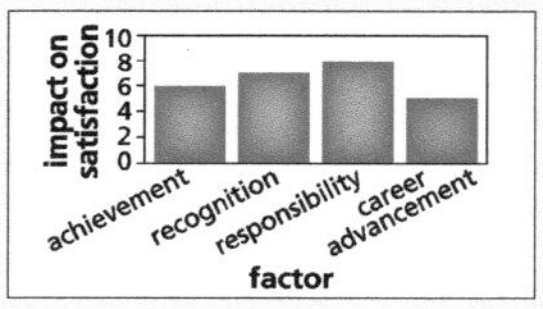

B

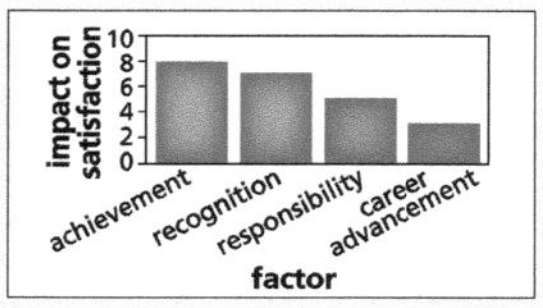

C

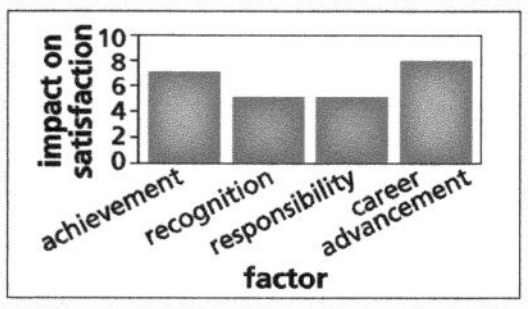

10 Factors affecting dissatisfaction

A

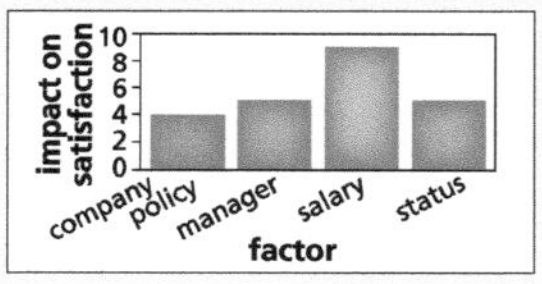

B

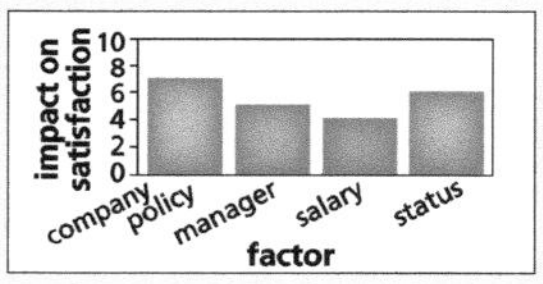

C

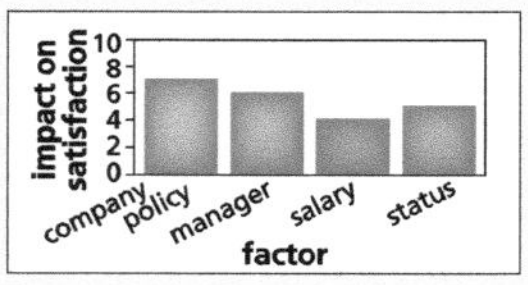

Section 4 2.23

Questions 11–14

Complete the notes. Write ***NO MORE THAN THREE WORDS*** *for each answer.*

Two-factor theory

Herzberg surveyed 203 **11** ....

Results: factors that lead to satisfaction and dissatisfaction are **12** ....

For most workers, it isn't enough to have things like a **13** ....

To improve **14** ...., companies need to think about both groups of factors.

Questions 15–20

Which factors does the speaker link to these behaviours?
Choose the correct letter, ***M***, ***H*** *or* ***P***.

15 Finding the work challenging
16 Employee effort
17 The effort and reward connection
18 Involvement in decision-making
19 Holiday allowance
20 Working relationships with others

M Motivation factor
H Hygiene factor
P Depends on personality

Speaking

Part 1 **EITHER**

a 2.24 **Listen and answer eight questions on two topics. After each question, you will have 15 seconds to respond.**

OR

b **Turn to audio transcript 2.24 on page 113. Ask and answer the questions with a partner.**

Part 2 **Prepare to speak about the topic on the card below. Think or make notes for one minute. Speak for between one and two minutes about the topic on the card. Record yourself or ask a partner to listen to you.**

Describe a recent achievement, eg an exam or competition that has changed your life.
You should say:
what you achieved
how difficult it was to achieve
who helped you with the achievement
and explain why it changed your life.

Part 3 **EITHER**

a 2.25 **Listen and answer 11 questions on three topics. After each question, you will have 25 seconds to respond.**

OR

b **Turn to audio transcript 2.25 on page 113. Ask and answer the questions with a partner.**

Writing

Task 1
You should spend about 20 minutes on this task. Turn to Task 8 on page 93.

Task 2
You should spend about 40 minutes on this task. Write about the following topic.

Increasing numbers of people are starting new careers half way through their working lives. What are the advantages and disadvantages of changing careers?

Give reasons for your answer and include any relevant examples from your knowledge or experience. Write at least 250 words.

This Writing task bank contains practice tasks for Task 1 of the IELTS Writing paper, linked to the Writing sections in Units 1, 3, 5 and 7 plus Test files 1–4. Sample answers for these tasks are available on pages 98–103. There are also 12 guided Writing tasks (unrelated to the units): four for Task 1 and eight for Task 2.

Unit tasks

Task 1

Unit 1, page 17; sample answer 1, page 98

The graph shows the percentage of university students who did educational activities by hour of day on weekdays in 2014.

Summarise the information by selecting and reporting the main features, and make comparisons where relevant.

Write at least 150 words.

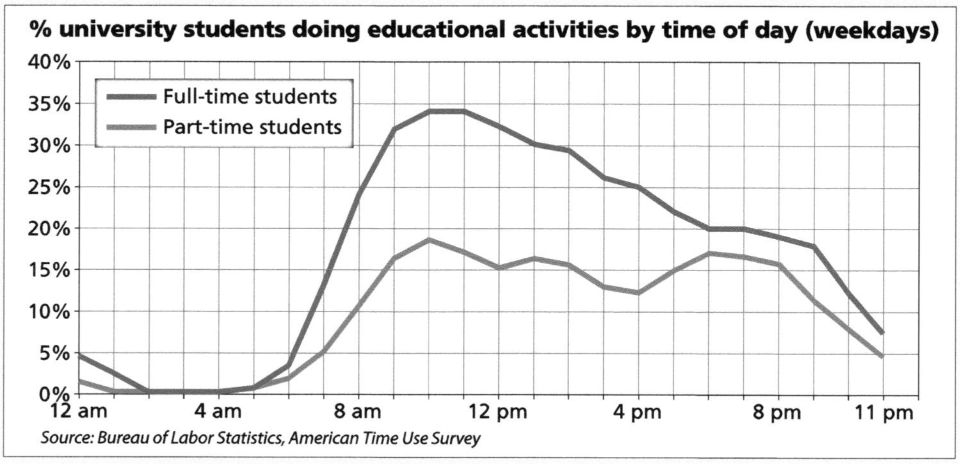

Task 2

Test file 1, page 29; sample answer 3, page 98

The line graph below shows the number of migrants living in an English-speaking country by language background.

Summarise the information by selecting and reporting the main features, and make comparisons where relevant.

Write at least 150 words.

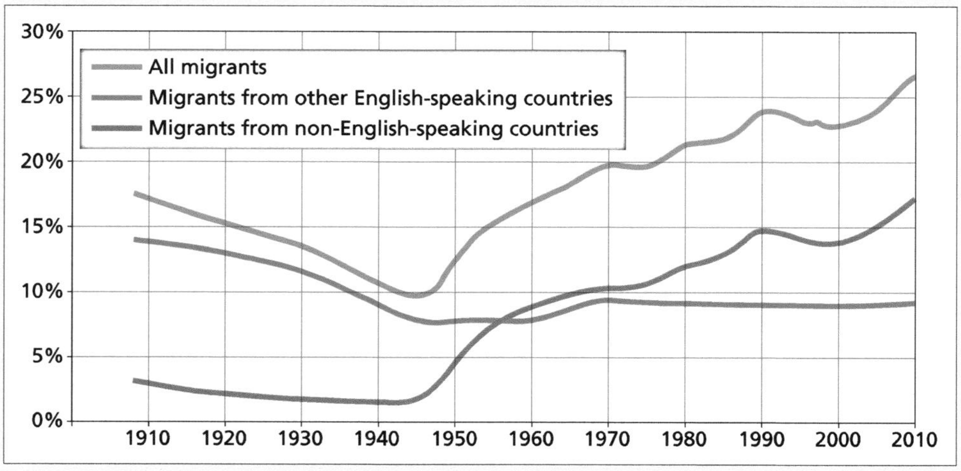

Task 3

Unit 3, page 37; sample answer 5, page 99

The chart shows both the number of girls and boys who received information about new music and video games from friends, and the number who gave the information to friends.

Summarise the information by selecting and reporting the main features, and make comparisons where relevant.

Write at least 150 words.

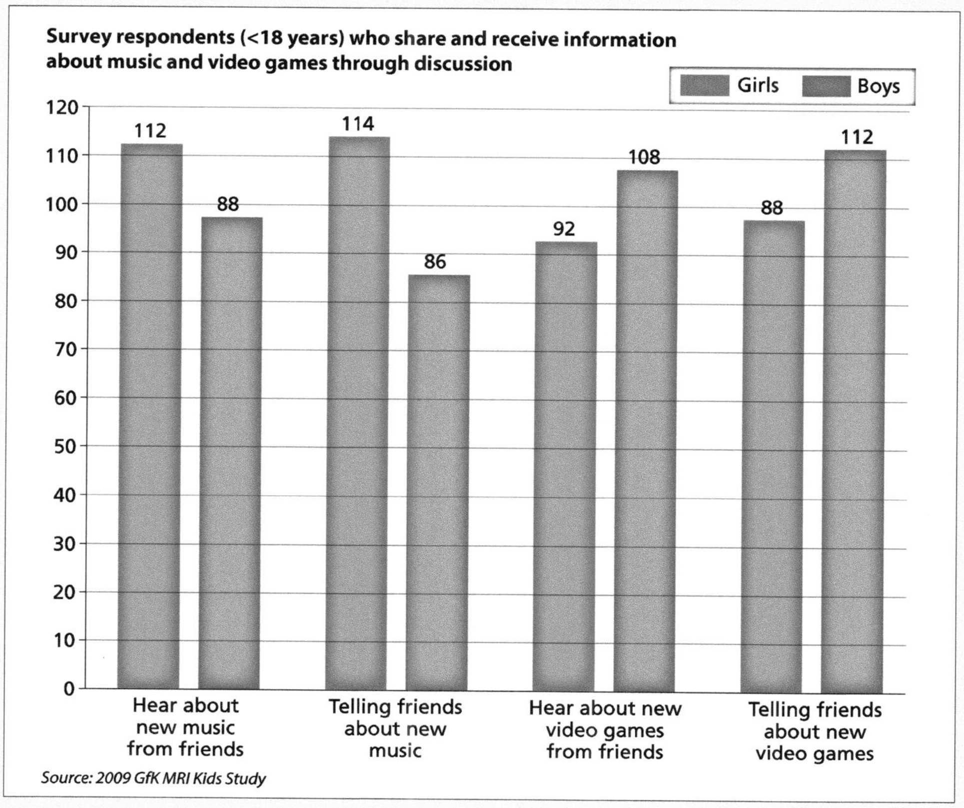

Task 4

Test file 2, page 49; sample answer 7, page 100

The table shows the top ten languages used for online content and the top ten native languages of internet users.

Summarise the information by selecting and reporting the main features, and make comparisons where relevant.

Write at least 150 words.

Language of internet content	Language of internet users
English 53.6%	English 25.9%
Russian 6.4%	Chinese 20.9%
German 5.7%	Spanish 7.6%
Japanese 5.0%	Arabic 5.0%
Spanish 4.9%	Portuguese 3.9%
French 4.1%	Japanese 3.4%
Portuguese 2.6%	Russian 3.1%
Italian 2.1%	Malay 2.9%
Chinese 1.9%	French 2.9%
Polish 1.9%	German 2.5%

Task 5

Unit 5, page 57; sample answer 9, page 100

The diagram shows the process by which four varieties of medicine are manufactured.

Summarise the information by selecting and reporting the main features, and make comparisons where relevant.

Write at least 150 words.

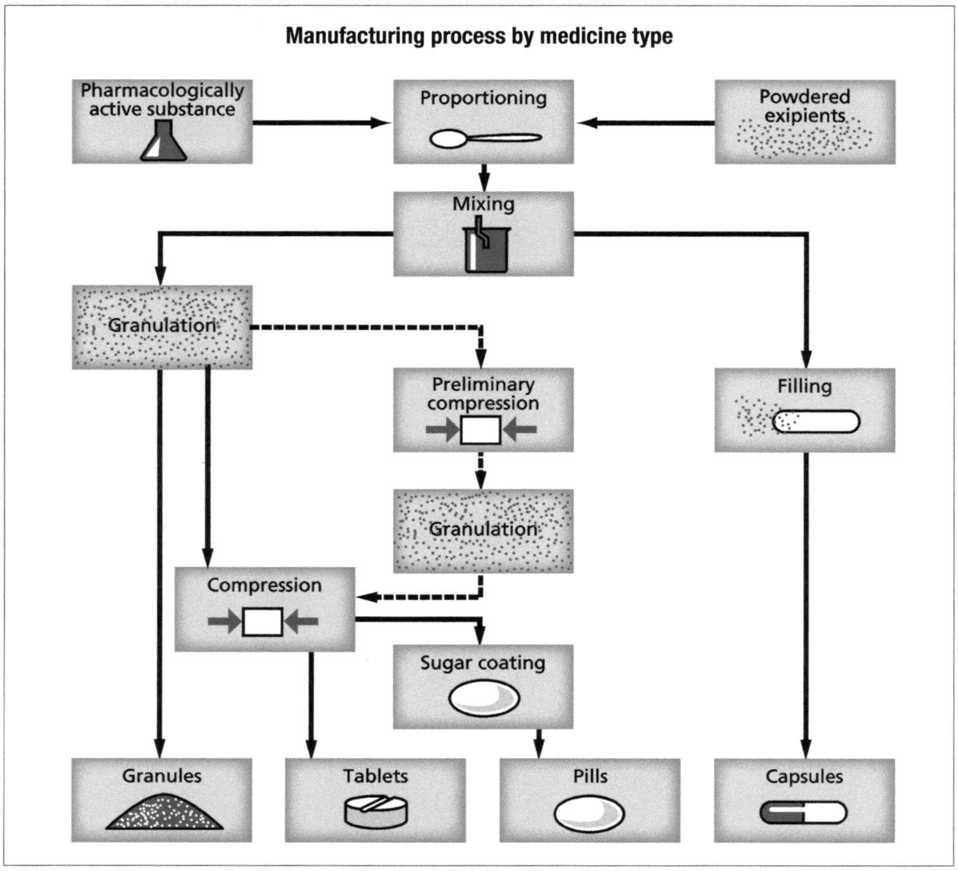

Task 6

Test file 3, page 69; sample answer 11, page 101

The diagram shows the main stages of recycling for various materials.

Summarise the information by selecting and reporting the main features, and make comparisons where relevant.

Write at least 150 words.

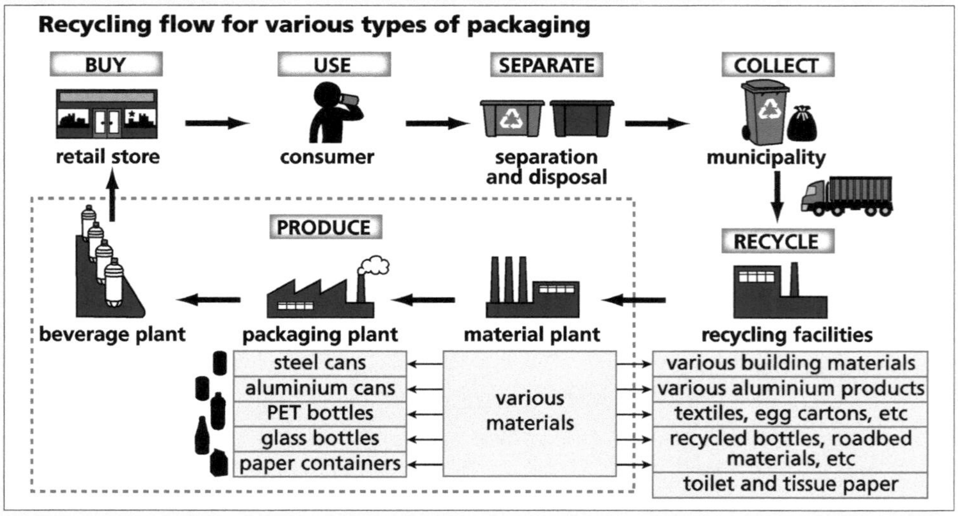

Task 7

Unit 7, page 77; sample answer 13, page 102

The diagram shows the changes that have taken place in the use of an office space over a five-year period.

Summarise the information by selecting and reporting the main features, and make comparisons where relevant.

Write at least 150 words.

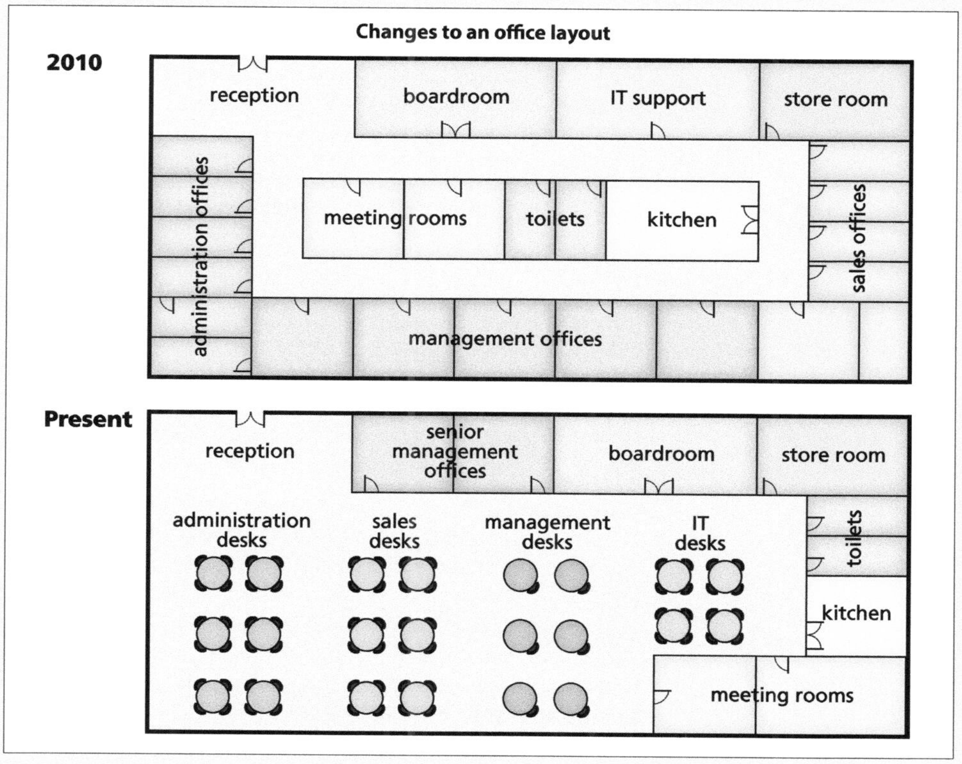

Task 8

Test file 4, page 89; sample answer 15, page 102

The diagram shows a design for a modern prison.

Summarise the information by selecting and reporting the main features, and make comparisons where relevant.

Write at least 150 words.

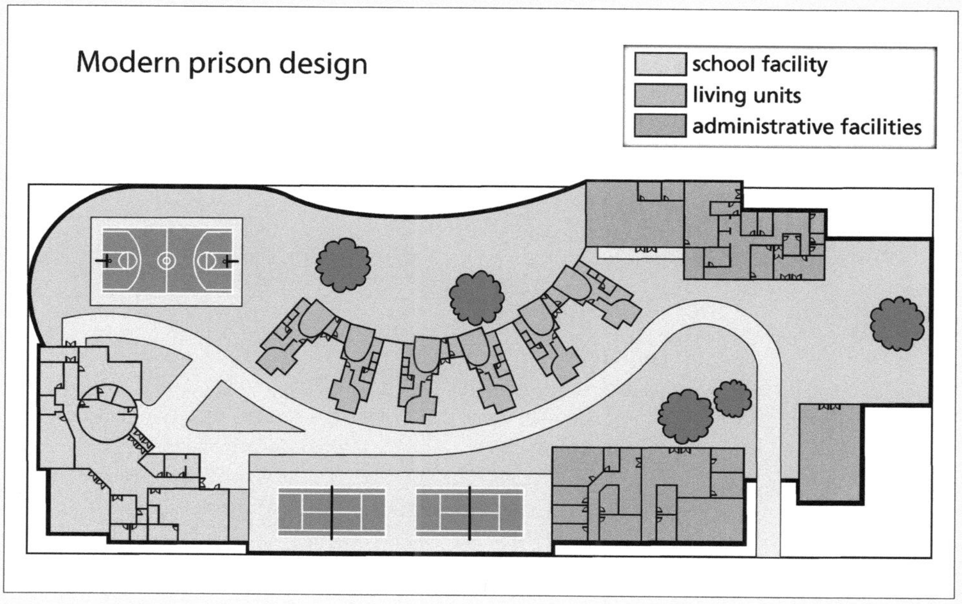

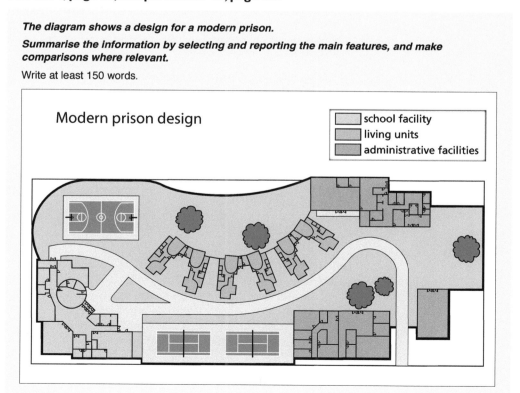

Guided writing tasks

Writing Task 1

You should spend about 20 minutes on these tasks. Write at least 150 words.

Task 9

The graph shows the changing size of urban and rural populations in rich and poor countries.

Summarise the information by selecting and reporting the main features, and make comparisons where relevant.

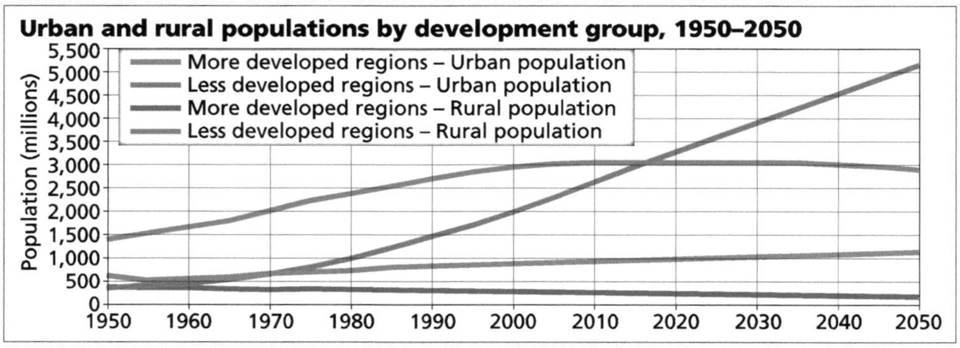

Guidance

Data type: trend

1 When you approach this task, avoid describing the shape of each line. Instead, ask yourself about the relationship between the categories of data. To write your overview, consider which categories of data show the most dramatic changes: those in developed regions or those in less developed regions? Write a sentence describing this general difference.
2 To focus on less developed regions, divide the data into two time periods. What is the relationship between urban and rural populations before around 2015? What is the relationship after 2015?
3 In developed regions, are urban or rural regions most populated? Is the gap growing or narrowing?

Task 10

The chart shows how often people of different age groups use mobile devices for texting and speaking.

Summarise the information by selecting and reporting the main features, and make comparisons where relevant.

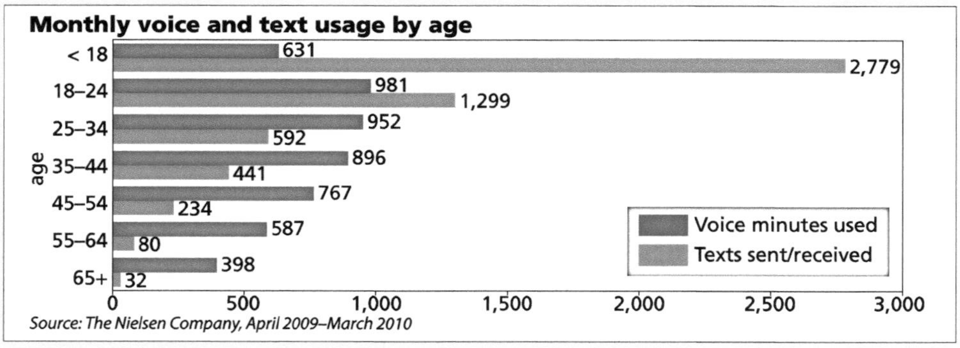

Source: The Nielsen Company, April 2009–March 2010

Guidance

Data type: comparison

1 For the overview, divide the age groups into two categories. Complete these phrases:
   a Age groups who use texts more than speech (people under ____)
   b Age groups who use speech more than text (people over ____)
2 Write a sentence comparing the two categories.
3 Consider these questions:
   a What happens to text use as age increases?
   b Do 'voice minutes' follow the same or opposite trend? Are there exceptions?

Task 11

The chart shows the stages of the application process for senior management jobs.

Summarise the information by selecting and reporting the main features, and make comparisons where relevant.

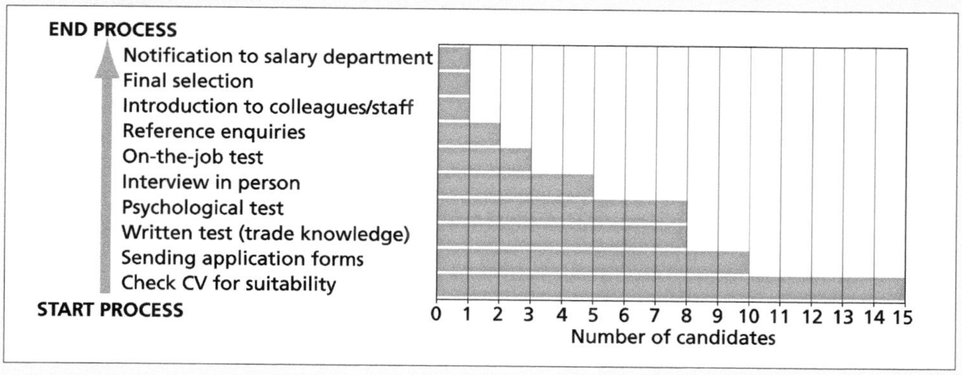

Guidance

Data type: process

This process is not represented by a flow chart, so you'll need to work out whether the process starts at the bottom of the chart or the top. However the style of writing should be the same.

1 For the overview, think of something interesting to say about the process. Is it really interesting that the later stages of the process have fewer people? Or is the complexity of the process more interesting?
2 Look for ways you can group the stages of the process. Perhaps you could consider the steps of the process that involve the same number of candidates as single stages?

Task 12

The diagram shows the features of a modern, energy-efficient home.

Summarise the information by selecting and reporting the main features, and make comparisons where relevant.

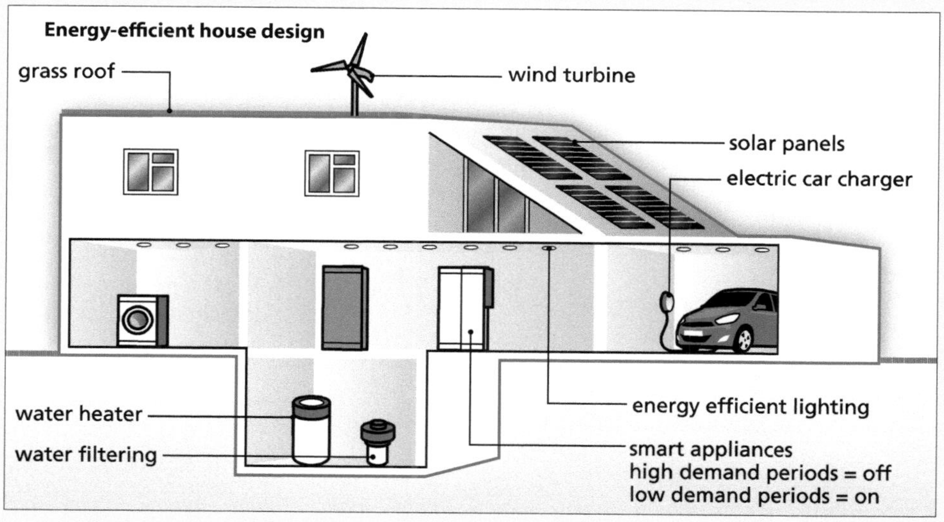

Guidance

Data type: diagram

1 What do you think when you look at this image? Perhaps you're impressed by the amount of technology in the house? Write a sentence about your general impression to create an overview.
2 To help you organise your description coherently, think of ways that you can group the features in the diagram. Match two features from the diagram to each of these categories:

External		**Internal**	
Underground		**On the roof**	
Energy production		**Energy consumption**	

3 Which categories help the reader to gain a greater understanding of the features?

Writing Task 2

You should spend about 40 minutes on these tasks. Write at least 250 words.

Task 13

Many tourist destinations, like beaches and mountains, have become overcrowded. How can governments control the number of visitors to popular tourist destinations?

Guidance

Essay type: solutions

1 How do you choose a holiday destination? Do you consider the cost, availability of tickets, advertising and advice, legal restrictions?

2 How could the government use these factors to stop you travelling to certain places? Make notes under these headings:

Cost	
Availability of tickets	
Advertising/advice	
Legal restrictions	

3 Develop each row of the table into a paragraph; then add an introduction and a conclusion.

Task 14

Health systems do not have enough money to care for everyone who needs treatment. People who choose to do dangerous sports should pay for medical care if they have an accident. To what extent do you agree?

Guidance

Essay type: opinion

1 To decide if a solution is good or bad, you need to think about a) the likely consequences of the solution, and b) how fair it is.

2 Think of the consequences and fairness of charging people who do dangerous sport for their medical care and complete the table.

Positive consequences	
Negative consequences	
Reasons why it's fair	
Reasons why it isn't fair	

3 Which side of the argument is strongest? Write your opinion clearly in the introduction, then create a paragraph for each reason that supports your view.

Task 15

Many people in society do not earn enough money to cover living expenses. Some people believe that the government should give more money to them. Others think they should work harder. Discuss both views and give your opinion.

Guidance

Essay type: discussion

1 Consider the two different solutions mentioned to the problem of low income:
- providing 'free' money
- working more hours.

2 For each solution, imagine you are these people and consider what they would think about each solution:
   a a businessperson who needs to attract workers to their business
   b an accountant who has a good salary because they've made the right choices in life
   c a mother who works 44 hours a week in a low-paid job and needs more time with her kids

3 Think of at least one positive and one negative view for each solution.

Task 16

Some people think the main purpose of education is to prepare people for work. Others think education makes us good citizens. Discuss both views and give your opinion.

Guidance

Essay type: discussion

1 We all need to work, and we all need to be good citizens. This question isn't asking you which is more important. Instead it's asking which should be the main aim of education. To consider this, ask yourself how far education can help achieve each aim and complete the table.

	How education can help	How other factors can help
Getting a job		
Becoming a good citizen		

2 Write a paragraph about each aim, including information from both columns. Then decide which role education plays most effectively.

Task 17

Many of the things that are good for us are not always popular, like doing exercise. Why do some people dislike doing exercise, and what can governments do to encourage them to exercise?

Guidance

Essay type: problem and solutions

1 Note that there are two parts to this question, and you'll need to answer both to achieve a high Task Response score. However, the two parts are related; if you can identify barriers in the modern word that stop people exercising, you can consider how governments can remove them.

2 Complete the table.

Barriers that stop people exercising	How governments can remove each barrier
1	A
2	B
3	C

3 Before you write, decide if you want to include ideas 1–3 first, then A–C, or whether you want to present your ideas as 1A 2B 3C? Which format might give you a higher mark for cohesion and coherence?

Task 18

Some people think the news is just a form of entertainment. Others believe the news helps us become better citizens. Discuss both views and give your opinion.

Guidance

Essay type: discussion

1 In this debate, the two views are closely related: if the news doesn't help us become good citizens, it must be a form of entertainment. This means that we can answer the question by considering whether news makes us good citizens or not. Complete the table with an example for each item:

News makes us good citizens	News doesn't make us good citizens
1 We learn about people who need help	A A lot of news is trivial (unimportant)
eg	eg
2 We learn about issues we must vote on	B News us designed to shock, not inform
eg	eg
3 We hear about events we can take part in	C News is biased towards our countries
eg	eg

2 In this case, it isn't easy to match ideas 1–3 with ideas A–C. So it may be better to put ideas 1–3 in one paragraph and ideas A–C in the next.

Task 19

Shop assistants work increasingly long hours at weekends. Should all shops close one day at the weekend so that staff can spend time with their families? Give your opinion.

Guidance

Essay type: opinion

1 This essay is asking you to decide if there are more advantages or more disadvantages to closing shops for a day at weekends. It's tempting to see this debate solely from the viewpoint of a consumer, but to improve your essay, consider the views of the other people mentioned in the table.

	Advantages	Disadvantages
Shop managers		
Shop workers and families		
Consumers (shoppers)		

2 Decide whether advantages outweigh disadvantages or vice versa before you start writing. Imagine you're trying to convince your reader why you're right.

Task 20

In many families, both parents work, do housework and care for children. It would make more sense for women to perform some roles and men others. Do you agree?

Guidance

Essay type: opinion

1 Should women perform some roles and men others? This isn't really a question about traditional social roles, because the viewpoint under discussion doesn't state who should do which role. Before planning this question, note the emphasis on *parents*. You should consider the effects of dividing roles on the parents *and* the children.

2 Complete the table.

	Positive	Negative
Effects on parents	Less pressure for each parent	
Effects on children		Narrow view of social roles

3 Remember, you can take a balanced view if you like, but state your position clearly in the introduction.

SAMPLE ANSWERS

Attempt to write your response to the Writing tasks in the units and in the Writing task bank on pages 90–97 before looking at the sample answers. Then use the questions to help you compare your response with the sample.

Sample answer 1
(Unit 1, Over to you, pages 17 and 90)

1 Underline the times of day that the writer has mentioned to illustrate key trends. Did you select the same times?

2 Underline the different past tenses that the writer has used. Did they use more or fewer than you?

The graph shows the proportion of students on further education programmes that were occupied with their studies at different times of the day over a 24-hour period. Not surprisingly, full-time students spent far more of their time studying than part-time students. By mid-morning, for example, when the greatest percentage of both groups are engaged in study activities, 35 per cent of full-time students were learning, compared to just under 20 per cent of part-time students.

However, the gap between the two groups narrowed in the evenings. By around 6pm, when normal office/school hours finish, the number of full-time students who were studying had fallen to around 20 per cent, while that of part-time students remained relatively constant at between 13 and 16 per cent until 9pm, despite a notable drop shortly before 4pm when schools finish. Interestingly, at no time during the day were more than 34 per cent of students, full-time or otherwise, engaged in learning.

[157 words]

Note how the writer reports a key trend in the graph before giving specific examples to illustrate that trend.

Sample answer 2
(Unit 2, Over to you, page 25)

1 Underline the sentence(s) that give background information about the topic. The next sentence states an opinion. Have you included both background information and an opinion?

2 Did you manage to avoid repeating key words from the question prompt? If not, can you find any synonyms in the sample answer that you could have used?

2 In many parts of the world, cities are growing rapidly as people move from the countryside to fulfil their dreams of higher wages and greater prosperity in the metropolis. The consequences of this mass migration are serious, both for the migrants and for the life of existing city dwellers, and city authorities urgently need solutions to address them.

3 In the modern, globalised world, mass-produced goods have largely replaced products made by hand, which are inevitably more expensive. At the same time, new materials are replacing old ones, like wood or ceramics, from which man learnt to create objects over many centuries. Such losses can only impoverish our culture and we must act now to protect them.

Notice how both the sample introductions contain some background information in the first sentence, then a clear opinion on the issue in the last sentence.

Sample answer 3
(Test file 1, Task 1, pages 29 and 90)

1 Did you present the features of the graph in the same order as the writer of the sample? Is the order you used more or less effective?

2 Compare the number of sentences in your answer and the sample answer. Note that longer, more complex sentences may earn higher marks for grammar.

The line graph shows the number of foreign residents in an English-speaking country during the century from 1910 to 2010. We can divide the data into two distinct periods: there was a decline in migrant numbers up to the middle of the last century, followed by a significantly greater rise in the latter period.

Turning to the period of growth first, the proportion of the population that was foreign-born rose threefold from the middle of the 20th century. All of this increase was accounted for by people from countries who don't speak English as their first language. While the level of migration from English-speaking countries remained constant from 1950 at around 8 per cent, that of immigration from non-English speaking nations rose from only 1 per cent to around 16 per cent.

The earlier decline in migration numbers that ended in around 1948 was evident in all categories of migrants shown, but was particularly notable among English-speaking migrants, whose numbers halved from 14 per cent to 7 per cent.

[169 words]

You may get extra marks if you put data into categories. Notice how the writer has done this by dividing the data into two periods of time. Why do you think they have written about the second period first?

Sample answer 4
(Test file 1, Task 2, page 29)

1. **Underline two places where the writer states their opinion. Did you give the same opinion?**
2. **How many arguments does the writer state to support their opinion? (Don't forget the argument used to reject the opposing point of view.) Did you think of several reasons to support your view?**

For young people, mobile phones have become not only the main tool of communication but a valuable tool for gaining information. It therefore makes absolute sense to allow this educational tool in the classroom.

Those who disagree would say that the ability of a teacher to control a class will be affected if students can use their phones. For example, they might check social media pages, chat with friends and generally disrupt lessons. This is a valid concern, but there are ways that teachers can get around this problem. Mobile phones could be permitted at certain times of the lesson and not others, so that when a teacher needs to gain the attention of class members, they are able to do so. The teacher could also insist that class members use mobile devices in pairs to reduce the chance that students will check their personal messages.

Besides, there are a whole range of advantages. Use of mobiles is more stimulating than textbooks or reference materials and will therefore engage students more in lessons. Admittedly, some modern classrooms will have equipment like tablet PCs and whiteboards, but students will enjoy using a tool that is familiar to them and which they are able to control easily. Allowing them to use their own equipment will prepare them better for independent study too and make them feel that they are in control of their learning.

In conclusion, while every classroom is different and while some groups of students will behave more responsibly than others, we should nevertheless find ways to permit use of mobiles in the classroom. It is the responsibility of the teachers to find ways of doing this that will encourage students to use this tool responsibly.

[286 words]

Notice how the writer uses the first paragraph after the introduction to focus on a different point of view. Criticising other views allows your essay to cover more ideas and sound more persuasive.

Sample answer 5
(Unit 3, Over to you, pages 37 and 91)

1. **Underline the overview statements (a statement that refer to all aspects of the data) that the writer has included. Have you included a similar overview?**
2. **Underline the structures used to make comparisons. Have you used the same structures or different ones?**

The bar graph shows the number of young people of both genders who, on the one hand, got information about either a new game or a new piece of music from friends and, on the other, the number who shared information about new music or games. We can see that information about new music is more likely to be passed on by girls than by boys. For example, 114 girls claimed to hear about music from friends compared to only 86 boys. However, the data shows the opposite trend for computer games, about which 112 boys shared information compared to just 88 girls. Interestingly then, it seems that boys and girls are equally as likely to share or get information through word of mouth, even if the type of information they pass on varies. It is also interesting to note that similar numbers of young people claim to give information about entertainment as claim to get it from friends: the difference is no greater than four respondents in any category. This emphasises how prevalent word-of-mouth advertising is among young people.

[180 words]

Note that the writer has written overview statements at the end of the report. It doesn't matter where you include an overview statement, as long as you include one.

Sample answer 6
(Unit 4, Over to you, page 45)

1. **The writer has chosen to take a very strong stance on this question. Is your position equally strong or is your opinion more moderate?**
2. **Do you think the essay would have been better if the writer had attempted to discuss another viewpoint, as in sample answer 4?**

Technology has helped bring the rest of the world into our living room and continues to do so. Not only can we watch documentaries and videos about the remotest regions of the world, we can even gain realistic experiences of other places through virtual reality. But impressive as these developments are, there will never be a substitute for real travel, for several simple reasons.

First, travel gives people time to lose themselves in a new environment, perhaps for many months. This enables them to immerse themselves in another culture and develop language skills, new ways of thinking and generally have more profound experiences. Occasional contact with other cultures through media is unlikely to have a long-term effect on our skills or our thinking.

Secondly, travel is not simply about the place; it is also a social experience. Whether we travel in groups or alone, an experience in a foreign country can help us to bond closely with travel companions or even with members of local populations, perhaps while sampling local food and drink. Such valuable personal interactions cannot be gained from consumption of digital entertainment.

Finally, the travel industry supports livelihoods worldwide. Locals gain valuable income from tourist arrivals, and travel and transport companies clearly depend on our willingness to travel. Such movement has helped many parts of the world to become integrated with the global economy and achieve a higher standard of living. Entertainment, by comparison, simply swells the profits of already-wealthy media companies.

In conclusion, the idea that technology may replace travel

fails to take into account the wonderful opportunities that travel provides for both personal and economic development.

[271 words]

Note that the writer has used some words that aren't very academic, like *immerse*, *swells*, *fails*, *wonderful*, etc. This 'emotional' language is acceptable for an opinion essay.

Sample answer 7 (Test file 2, Task 1, pages 49 and 91)

1 **The writer has avoided including all the data in their description. Did you highlight the same data in your description?**

2 **The writer has grouped countries by referring to 'European' nations. Did you place the countries into categories of your own?**

The table shows the percentage of text on the internet that appears in different languages and the most common languages of internet users. In general, we can say that English dominates web content, accounting for over 53%, but that the languages of the users are understandably much more varied. In terms of the content, the internet is very much dominated by languages of European origin, whereas internet users include a much wider range.

Another interesting point is that nearly 80% of the content of the internet is written in a European language. It is also notable that while just 1.9% of the internet is in Chinese, over 20% of users speak Chinese. Furthermore, nearly 8% of users speak Arabic and Malay, yet these languages are not in the ten most common for content.

To conclude, there is clearly a mismatch between the language used on the internet and the native language of its users, suggesting that many will be disadvantaged when it comes to accessing web content.

[167 words]

Notice how the writer has chosen to add a concluding sentence. Although this is not necessary, the ideas in the conclusion help to highlight important features of the data.

Sample answer 8 (Test file 2, Task 2, page 49)

1 **The writer discusses views different to their own in both paragraphs. This means that the main idea of the paragraph is not stated until later. Do you think this style is effective?**

2 **Underline the pronouns (*this*, *they*, etc) the writer has used. Have you used similar words to refer to previous ideas?**

Modern families often lack time and seek ways to make everyday tasks quicker and simpler. One such task is commuting, and consequently many people have developed an overdependence on their car. School authorities should act to discourage this trend.

Many people would disagree with this stance, arguing that they have the right to travel to school in the manner they choose. Often people take their children to school while on their way to work, and walking or cycling would not be practical. This may be true, but travel should not only be about convenience. Walking can help students improve fitness levels, especially if they avoid main roads. This will have a benefit for the school, since children who are healthy and active are likely to be better behaved in class. It can also have a significant positive impact on family life, giving more time for families to talk.

Another argument put forward by those who believe we should take children to school in cars is that they are safer inside vehicles than they are on the pavements. But while these particular children may be safer, others, whose parents cannot take them in the car, suffer from the impact created by the parent drivers. A higher level of congestion on the roads leads to an increase in NO_2 and other exhaust emissions that have serious effects on the health of pedestrians and cyclists. Encouraging parents to walk their children to school would reduce this impact.

In conclusion, encouraging more people to walk to school would transform young people's quality of life, and school authorities should take urgent action.

[267 words]

Notice that the writer has not used linking words before *Walking* ... and *A higher* ... because the connection between the sentences is already clear.

Sample answer 9 (Unit 5, Over to you, pages 57 and 92)

1 **Underline the overview statement that summarises the information. Did you remember to include one?**

2 **Underline the passive structures. How many tenses did the writer use? Could you amend your sample to include more passive structures?**

The diagram shows how four types of medication are made. The number of stages involved depends upon the type of medication being manufactured, but the process is fairly simple, involving as few as three steps. In all cases, the process begins with proportioning, during which powdered 'excipients' and pharmacologically active substances are carefully measured. Once the correct amounts have been obtained, they are then mixed together. The next stage in the procedure will depend on what is being produced. To make granules, tablets or pills, the mixture will then be granulated, and this will in fact be the final stage in the production of granules. Capsules, by comparison, may be filled directly without granulation. Tablets and pills require a little more finishing. Both require a degree of compression, which may also include additional stages of granulation. Tablets will then be ready for packaging whereas pills will first have to be sugar-coated.

[151 words]

Notice how the writer has often separated passive structures with adverbs like *carefully* and *then*.

Sample answer 10
(Unit 6, Over to you, page 65)

1 **How many effects of supermarket shopping has the writer thought of? Did you think of different consequences?**

2 **Underline examples of technical vocabulary, like *purchasing power*? Did you manage to use some precise or less common vocabulary?**

3 **Each effect has been separated by a paragraph break. Did you use paragraphing adequately?**

Previously, many businesses were owned and run locally. Meat was purchased from a butcher, bread from a baker and so on. Yet today, the vast majority of purchases are made from huge supermarkets that supply a whole host of goods. This growing trend has had both positive and negative impacts on our lives.

One positive effect is that the price of goods has generally come down. Supermarkets have incredible purchasing power and can use this to source suppliers from all around the world. They can then demand lower prices because of the volumes they are buying and hopefully pass this onto the end consumer.

Furthermore, we now have more choice. Goods were often reliant on seasons, and for example, tomatos might only be available for two months a year. But supermarkets tend to supply products from around the globe and so it is possible to have almost any item at any time of the year.

While both of these points may be true, these exact same behaviours have had a negative impact on our lives. By sourcing supplies from across the globe, smaller local farms and stores have been put out of business. This has led to decline in certain local industries and lack of investment in some areas. Equally, the potentially lower price is not always passed onto the consumer.

There have also been environmental consequences. Flying these foods around the world produces more carbon emissions, which leads to increases in air pollution. Furthermore, out-of-town supermarkets have often caused an increase in road traffic and congestion locally.

In conclusion, supermarkets have increased the choice of food on offer at different times of the year, but they have arguably put local companies out of business and damaged the environment.

[289 words]

Notice how the author has used the present perfect to talk about results that you can still see in the present.

Sample answer 11
(Test file 3, Task 1, page 69)

1 **Underline the four sequence markers (eg *first*, *after*, etc) that the writer has used. Have you used a similar variety?**

2 **The writer has chosen to put a paragraph break after the overview statement. Do you think this makes the answer clearer?**

The diagram shows what happens to different kinds of packaging during the recycling process. We can see that the processes don't simply result in the reuse of packaging but produce a wide range of other materials.

After all products are bought and consumed, they have to be separated and disposed of in recycling containers. At this stage, they are collected by local authorities and taken to recycling facilities. They will then be sent to a materials plant where most of the decisions about their future 'use' are taken. Many products will subsequently be returned to packaging plants and reused by drinks companies and so on, who will, in turn, refill them and return them to the shops. These include plastic and glass bottles and also cans. However, other materials are turned into a range of products. These range from domestic products like clothing and toilet paper to aluminium products and materials for construction.

[153 words]

Note how the writer uses the future tense to refer to regular habitual actions.

Sample answer 12
(Test file 3, Task 2, page 69)

1 **Which threats did the writer identify? Did you focus on similar ideas?**

2 **Create a table of problems and solutions, combining the ideas in your essay and the sample. Make sure you include some high-level vocabulary from the sample.**

These days, we are exposed to a growing range of threats to our health. This essay will decide which of these threats is most difficult to protect against and ask what we can do to protect ourselves from them.

One of the most difficult issues is air pollution. For the many people who live and work by busy roads, it is almost impossible to shield them from it. This is especially true in poor countries where traders work informally in the streets, cleaning cars and selling to drivers. Wearing masks can help reduce these effects, though they can be costly.

Traffic is also increasing the risk to our safety, and cyclists and pedestrians face many dangers as they attempt to use ever-more congested transport networks. While wearing a helmet might constitute a fairly simple safety measure, there are limits to how far protective clothing can actually protect you when faced with the power of a bus or lorry.

High-calorie food is a further modern threat. It is very difficult to change people's eating habits, and such foods have become a central part of our diets now, affecting young people especially. In contrast to air pollution, this issue is as big a problem in richer parts of the world. Individuals can either try to exercise more to combat weight gain or experiment with diets, but attempts to vary lifestyle are often short-lived.

In conclusion, traffic and diet are the two most intractable problems of our age. The extent to which individuals can protect themselves from both will largely depend on whether they have the financial resources and perhaps education to respond to the threats.

[273 words]

Notice how the writer has chosen to offer a solution to each problem before moving on to the next problem. This has allowed them to link problems and solutions effectively.

Sample answer 13
(Unit 7, Over to you, pages 77 and 93)

1 **The writer described physical changes to the office before considering the (less important) changes to the function of rooms. Have you included both sets of features?**

2 **Underline the sentences where the writer has highlighted continuity instead of change.**

The two plans show the changes that have taken place recently in a company's office space. The most significant change is that the vast majority of the office is now open plan, allowing staff members to collaborate more effectively. Over two-thirds of the original rooms have been knocked down and replaced by the one large space. People are still located in teams, but they no longer enjoy much privacy. What is more, there are now only two offices, for senior management.

The function of many rooms has also been adapted. Next to the senior management offices, the IT support room has now been transformed into the boardroom. The only room that has retained its original function is the store cupboard in the top right-hand corner of the plan. Meanwhile, the toilets and kitchen have been relocated to the right-hand side, and the offices in the bottom right-hand corner are now meeting rooms, where staff can hold discussions.

[157 words]

Note how the writer has highlighted important changes by commenting on the implications of some of the changes.

Sample answer 14
(Unit 8, Over to you, page 85)

1 **Which side of the debate has the writer chosen to agree with? Did you come to the same conclusion?**

2 **How many lines of text has the writer dedicated to each argument. Is your essay similarly balanced?**

The productivity of workers is essential to boosting the competitiveness of companies and economic growth. But the best way to achieve greater productivity is a question of debate.

Many would argue that pay is by far the simplest solution. Financial rewards can be linked to obtaining performance targets, and such incentives have long been known to make people work harder. Furthermore, rewarding staff with pay is an effective way of making workers feel that their efforts are valued, increasing their commitment. Finally, in the modern world, there is downward pressure on pay due to competition and the availability of cheap labour from other countries, so workers are likely to respond to financial incentives in this climate.

Yet there are those who believe that pay is not the most effective way to raise production. It can make people resentful of colleagues and undermine collaboration, and it can also attract people who are concerned with rewards rather than those who love their job and enjoy teamwork. It would be better, then, to develop commitment between colleagues by creating social areas or invest in team-building events, for example, or to improve training. This will increase the exchange of ideas and make workers feel they are free to take risks rather than simply follow the steps that will lead to reward.

In my view, the arguments against increasing pay seem to show a greater understanding of both business and personal needs, and I would recommend that employers focus on building stronger relationships at work.

[250 words]

Note that although the writer has not indicated their opinion until the conclusion, they have still focused on the argument they agree with second, creating a logical link to the conclusion.

Sample answer 15
(Test file 4, Task 1, pages 89 and 93)

1 **Underline ways in which the writer makes connections or comparisons between features. Did you attempt similar comparisons?**

2 **Underline all the structures that contain the verb *be*. Did you use any of them too?**

The drawing illustrates an architect's view of what a prison might look like. In general, they are envisaging a space in which there is large number of separate buildings and leisure facilities separated by large areas of green space. In the centre of the drawing are the blocks where the prisoners would have their cells. These are arranged in a radial pattern so that rather than facing each other directly, the windows would look out over more green space. Parkland and trees are visible from all four sides of each block. There are also separate school facilities (at the top left of the diagram) of a more or less equal size to the living areas, and administration facilities are located at various locations. Between them are areas where prisoners could do exercise and play competitive sports like tennis and basketball. To go from one facility to another, prisoners and staff would have to walk some distance, following a meandering path.

[160 words]

Notice how the writer puts some preposition phrases at the front of sentences, increasing the complexity of grammar structures.

Sample answer 16
(Test file 4, Task 2, page 89)

1 **Underline the linking expressions the writer has used to connect all the advantages advantages in one paragraph. Have you used similar expressions?**

2 **What cautious language has the writer used to suggest something might be true?**

Many people now work until they are 70, meaning that people often have working lives in excess of 50 years. With such long careers, it is not surprising that many people now frequently change their career. This essay will discuss the positive and negative consequences of making such a change.

There are a number of disadvantages to changing your career midway through. Firstly, any career change often requires retraining, which can be both expensive and time consuming. In addition to this, people's salary often falls as they have to take an entry-level position, whereas previously they may have been in a more senior position. Finally, depending on the stage of the applicant's life, some employers may be averse to hiring an older person in a lower-level position.

While these are valid concerns, there are also numerous advantages to changing professions. After a long period of time in one field, people can often become bored and unmotivated. The job is so familiar that it is no longer challenging or stimulating. By changing career, people's interest in their work can be raised and they can feel reinvigorated. This new positive feeling can have a favourable impact on many parts of someone's life. It may also allow people to move away from a career that they chose whilst young and with very little knowledge of what they actually wanted to do.

In conclusion, while changing careers can be time consuming and expensive, it can also make people feel more engaged with their working life. By not feeling depressed or uninterested in their work, it may also give them a more positive outlook on life in general. It should therefore be encouraged.

[278 words]

Notice how clearly the first sentence of each paragraph states the paragraph purpose. The last sentence of the introduction also helps the reader understand the intention of the writer.

Track 1.2 (Unit 1, Listening, Exercise 4)

1 17 **2** UAE **3** BPY **4** 111 **5** 30th

Track 1.3 (Unit 1, Listening, Exercise 5)

You will hear a conversation between an administrator and a student. Listen and answer Questions 1–3.

A Hello?
B Hello, this is the university accommodation department. You asked us to call you back about a student room.
A Oh, yes, I did. Thank you.
B So, how can we help?
A Well, I'm starting a course in January, on the 12th, but I missed the deadline for internet applications.
B Is this for an undergraduate course?
A No, post-graduate.
B Then yes, you have. But we still have some options available. Can I take some details first of all?
A Of course.
B So your name is ...?
A It's Husham Osman.
B Is that H-i-s-h-a-m?
A No, H-u, actually.
B One moment ... You're from Sudan, right?
A Yes, that's correct.
B Great, yes, I see you've accepted a place in the faculty of Commerce and Law.
A That's right, I'm doing a course in global business.
B Yes, that's a popular programme. So let's see what accommodation we can offer.

Track 1.4 (Unit 1, Listening, Exercise 6)

Now listen to the rest of the conversation and answer Questions 4–10.

B Well, you still have two options. There are two rooms left in the student village.
A Where's that?
B It's by the Westwood campus, which is where your faculty is located.
A Mm. How much do the rooms cost?
B Let me see, they were £150 a week last year, but now they're ... £160.
A That seems expensive.
B Well, it does include all your meals.
A Sorry?
B I mean there's a place to eat there, like a restaurant, so you don't have to cook. There are also other facilities, like a laundrette and a games room.
A Oh, right. Actually, I quite like to prepare my own food – you know, dishes from my country.
B OK, well, you might prefer to live in a private house in the town centre. There's a house on Greenfield Lane with rooms for £110 a week. Are you happy to share with three other male students?
A Yes, that would be great. Do I have to contact a landlord about it?
B No, we can organise it. So, it has four bedrooms, a shared living room and a kitchen.
A Do the rooms have bathrooms?
B No, you have to share one. But the house is furnished and you can access high-speed internet from all parts of the house.
A Good – that's really important so I can send in my essays.
B Yes, we don't want you to miss any more deadlines!
A Mmm. And is it easy to reach the campus?
B It's about 3 kilometres by road. Buses run close to that area every ten minutes. But we recommend you go on foot. It only takes 20 minutes if you take the path over the railway bridge.
A Great. Can I book it? Who do I pay?
B Don't worry, we deal with all that. We add the accommodation costs to your university fees and then we pay the landlord directly.
A That's great. So how do I get the keys?
B You come to our offices near the main library any time between 9am and 6pm.
A Can I have the address now?
B Not yet, we have to contact the landlord first, but when they've accepted, we'll text you all the details, if that's OK?
A That's great. Thank you!

Track 1.5 (Unit 1, Speaking, Exercises 6 and 7)

Examiner What do you enjoy doing in your free time?
Candidate 1 Well, I mostly enjoy doing outdoor activities, yes.
Examiner What sporting activities did you enjoy at your secondary school?
Candidate 1 Football, of course. I liked football very much.
Examiner Mm. After class, do you prefer to spend time alone or with others?
Candidate 1 Actually, I like to be alone. It's best, I think.
Examiner Is there an interest or hobby you would like to try?
Candidate 1 Oh yes! I'd like to try caving.

Track 1.6 (Unit 1, Speaking, Exercises 6 and 7)

Examiner What do you enjoy doing in your free time?
Candidate 2 I love watching films. I really enjoy horror and science-fiction movie. I go to the cinema every Friday night and in the summer I go to local film festival.
Examiner What sporting activities did you enjoy at your secondary school?
Candidate 2 I enjoyed doing athletics. I was in an athletics club at school. We ran most lunch times, and we often go running in the evenings. I won a big tournament when I was 13.
Examiner After class, do you prefer to spend time alone or with others?
Candidate 2 I like to be alone for a while. Is good to have time to do homework or to chill out and play music.
Examiner Is there an interest or hobby you would like to try?
Candidate 2 I'd like to have a go at painting. There are classes at a local college and I'd really like joining. Unfortunately, I often don't have enough time.

Track 1.7 (Unit 1, Speaking, Exercise 9)

1 I enjoy films most of all.
2 I see films at my local cinema.
3 I go to the cinema every Friday if I can.

Track 1.8 (Unit 2, Listening, Exercise 4)

You will hear someone giving a presentation about a new housing development. Listen and answer Questions 1–5.

Good morning, everyone. Glad to see so many people have come to hear about our plans to redevelop this part of the city. My name's Mike Ryan and I'm the lead architect. In your pack, you have most of the information you'll need, but I'm just going to highlight some of the key features. So let's look in more detail at the map in your packs.

When designing this development, we wanted to focus on the things people find most important in a new neighbourhood. When you enter the development from the south, along the road that you can see at the bottom of your maps, there are some wide open spaces. Directly in front of you are the public gardens and behind them are the tennis courts. We've made the centre of the development the focus of social life, with wide open spaces and lots of facilities. Behind the tennis courts is the main square in which we have a street market twice a week. The main road leading off this square has restaurants, cafés and bars to suit a wide range of tastes. To the north-west of this area, we have some flats constructed for young professionals. As many young professionals are likely to need to commute for work, we've chosen to place the central bus station just south of here, just north of the library. The large area in the bottom left of the map is the main retail hub with the new shopping centre. This was another reason for placing the main railway station here, near the edge of the development. Obviously, this area of the development is one of the more lively parts. To the east of the development, you'll find a quieter part of the neighbourhood that's much more family focused. There's a nursery and a small primary school, and between the school and the main family housing area, we have a small medical practice that contains a doctor's surgery and a pharmacy.

Track 1.9 (Unit 2, Listening, Exercise 5)

Now listen to the rest of the presentation and answer Questions 6–10.

Now, I'm sure the primary school will be of interest to many of you. It will have enough places for up to 250 children, and once they get to high-school age, there's the excellent Highdown School nearby. In the family housing area, there'll be houses for all sizes of families. There'll

be a number of small two-bedroom starter homes. The largest homes in the area will have five bedrooms. Prices will range from £150,000 to £800,000. The green area that you can see in the bottom corner is a small children's playground to keep the kids active.
As many of you know, we have a lot of green targets for this development. Rain water will be recycled for use in the public toilets. There are numerous recycling points throughout the town and allotments for people to grow their own food. In terms of electricity, all houses will have solar panels. Studies show that these can provide 50% of the energy that the settlement is likely to need. To reduce car use and keep people fit, there are also free bikes for residents to use to get around. If things aren't in walking distance, then people can quickly cycle around town. Now, I'd just like to look at one more part before we present the alternative plans for the layout of the complex.

Track 1.10 (Unit 2, Speaking, Exercises 3 and 4)

Candidate 1 My grandmother is the person I admire the most. When I was young, she was, like, always there, so perhaps I didn't think about her much. I certainly didn't think about the life she had before I was born. But then I had a chat to her once when I was about 14 and I found out that her life had been very interesting. She was born into a poor family, but certainly didn't let that stop her. At a young age, she went onto the street to sell fans that she'd made.

Track 1.11 (Unit 2, Speaking, Exercises 3 and 4)

Candidate 2 A person I know well that I admire is my teacher. I really look up to him. My relationship to them is ... well, I was his pupil. He was the most inspirational teacher I had. How they have spent their life is, well, in school, of course. He was so passionate about his job. And what they are like ... he is really resourceful and dedicated to his work. And now I am going to explain why I admire them.

Track 1.12 (Test file 1, Listening, Section 1)

You will hear a conversation between a receptionist and a member of the public. You now have some time to look at Questions 1–5.

***

Now listen and answer Questions 1–5.

A Hello, Hunton Community Centre.
B Hi – yes, I'm thinking of joining the youth club.
A Sure – in fact, there's a website for the youth club – everything you need is on there, application forms, programmes ...
B Actually, I don't have internet at home at the moment.
A OK, no problem. What do you need to know?
B Well, firstly, I'll be 19 next week. Am I too old to join?
A Not at all, 19's fine. In fact, we take people up to the age of 21, and even after that you can get involved as a youth leader.
B Great. Is there a separate group for older members?
A Yes, there is. Both groups used to meet on Fridays, but now the 15 to 21s meet on Wednesdays – that'll be your group – whereas the younger members, from ten to 14, meet on Mondays.
B Do they meet at the same time?
A No, the older group meets at 7pm – that will be your start time – and finishes at 10pm. The younger group has a 6pm start.
B Is there any space at the moment?
A Ah, let me see – yes, we have plenty of space in the older age group. If you just give me your name and contact details, I'll let them know you're coming.
B OK, that would be great. It's Daryl Greene, D-A-R-Y-L, and then Green with an *e* on the end.
A Mm-hm. Thanks, Daryl, and can I take a phone number for you, just in case?
B Sure – my mobile is 07892 556250.
A ... 2-5-0 – that's great. We'll see you on Wednesday.

You now have some time to look at Questions 6–10.

***

Now listen to the rest of the conversation and answer Questions 6–10.

B Actually, before I go, can I ask you some questions about the club?
A Sure.
B My younger brother is interested too, so it would be good to know about both groups.
A That's fine. What would you like to know?
B Well, firstly, do members have to bring anything? What about payment?
A Oh, yes. Bring along £1.50 for yourself. Your brother wouldn't need to bring anything because it's free for him. You don't really need anything else.
B What's the payment for?
A It covers the cost of snacks – you get a piece of fruit in the younger group, and there are normally some hot snacks for the older ones, like noodles.
B And what kind of activities are there?
A Well, it's up to you, really. The ten to 14s normally play sports, especially football or basketball, and then watch a film. There would be more opportunities for you, though. There's often a chance to prepare simple meals in the kitchens, like pancakes or fruit salad. Some of our members like to do street dance, too.
B Is all the equipment provided?
A Absolutely. We have sports equipment for everyone – things like coloured vests or table-tennis equipment. Then there are craft materials for the younger ones – and we have gym equipment like crash mats for the older ones. You just need to make sure you wear comfortable shoes.
B That's great. Thank you – see you next week.

That is the end of Section 1. In the test, you will now have 30 seconds to check your answers.

Track 1.13 (Test file 1, Listening, Section 2)

You will hear a student induction talk. You now have some time to look at Questions 11–15.

***

Now listen and answer Questions 11–15.

Welcome to this open day for the Faculty of Science here at Joseph Wallis University. Please take your seats quickly if you haven't already. Thank you. Now, in a moment I'm going to hand over to the Dean of the Faculty, Janice Pembrook, who will give you a short introduction to the faculty's teaching and research, but first let me just tell you about the programme for the afternoon. It will be useful if you can look at your map first. So we're now in the Auditorium, and here there will be a programme of talks by heads of department who will all try to persuade you that their courses are the best. However, we don't expect you to stay for all of them! Instead, we invite you to look around our beautiful faculty building and talk to members of our various departments. In the Atrium, just opposite as you leave this hall, there are some permanent stands where you can pick up literature and ask any questions you might have. On the right is the stand for the computing department, in the middle of the space you can meet members of the faculty of medicine, and on the left there's dentistry. Just behind the dentistry stand, there's the admissions desk – feel free to head there with any questions you might have. At the far right of the building, to the right of the auditorium, we have our main resources centre. You'll enter via the IT suite and if you continue through that, you'll find the faculty's extensive library. Of course, the main university library has the widest selection of science books, but you'll find a range of more specialist publications here. Toilets are just outside the resource centre, and if you need a break to digest the information, you'll notice our modern cafeteria is open all afternoon. That's the large space just above the toilets. Finally, if you walk towards Hall 1, in front of you you'll see an exhibition for our many 'study abroad' programmes, with posters and photos of our partner institutions.

You now have some time to look at Questions 16–20.

***

Now listen to the rest of the talk and answer Questions 16–20.

The 'study abroad' programmes are a particularly important part of life in the science faculty. We expect all second-year students to spend some time studying at a foreign university if they can, and in fact 80% of our students – over 300 – do just that. We're lucky to be working in partnership with a number of prestigious overseas institutes, and a period abroad shows employers that you're independent, and so you'll find it easier to attract attention from large organisations in the jobs market. So we suggest that all of you spend a while this afternoon exploring these opportunities.
We understand, however, that our 'study abroad' programmes will cost extra money, so we do provide financial help to our students. You can find details about financial support at the admissions desk, marked on your map. Also some of the overseas courses will be taught in a foreign language, so all students will be required to develop their language skills during their first year here. If you'd like to visit the modern languages department, where these courses are held, it's just opposite this faculty.
When you're finally ready to leave for home this afternoon, remember the shuttle bus can take you directly to the central bus station. But please feel free to stay as long as you like! So, let me now introduce you to Janice ...

That is the end of Section 2. In the test, you will now have 30 seconds to check your answers.

Track 1.14 (Test file 1, Speaking, Part 1)

Let's talk about your home town.

1 What do you like about your home town or city?
2 What was it like growing up there?
3 How has the town changed?
4 Where will you live in the future?

Let's talk about family.

1 Can you tell me about your family?
2 What did your family do at weekends when you were a child?
3 Who do you get on best with in your family? Why?
4 Would you like to spend more time with your family?

Track 1.15 (Unit 3, Listening, Exercise 4)

You will hear a conversation between two students. Listen and answer Questions 1–6.

Noel OK, shall we get started? We've only got a week left to do this presentation.

Wei Don't worry! The topic is easy: 'Effective communication'. I could write a presentation on it now and it would be fine.

Noel I don't think it's that obvious. I think the tutor is going to want us to base this on things we actually find out, not just our common sense. He's going to want us to look into the actual theory and not just summarise our best ideas from a quick brainstorm.

Wei OK, so where would be a good place to start?

Noel I think marketing or media-studies websites could be a good place. They'll have lots of information.

Wei Really? Why?

Noel Well, communication is a skill used in marketing a lot. Adverts on TV or radio and so on are largely about how you get your message across effectively and engaging your audience with what you're saying.

Wei OK, but I think that's true for media studies as well. News stories need to be put across clearly, effectively and accurately. I've got some useful textbooks I can look at.

Noel Right, that sounds like a good idea, then. Let's go and do some research in the library and meet later.

***

Noel So how did you get on with your research?

Wei There's actually an awful lot of information out there. It's difficult to summarise it all, really.

Noel Well, how would you summarise the main point? What does it mean to communicate effectively?

Wei Well, there are loads of definitions, but I guess it can be best summarised as getting your message across clearly.

Noel Mm. What exactly does that mean, though?

Wei A couple of different things, really. One of the key things is your audience. You have to think about who they are.

Noel Anything specifically?

Wei Well, what their background is, how much knowledge they have, why they're there, and what they hope to get out of your talk.

Noel Interesting. I'd always just thought effective communication was about the style of delivery. You know, things like having a clear, loud voice.

Wei I suppose that's key as well. In presentations, for example, people are often very nervous and speak too quickly, which makes it hard for people to understand you. But we'll always be nervous, so I don't think we can avoid that.

Noel Mm, I'm not sure. You can control your speech if you stress key words or pause at the right point. It gives people time to take in the things you just said.

Wei I guess we'll have to include both aspects in our talk, then.

Noel I think you're right. What about speaking from notes or cards? Is that a good idea?

Wei It depends on the person a bit. If you can do it without any notes, it's good, but it's really hard. The main thing, though, is not to read your whole talk word for word. It makes the delivery boring.

Track 1.16 (Unit 3, Listening, Exercise 5)

Now listen to the rest of the conversation and answer Questions 7–10.

Wei Let's decide what we need to prioritise.

Noel OK, well, I guess it's important to get the introduction done urgently.

Wei Actually, we can probably do that at the end when we know what points we want to make. I don't think we should worry about finding lots of images either. They can be distracting.

Noel Really? They may not be vital, but I'd say they'd give our presentation a little more impact. Video clips would be fairly useful too.

Wei All right, I agree that would be nice, but let's decide what to type on the slides first, starting with the headings. I mean, that's essential.

Noel Fine. Are we going to add some quotes too, from the textbooks?

Wei Well, that will take time. I don't think it matters much, really.

Noel OK. By the way, I have a friend who designs slides. Shall I ask her to help us?

Wei Absolutely, that will really impress the others. Let's make sure we get her help.

Noel OK, I'll call her now.

Wei Great. I'll start thinking about those slide titles while you do that.

Track 1.17 (Unit 3, Speaking, Exercises 5 and 6)

1 Well, obviously there are the things people put on ... er ... social media ... er ... These can be anything from photos to their ... er ... opinions to contact details. Many people also have online professional ... er ... profiles on sites such as LinkedIn. This is essentially your online career history and your ... er ... your ... er ... CV.
2 I think it really depend. Not enough people is careful about who do they share photos with and what can people see in those photos. So, for example, university friends are sharing photos from a night out together on Instagram. At the same time, this person is looking for a job and their potential employer see the photos. The photos are give a really negative impression of the person. You need make sure you will be happy for anyone can see them.
3 Well, there are lots of crimes. First, there are people that take your bank information – like the number on your card. Sometimes they send you an email and they ask you to give this information. There are also people who try to get into government websites or company websites.
4 There are a wide range of reasons to change your password, but the main reason is that people are concerned about internet security. If people can access your password, they might attempt to access your bank account or buy things from any of your online shopping accounts. Sometimes computer systems make you change your password. When this happens, people often forget their passwords because they have so many that they've changed.

Track 1.18 (Unit 3, Speaking, Exercise 8)

If people can access your password, they might attempt to access your bank account or buy things from any of your online shopping accounts.

Track 1.19 (Unit 4, Listening, Exercise 3)

You will hear a lecturer talking about ecotourism. Listen and answer Questions 1–6.

Good morning, everyone. Today, we're going to be looking at how ecotourism has developed from its origins to present day.

First, let's look at how it all started. In the fifties and sixties, people couldn't get enough of tourism. It seemed like there were no limits to its benefits. Then, in the 1970s, some started to worry about the damage that all the big, foreign hotels were doing to local cultures, to the environments, and to the economy too – after all, tourists come and go again, so you can't rely on them. In the following decade, a movement emerged called 'ecotourism'.

So what does ecotourism in its original form look like? Well, I want you to imagine a village in Africa with a growing population. It's the kind of place where people might have to cut down more trees to create more farmland or where they might hunt more animals, either to sell or eat. But instead, 80 of the locals invite foreigners to come and stay with them. They protect the beautiful wildlife because tourists are interested in it and they make crafts and clothes that the visitors can buy. This village I've just described to you is called Bigodi in Uganda. Since 1992, it's provided a model of an ecotourism project. And with the money it's generated over the years, the locals have built a school and set up a range of health services.

So, to define ecotourism, we must recognise that it's not simply about tourism in wild areas, though it does take place in nature and attracts educated city dwellers who like adventure tourism in general. It's essentially tourism that helps engage local people and protect nature. If well-planned, it gives locals a lasting income, and lets them take management decisions about the tourism projects. And it gets tourists or locals to maintain their environment into the long term.

Despite the success of Bigodi, ecotourism projects have faced a variety of challenges and not all are as successful. Sometimes the income from the projects is not spent as wisely. For example, money might be spent on funding a local male football team, therefore benefitting only a few. Corruption and community divisions sometimes result, and many projects are short lived.

Besides, there are several ways in which tourism might also damage the local communities in the long term. Protected animal populations may become very successful and start to destroy crops, for example. Or Western tourists might start expecting access to refrigerators or cars which cause pollution or damage to the environment. Some also argue that living with Westerners causes the young to gradually adopt their values and increase the demand for importing goods and lifestyle. And jobs for locals are often fairly unskilled and unreliable too.

One final issue is scale. Most of the projects are small-scale in nature, and this makes them difficult to manage and regulate. Governments often fail to take ecotourism seriously and prefer larger projects that can generate greater investment in infrastructure and skills development. Besides, today's environmental challenges, like global warming, are arguably greater than the challenge of protecting local wildlife.

Track 1.20 (Unit 4, Listening, Exercise 4)

Now listen to the rest of the lecture and answer Questions 7–10.

For these reasons, in modern times, there has been a shift of emphasis in modern ecotourism with governments often asking how they can use the principles of ecotourism to make mass tourism more eco-friendly. For example, they might encourage hotels to source products like soaps or towels from local businesses or work with local environmental agencies to arrange tours. Of course, governments are also asking how they can reduce the environmental and energy costs of large tourist complexes. An example of a solution comes in the form of water air-conditioning systems which have helped reduce hotel energy costs in coastal areas. You can see a diagram on the screen here.

The system is simple. A pipeline is installed that leads into the ocean at a depth where there is ice-cold water all year round. This water is then pumped up into a cooling station. At the same time, fresh water is continually being distributed through the hotel's air-conditioning pipes in a closed loop system. This water passes back through the cooling station at a temperature 12 degrees higher than when it left. This extra heat is then transferred to the sea water, which flows out of the cooling station and into the sea as effluent. With such a system, electricity costs are a tenth of normal air-conditioning costs and there's no need for the use of fossil fuels or CO_2 emissions.

The adaptation of mass tourism in eco-friendly ways seems to represent the future of ecotourism.

Track 1.21 (Unit 4, Speaking, Exercises 6 and 7)

1 Generally, I prefer going by myself. Always it's more relaxing. Going with friends is stressful because you have to think about what they want to do as well.

***

I have. Typically, they are other countries in the Middle East. We go usually to Oman in the spring. The weather's perfect then.

***

I'd love actually to go somewhere really remote and peaceful. The idea of trekking through a jungle or climbing an isolated mountain range is really exciting.

Track 1.22 (Unit 4, Speaking, Exercises 6 and 7)

2 I don't like to do much at all. I always go on a beach holiday and I spend most of my time on the beach sunbathing, swimming and eating.

***

I find travelling stressful. I like travelling by plane because it's usually the quickest way to get anywhere.

***

I don't. My parents don't like flying, and we live in the Philippines. But I want to go abroad. I will go abroad next year, I think.

Track 1.23 (Test file 2, Listening, Section 3)

You will hear a conversation between a tutor and two students. You now have some time to look at Questions 1–6.

***

Now listen and answer Questions 1–6.

Tutor Hi, Rehab and Dev. Come in. Take a seat. So, you have some questions you want to ask me about the essay on Renaissance architecture?

Rehab Yes, we do. They're probably really obvious, but this is the first essay, so we want to check a few things.

Tutor Sure, Rehab, no problem.

Rehab So Dev and I aren't really sure about how to include other people's ideas.

Tutor Have you found any relevant books and articles yet?

Dev Yes, we've found two of each already. We've been very organised, but we're not really sure how to refer to them in the essays. How do we include quotes and a bibliography?

Tutor You have to follow something called Harvard Style. There are lots of books on this topic, and there's also a useful sheet the library produces about plagiarism.

Rehab Where can we get those?

Tutor I think the sheets are in the self-study area on the first floor. You'll have to ask about the books.

Dev OK, thank you. We'll take a look. I'm also not sure about using the online submission system. The instructions say we don't print out the essay to submit. Is that right?

Tutor Yes, that's right. Give me a moment and I'll email you a link. It shows you how to upload essays and how to check your work ... There. So, er, what about the content of your essays? Do you think you've included enough evaluation and not simply written a descriptive essay?

Dev Um, I think so, but it would be useful to read a sample essay to make sure.

Tutor If you take a look at the online course website, there are a few from last year. Print one out and try to highlight all of the evaluation so you can see how much there is. Bring it to our next tutorial and we can look at it together.

Dev OK, that would be really helpful. Thank you.

Rehab Can you print one off for me as well, Dev?

Dev Sure, Rehab, no problem.

Tutor And I think you might need some more sources, too. I suggest you go to the library this afternoon and pick up a couple more books.

Rehab I'll do that.

Dev Could you get one of those plagiarism sheets, too?

Rehab Actually, I think I've got one on my desk already. You can borrow it, Dev.

Dev Ah, great. Thanks, Rehab.

Tutor And if you wait a few minutes, I'll get you a sheet with updated information about the books you need to read for the course. When you go to the library, try looking at the books near these on the shelves. They'll give you more relevant sources.

Dev / Rehab Thank you. / Thank you, sir.

You now have some time to look at Questions 7–10.

***

Now listen to the rest of the conversation and answer Questions 7–10.

Tutor So you've looked at a range of sample essays, then?

Rehab Yes, we have. Can we ask you one question about this essay?

Tutor Sure.

Rehab We're not really sure why it's got a bad mark. There are lots of references in there, and I think it answers the question.

Tutor You're right, it does, and everything is related to the question.

Dev So why did it get such a bad mark?

Tutor One thing you have to be careful with about looking things up online is the quality of the information you find. Take a look at the reference list. What type of information have they used?

Dev Oh, I see. It's all media information and blogs.

Tutor Yes, they're not very reliable sources.

Rehab Is this the most common thing that goes wrong?

Tutor No, actually, lots of students are good at finding information.

Dev I imagine not everyone knows how to organise their work, though.

Tutor That's not actually too bad, either. It's more about your thinking. We want you to challenge ideas. To think about strengths and weaknesses. Not to simply describe and repeat all the things you read.

Rehab Like in essay A?

Tutor Exactly!

Dev Sir, when will we get our marks?

Tutor I'll give you the marks within two weeks. Log in to the university learning website, and you'll find them there. Read the online tutorial if you need help.

Dev OK. We're really stressed about getting good marks for this essay.

Tutor Don't worry too much. It's only 15% of your mark for the term. The main thing to do is use what you have learnt in future work.

Rehab Do you mean for the presentation?

Tutor Less so. The feedback will be most helpful for the essay in the exam next month. It's a similar topic to the research you're doing now.

Rehab OK, great. Thank you. One more question ...

That is the end of Section 3. In the test, you will now have 30 seconds to check your answers.

Track 1.24 (Test file 2, Listening, Section 4)

You will hear a lecturer speaking about the history of communication. You now have some time to look at Questions 11–16.

***

Now listen and answer Questions 11–16.

Human communication has developed dramatically over the centuries. From the simple cave paintings of early man, we are now able to send multiple messages simultaneously to thousands of people around the world. Some would actually say we've gone backwards – I certainly feel like that when I look at all of the emojis in my daughter's text messages! Today, we're going to look at the key moments in this development. Some of the first known people to move beyond simple pictures to communicate information were the ancient Egyptians. They started using what we call hieroglyphics. This system was a mixture of symbols and simple drawings: not really a language as such, but definitely a means of communication. The first alphabet as we would recognise it actually came from the Phoenicians – an ancient empire based around the eastern Mediterranean sea. The alphabet contained 22 letters, and all were consonants. However, although they had an alphabet, they didn't have anything cheap and available to write on. Another 1,500 years would pass before the Chinese inventor Cai Lun created paper in around AD 105. Up until then, people wrote largely on animal skin. Another problem was that it was difficult to reproduce texts. Whenever anyone needed anything copied, it was done by hand. Well-educated people were paid to copy out whole books page by page for another 1,000 years. Then, around 700 years ago, the speed of this process increased dramatically with the invention of the printing press. These huge contraptions needed several people to operate them and could only produce a few thousand pages a day. They were also the size of a room. This press, however, was perhaps one of the greatest inventions because it changed the power balance in the world. In Europe, there was a large increase in the educated middle classes, who started to take some power away from religious and political organisations. The process this machine allowed really was the first period of time where mass communication was possible. Printing was still obviously limited to companies, but increased literacy meant that more people could read and write. Writing tools did not develop as quickly. In Europe, for nearly a thousand years, people used quills – bird feathers – to write with. Metal quills actually have their origin in ancient Egypt. However, the quality of writing that could be achieved was low. Pens were expensive and in their infancy. The original version of a ballpoint pen was only invented around a century ago, and even that took some 50 years to become similar to today's pens.

You will now have some time to look at Questions 17–20.

***

Now listen and answer Questions 17–20.

Let's look a little more closely at the development of pens. One of the problems with a quill was that the point would blunt quickly and need to be sharpened. This did not improve much until 1822, when John Mitchell set up a pen factory in Birmingham, England. Mitchell's early pens stayed sharp for longer because they had steel nibs, like the one you can see on the left here. At the bottom of the nib, there's a hard point, and then leading from this tip is the feeding system, which appears as a line or slit on the diagram. The ink flows down from the body of the nib, at the top, through a series of channels that control the amount that can flow out. And through the vent hole at the top of the slit the amount of air that can flow back is also regulated. This system was quite complicated and sophisticated. Early pens needed to be filled by hand, and ink could frequently flow out more rapidly than intended, thus ruining the document. While the steel nib did not blunt, it was also not very good at writing on many surfaces. In fact, when John J. Loud submitted his patent for an early ballpoint pen, shown on the right of your diagram, he stated that he wanted something that would be able to write 'on rough surfaces such as wood, coarse wrapping paper and other articles'. In much the same way as a fountain pen, the ink is stored in a well. When pressure is applied, the spring just by the ball releases the ink from the chamber. The movement of the ball at the same time allows ink to cover it and writing to flow. This means that the ink does not spill out onto the page. The spring pushes the ball back when pressure is released and the ink no longer comes out. It seems a very minor change, but it was one that transformed how the pen can be used.

That is the end of Section 4. In the test, you will now have 30 seconds to check your answers and ten minutes to copy your answers to the answer sheet.

Track 1.25 (Test file 2, Speaking, Part 1)

Let's talk about contacting friends.

1 How do you contact friends?
2 Are there times when you shouldn't send messages to friends?
3 Do you prefer chatting on the internet or talking in person?
4 Would you like to have more friends in the future?

Let's talk about city centres.

1 How much time do you spend in city centres?
2 What did you do the last time you visited a city centre?
3 Do you prefer ancient or modern cities?
4 Would you like to live in a city centre when you're older?

Track 1.26 (Test file 2, Speaking, Part 3)

Let's talk about long journeys first.

1 What kind of long journeys do people in your country make?
2 Why do some people prefer not to go on long journeys?
3 Some people think travelling is more exciting than arriving at a destination. Do you agree?

Let's talk about travel choices now.

1 What's the best way to choose a holiday destination?
2 Is it better to go on a long journey alone or with other people?
3 Will people choose to travel less in the future?

Can we talk about foreign travel?

1 Why do governments try to attract foreign travellers to their countries?
2 Should everyone travel to foreign countries?
3 What can governments do to increase or reduce movements of people between countries?

Track 1.27 (Unit 5, Listening, Exercise 5)

You will hear the first part of a conversation between a student and a doctor's receptionist. Listen and answer Questions 1–5.

Reza Hi, I'm a new student. What do I need to do to register with the practice?

Receptionist It depends. If you're here for less than three months, you can do a temporary registration.

Reza No, I'll be here until June I hope, if I qualify as a psychiatrist then.

Receptionist I see. Then yes, you should go through the normal registration process. Don't worry, it's simple.

Reza How many doctors do you have here?

Receptionist Er ... we have eight full-time GPs in total: five are male and the other three are women.

Reza Wow, that's a lot!

Receptionist Well, most of the students from the university register with us, and we also serve some of the local residents, too. We're very busy.

Reza As you can tell, my first language isn't English. Do you have any doctors who speak Farsi?

Receptionist Farsi? Yes, Dr Qazwini is from Iran. We could register you with him.

Reza That would be great. How is that surname spelt in English?

Receptionist Q-a-z-w-i-n-i. He only works here part time, though.

Reza What day does he have his ... what's the word, clinics?

Receptionist That's right – his are Tuesdays and Thursdays at the moment. The precise days might change, but he'll always do two days a week here.

Reza And if I need a doctor urgently, is it possible to see one?

Receptionist Yes. I mean, you can book up to two weeks before you want an appointment, so that's best, but in urgent cases, we ask you to call at 8.45 – those appointments go very quickly – or you can see if there are cancellations at 1.45 pm. There's also an after-hours service.

Reza Can I have the number for that, just in case?

Receptionist Sure, it's a local number, so use the local code, 01345, then 433 22 20. There's a leaflet about it here. And we also have a fact sheet about the health system in this country.

Reza Thank you. So, how do I register?

Track 1.28 (Unit 5, Listening, Exercise 6)

Now listen to the rest of the conversation and answer Questions 6–10.

Receptionist Well, the first thing to do if you're a student is to download form SA1 from the website and complete it.

Reza OK, got that. Then what should I do?

Receptionist Well, you can either bring it in or, if that's difficult, you can post it to us.

Reza I'm close by, so I should be able to bring it. Then is that it?

Receptionist Not quite. There's a medical questionnaire on the back of the form. It's about your lifestyle – you know, how much exercise you do, etc. If you score over 16 points on that, we ask you to arrange an appointment here so you can have a talk with the nurse.

Reza Oh, I see.

Receptionist Even if you don't, you should make an appointment within three months. On your first visit, we require you to show some photo ID – perhaps a passport – but we'll remind you of that closer to the time.

Reza Great – thank you very much.

Track 1.29 (Unit 5, Speaking, Exercise 3)

1 I think this includes races up to 400 metres. My best distance is the 200-metre race.
2 After a short run, you have to launch yourself as far as possible into the sand.
3 You need strong winds to reach a fast speed over the water.
4 This is usually played in teams of 15, but it can be played in teams of seven.
5 At first you practise in a pool and then gradually you can go deeper and deeper in the ocean.

Track 1.30 (Unit 5, Speaking, Exercise 5)

1 Ice hockey is a popular physical activity in Austria. You learn to play it in school and some people even learn to play before school, which is one of the reasons why I think it's popular. Ice hockey is a team sport and of course it's played on ice usually in teams of six people. Basically, you have to get a little rubber thing in the net using these special sticks. It's usually more popular with men as it can be quite an aggressive sport. Anyway, everyone plays it at some point and we have ice rinks everywhere.

Track 1.31 (Unit 5, Speaking, Exercise 5)

2 There are lots of sports that are popular in my country, but the three most popular are probably football, cricket and hockey. I know how to play cricket the best, so I'm going to focus on that sport. It can be played by anyone and we have men's and women's teams, and families and friends also often play together in mixed games. It's usually played on a pitch with an area of grass called a wicket, but you can play it on any flat land, like the park or on the beach. The equipment is quite basic – you have a bat, a ball and three sticks, called stumps, and if you want to play it properly, there a lots of detailed rules, but the basic rules are quite simple really.

Track 1.32 (Unit 5, Speaking, Exercise 6)

1 Some people just do it to get fit, but others do it to protect themselves.
2 You need regular classes, and it takes a long time to prepare for the assessments.
3 Martial arts, such as karate, judo and taekwondo, are popular in my country.
4 Anyone can do karate, but it's not popular with older people because you get lots of injuries.
5 Lessons often happen in gyms or sports halls which have the special equipment we need.

Track 2.2 (Unit 6, Listening, Exercise 4)

You will hear a presentation by a school headteacher. Listen and answer Questions 1–5.

Good evening, everyone. It's nice to see so many parents here – and a few pupils too, I see. Now, at todays's meeting we're going to be discussing the new development plans of the council, which you've probably heard about by now. As we know, the council has a shortage of houses, a serious one. They have a number of different proposals for new housing, but the one that would affect us the most is the plan to build a new block of flats right next to our school. This would have a number of consequences. First, there is the potential loss of the nature area behind the school art block. Now, this land doesn't actually belong to the school and is owned by the local council, so we can't actually stop them from doing anything they want, but currently we use the space as an outdoor educational area, so the land is important to us. The younger students conduct a number of nature projects there each year. In fact, a number of geography and biology lessons happen there, too. Secondly, there's the playing field. In order to build the planned housing development, the council would need to place an access road through part of the lower school field. It wouldn't be all bad, though. Obviously at this school we're blessed with a lot of space, and in return for losing the ground for the access road, the council have offered to invest in developing the other outside areas. These proposals include adding three all-weather football pitches with floodlights and adding a running track. Now, these facilities wouldn't just be for school use, but also for local community use. In the evenings and weekends, these would be bookable via the local sports centre. This would obviously be a welcome development for the school, but of course there are the major downsides I mentioned earlier.

***

Now listen and answer Questions 6–10.

Now, the students have been discussing this development and, despite the benefits I've just mentioned, they are very keen to campaign against the proposal. So this evening I'd like to put forward a number of suggestions for action you can take to persuade the council to leave our field alone! So the council has proposed three different developments. We believe the Moreton development on the edge of town is the better option. More houses can be constructed there and in the long term, a school and other facilities can be built there too. So one way you can act directly is to vote for this option online. However, we can also explain why the nature area is so important. As many of you know, it's not just used by the school. People walk dogs there, play games and relax. We're looking for volunteers to count how many members of the public use the area in a day and what they do. We can then present this data to the council. As far as we know, there aren't any rare plants or animals in the nature area, but it is a very diverse space, and we're going to record the different plant and animal species present there. If anyone has time or expertise to help with this, it would be greatly appreciated. Next, as with everything these days, social media plays an important part in getting our message across to the wider community. I know many of you have skills in this area, and we'd like help in developing a blog and social media presence. Please see me afterwards if anyone would like to discuss this. Finally, the school is raising money to pay for the printing of leaflets. These leaflets will detail the reasons why we're against this plan and will be delivered to over 5,000 houses in the area. If you have any ideas to help raise the money, we'd love to hear them too. Now, does anyone have any questions?

Track 2.3 (Unit 6, Speaking, Exercises 7 and 8)

1 Less, definitely. People didn't use to have running water in their homes, so they would have had to carry all the water that they used. There wasn't any electricity or sewerage either. If they'd had hot water on tap, they would have washed themselves and their clothes a lot more regularly, I think!

Track 2.4 (Unit 6, Speaking, Exercises 7 and 8)

2 Well, that's a good question. I mean, often it's quite windy by water. I'd say the views attract people the most. Yes, you get beautiful views. Um ... what else? Actually, it's also easy to walk there. You see, the land is flat in those areas, generally speaking, or quite flat anyway. That's pretty important, especially for old people and kids.

Track 2.5 (Unit 6, Speaking, Exercises 7 and 8)

3 For me, there are two key things. Most importantly, they need to insist that people pay for the quantity of water they use. That way, they would be more careful. Besides that, it's important to educate people. We need to encourage them to use dirty bath water on their gardens or use 'quick wash' cycles on washing machines.

Track 2.6 (Unit 6, Speaking, Exercise 12)

1 Do people drink a lot of water in your country?
2 Why do some people need to drink more water than others?
3 Is it better to buy water or drink water from the tap?
4 What activities do people enjoy doing in water?
5 Why do some people like swimming in rivers, lakes and seas?
6 Was it safer to swim in rivers, lakes and seas in the past?
7 Why are boat trips and cruises so popular?
8 What industries or businesses need water?
9 Why do some countries have more water than others?
10 How can governments or individuals increase their water supplies?

Track 2.7 (Test file 3, Listening, Section 1)

You will hear a man enquiring about a visit to an activity centre. You now have some time to look at Questions 1–5.

***

Now listen and answer Questions 1–5.

Receptionist Hello, Jungle Jim's Activity Centre.

Man Oh, hi. Yes, I wanted to know if you had space on the tree-top adventure course next week for a group of 12. It's for a birthday.

Receptionist That should be fine. We're very busy on the Saturday morning, but there's space on Thursday and Friday evenings and Sunday mornings.

Man OK, I'm sure one of those will be fine, but I'll check and confirm later. Could you tell me a bit about the tree-top adventure, like how long it takes?

Receptionist Sure. Well, there are 30 separate obstacles, like bridges between the trees and climbing nets. It usually takes around 90 minutes, but you'll need to leave another hour for booking you in and preparation.

Man Is the course difficult? Some of us aren't comfortable 30 feet off the ground.

Receptionist Well, some parts are challenging, but if you can climb a ladder without help, you should be fine. We grade all parts of the course like a ski run. So you can take the easy blue route if you like, but stay away from the black route!

Man OK, that sounds good. Do we have to bring anything, like a helmet or something?

Receptionist No, all the safety equipment is provided by us. But sun cream is also a good idea, as well as protection from the rain.

Man OK, can we wear what we like?

Receptionist No, there's a dress code. You have to tie your hair back, remove jewellery and make sure all areas of your skin are covered. We also recommend trainers rather than loose sandals – you don't want your shoes to fall off!

Man We've got a couple of 17-year-olds too. Is that OK?

Receptionist Yes, but they'll need signed permission from their parents or guardians.

You now have some time to look at Questions 6–10.

***

Now listen and answer Questions 6 to 10.

Man So what will happen on the day?

Receptionist On arrival, you'll spend a few minutes filling in and signing documents – you know, for legal purposes. Once that's finished, your personal instructor will then provide you with your safety equipment and take you over to our Induction Zone.

Man Induction Zone? That sounds very serious.

Receptionist Well, it's certainly important. It's where we show you a short video and listen to a talk from our instructor. It doesn't take long, but you do need to complete the induction activities safely. There's a short test for everyone.

Man And then we begin the course?

Receptionist Absolutely, we take you to the first of 30 obstacles and the fun begins. But the instructor stays with you and sets a few surprise tasks on the way! You'll be in good hands.

That is the end of Section 1. In the test, you will now have 30 seconds to check your answers.

Track 2.8 (Test file 3, Listening, Section 2)

You will hear a radio presenter talking about safety in the countryside. You now have some time to look at Questions 11–15.

***

Now listen and answer Questions 11–15.

This week, on *The Great Escape*, we're in the beautiful hills of Grimswick. With summer fast approaching, many of you will be thinking about weekends away in places just like this. And there's no reason why you can't have a very safe and enjoyable experience out here in the wilds. But of course there are dangers lurking in the countryside, often from the least expected sources. Let's look at some of them.

You'll find beautiful lakes out here in the country which can be very inviting on a hot day. But there can be all sorts of dangers with open water, especially unexpected objects under the surface. However, walkers wanting to cool down are not the greatest cause of accidents. Most of those who die in water don't mean to go in – they fall as a result of running or cycling too close to the water. If that happens to your friend, don't dive in, even if it's a child you think you can drag out – try to offer them a stick or lie flat as you reach out to them.

It's always nice to stop and have a picnic in a place like this. But what dangers could possibly be linked to a picnic? Well, what about that glass bottle that you've finished with? You won't find many bins in the countryside, so it's tempting to leave them rather than carry them back in your heavy packs. Remember, however, that aside from being a danger to walkers, glass can concentrate sunlight and accidently start fires. Once started, they can be very difficult to put out.

Animals are another attractive feature of rural areas. But local farmers have also reported an increasing number of incidents with farm animals. Taking dogs with you, for example, is not a good idea. Often it's your dog who will come off worse in a confrontation with cows or horses. Humans have to be careful, too. Although you might want to go as quickly as you can through the field, you should avoid walking between cows and their young. Mothers will chase you off if they feel you're a threat to their family. Go around their territory.

Of course, if you're walking longer distances, there's a lot you'll need to think about. It's important to remember that shops and medical services are not as close and you'll be spending a long time away from civilisation. So what you set out with is all you'll have to help you deal with any emergency. There are lots of things that some people like to take, like survival blankets or fire starters, but it's the basics you need to remember. Make sure your phones are fully charged before you set out. And while keeping sweets with you may not be a good idea generally, you'll be glad of them here. Calories can give you much-needed energy for outdoor activities and help you stay warm, too. Clothing is very important, and you can forget fashion. Light-weight trousers are a must, and you'll need something to keep the hot sun off your head and the rest of you – whatever you wear on the top half, make sure it has long sleeves and a collar.

You now have some time to look at Questions 16–20.

***

Now listen and answer Questions 16–20.

Your biggest enemy will be the weather. The rain, for example, will make your maps quite unreadable. And then there's the cold. It can still get pretty cold at this time of year. In fact, the owner of the local hotel was telling me about a young couple who got into severe difficulties here just last week. They were passionate walkers apparently and had come here on honeymoon. They had checked the weather forecast and seen that it was going to be a nice day, so they set out after lunch. They had plenty of water and all the equipment you could need, including good strong boots and hiking poles. But it's often the basic things you forget. At around four in the afternoon, on the last leg of their journey, the young lady twisted her ankle, which slowed down their progress, and it started to get dark before they could make it back. It was then that they realised that their torch battery was fading and they hadn't packed a spare. Walking in complete darkness is simply impossible in these hills. You have to be able to see where you're putting every footstep. So they decided to stop and stay where they were for the night. With clear skies and no tent, they quickly got very cold. The young man was able to jump up and down to keep warm, but with an ankle injury, his wife could do very little to fight the cold. By the time dawn broke, she'd started suffering from hypothermia and couldn't walk. Fortunately, the hotel manager noticed they hadn't returned and alerted the emergency services. The rest of the trip was spent at the local hospital. But they were still glad they'd stopped. Just ten metres from where they spent the night, there had been a cliff edge with a 30-metre drop the other side!

That is the end of Section 2. In the test, you will now have 30 seconds to check your answers.

Track 2.9 (Test file 3, Speaking, Part 1)

Let's talk about sport and exercise.

1 How often do you exercise?
2 What sports do you like to play?
3 Do you prefer playing team sports or individual sports?
4 Would you like to do more exercise in the future?

Let's talk about staying healthy.

1 What are your favourite foods?
2 Do you try to eat healthily?
3 Do you think diet or exercise is more important for health?
4 Would you like to change anything about your lifestyle?

Track 2.10 (Test file 3, Speaking, Part 3)

Let's talk about competitive sports first.

1 Which groups of people in society enjoy competitive sports the most?
2 Why do some people prefer to watch sport rather than do sport?
3 Some people think competitive sport is bad for you. Do you agree?

Let's talk about success in general.

1 What's the best way to become successful in something?
2 Is it better to be successful in work or in other areas of your life?
3 Some people think that in order to succeed, it's acceptable to behave selfishly. Do you agree?

Can we talk about sporting events and sports stars?

1 Why do governments try to attract big sporting events to their countries?
2 Should salaries of top sportspeople be limited?
3 How can we encourage sportspeople to play fairly and follow the rules?

Track 2.11 (Unit 7, Listening, Exercise 4)

You will hear a conversation between a careers advisor and a student. Listen and answer Questions 1–7.

Advisor Hi, it's Mark, isn't it?

Mark Yes, that's right.

Advisor Good to meet you, Mark. Take a seat. So you wanted to meet today to talk about your future career.

Mark Yes, that's right. I'm just finishing my second year in Business Studies. I need to think about my summer job and then the modules to take next year, but I'm really not sure what career to go into.

Advisor So what have you enjoyed studying so far?

Mark Well, I like some of the more creative modules like marketing, advertising and sales.

Advisor Careers in marketing can be very creative. Especially, if you're good with language or design.

Mark Yes, I was thinking about copywriting – the language of advertising.

Advisor Bear in mind, though, that a good marketing role can be difficult to get. In particular in a field like copywriting. I'll email you some information about short courses and training programmes. Are there any other careers you would consider?

Mark Well, I'm good at maths and I've taken some accounting modules.

Advisor Accounting can be a good choice. There's a lot of career stability, and financially speaking the pay is very high.

Mark What are the downsides?

Advisor There are a lot of difficult exams to pass, and training is a very lengthy process – nearly five years.

Mark Do you have any other suggestions? I like working with people more than data.

Advisor Have you considered human resources?

Mark No, not really. What types of role can you have?

Advisor There are a wide variety of roles. Also, one of the main benefits in HR is that you can work for a wide range of companies. It's also not limited to particular areas of the country or specific sectors.

Mark What are the main areas you can work in?

Advisor Well, one is training staff and another is recruiting new staff and dealing with staff leaving.

Mark The training might be interesting, but I'm not sure about working in recruiting and I can't imagine telling someone they've lost their job.

Advisor Yes, you have to make a lot of challenging decisions. Have you thought about a career outside of business? Are there any other areas that interest you?

Mark Well, I quite like the idea of being a lawyer, but I haven't studied law.

Advisor Well, that's not necessarily a problem. You can do a law conversion course after your degree. It would take an additional two years to complete.

Mark I wouldn't mind that.

Advisor Well, the profession is certainly respected and it pays well, but that also means lots of people want to do it. When you finish your course, you still need to do more training and it can be hard to get your articles – that means a trainee position. It's also incredibly competitive. There are many candidates for each job.

Mark So there's no guaranteed job?

Advisor Definitely not. Lots of people who re-train in law can't get a job in law.

Track 2.12 (Unit 7, Listening, Exercise 5)

Now listen to the rest of the conversation and answer Questions 8–10.

Mark So how competitive is the jobs market?

Advisor Well, it's changed a lot in recent years. Ten years ago, half of our graduates had full-time jobs within six months.

Mark But it got much worse a few years ago, didn't it?

Advisor It did. So ten years ago, about 70% had jobs within a year. Four years ago, only 50% got jobs in this timeframe.

Mark And today?

Advisor It has got better. Here, look at this chart. Two-thirds get a job in their first year after graduating.

Mark And about a third have secured one within six months.

Advisor That's right.

Mark And what about salaries?

Advisor Well, that very much depends on the sector. Some jobs have seen a steady increase, in particular the financial sector. Others, such as teaching, have seen a gradual decline.

Mark In general, how have they changed?

Advisor Not a lot really. Here, look at this graph. It shows the last ten years of graduate salaries. There's some fluctuation up and down, but it's remained fairly constant.

Mark I'm thinking about taking a gap year, but I'm worried it'll be bad for my career.

Advisor I think that depends what you do. Lots of people still take a year out, but what they do has changed. In the past, most people just travelled.

Mark What do they do now?

Advisor More and more work or volunteer.

Mark Working? Is that a gap year?

Advisor Yes. People often work, but not in their future career. Perhaps they work to travel or they work to help others. Take a look at this graph.

Mark So travelling is the most popular.

Advisor It is, but if you add working and volunteering together, they're more popular.

Mark One more thing I'd like to ask ...

Track 2.13 (Unit 7, Speaking, Exercises 5 and 6)

1 I imagine I'd have to get up very early and clean out the, you know, spaces where the animals live. Lots of people wouldn't like that, but I don't mind getting dirty. I think I'd be good at the job because I'm ... you know, never late and you can trust me – I wouldn't forget to close any doors behind me! I'm also quite good at working as part of a team, which I think would be important. I'm generally, er, sensitive to the needs of others, both humans and animals, so I'd be happy to help colleagues out and chat to the visitors. Yes, I think I'd be a good team member.

Track 2.14 (Unit 7, Speaking, Exercises 5 and 6)

2 In this job, people tell you to go away a lot↘, but you can't take it too seriously↘. You have to just call↗ and call↗ and call↗ until someone buys whatever you're offering them↘. And then↗, well, you have to do it all over again!↘ I know it's a strange choice, but I think it's a good job for me↗ because I'm tough like that↘, and I like having clear targets↘ – it's more satisfying↘. There are also some good perks, ↘ especially the bonuses!↘

Track 2.15 (Unit 7, Speaking, Exercise 8)

1 I'd absolutely love to have my own office↘. I'd have plants↗, photos of my family↗ and a huge desk↘.

2 The other day↗, I was in the supermarket↗ when I met my old boss↘. It was awkward↘.

3 The best thing about my current job is↗ ... No, I can't think of anything↘.

Track 2.16 (Unit 8, Listening, Exercise 5)

You will hear a lecture by a psychology professor. Listen and answer Questions 1–4.

I'm going to start this lecture by making three guesses. First, that most of you would be very grateful for a cup of coffee right now. Second, that you didn't get up early enough to make one before this lecture. And third, that you haven't really got the money to buy one. Am I right? Now, in front of you there's a cup of cappuccino. And I'd like to give you a choice. You can buy it now for £3 or wait and make one for free when you get home. In other words, act on impulse or wait and save the money. You may not think the choice is so important really, but researchers would disagree with you.

To understand why, let's look in a little more detail at what we mean by impulsive behaviour, or impulsivity. Impulsivity involves acting rapidly without any kind of plan or conscious thought. It can make people seem very spontaneous and attractive. But on the other hand, it makes it more likely that you'll do things you might regret later, from shouting loudly to being physically aggressive. Impulsivity is caused, in part, by low levels of activity in the control centres of the brain. To illustrate: imagine a professor reduces your assignment grade because you handed it in late. Our *natural* reaction is to argue and say how unfair they are. But part of you will try to supress that response because, well, you have to show us professors respect, right? So your control centres police your reactions. Impulsivity has a second cause, too: a tendency to forget about long-term aims and strategies for achieving them. To return to the example of our mean professor, a further reason why we may not shout back is that we don't want to be thrown out of university. Accepting the low mark is a small sacrifice when you think that controlling your behaviour may stop you being removed from the course. So impulsivity can lead people to make decisions that are against their interests. In extreme cases, it can also make it more likely that a person will do things that break the law, which is why it's of interest to psychologists and criminologists. The thought of bad behaviour is present in everyone and we need a degree of self-control or forward thinking to stop it.

Track 2.17 (Unit 8, Listening, Exercise 6)

Now listen to the rest of the lecture and answer Questions 5–10.

So there's a higher risk that impulsive people may engage in poor behaviour, but this doesn't mean that impulsive people are dangerous, for two good reasons. Firstly, levels of impulsivity are wide-ranging. A moderate degree of impulsivity throughout life might be a factor in relationship break-ups or poor career decisions, but it rarely results in problem behaviour. Also, levels of impulsivity do fluctuate throughout life quite naturally, without leading to criminal acts. Many children are very impulsive at a young age, but learn to develop self-control and forward thinking as they grow up by exercising the control centres of the brain. This process is often interrupted during adolescence when young people may be attracted to risky thrill-seeking behaviour when they are with peers, even creating minor damage to property perhaps or stealing small items from shops. But this kind of anti-social behaviour doesn't normally include violent acts and will quickly disappear in adulthood, when all those adolescent chemicals settle down. Later in life, we also have far more to lose in terms of possessions or career, so even if we're a little impulsive by nature, we make an effort to check our instincts.

But there are people who demonstrate the kind of severe impulsivity from a young age that doesn't seem to alter. Some young children may, for example, show a greater tendency towards biting or hitting than others and may go on to bully other pupils and later to get in trouble with the law, without any changes to behaviour. In such cases, impulsivity may have a strong biological cause. Prisoners, for example, are far more likely to have a genetic make-up that makes the control centre of their brains less active, and criminals are often described as having quite child-like reactions that show lack of maturity and development. Childhood impulsivity and serious crime are both far more common among males too, further supporting the idea that there is a common biological basis.

Even in these cases, good parenting techniques, like creating reward systems and clear boundaries, may help self-control to develop. But because the parents themselves often have impulsive characters and resort to aggressive measures of control, the opportunity to practise exercising self-discipline is often lost, and the child may go on to develop very stormy relations with parents in their teenage years. If impulsivity goes uncontrolled, it may also prevent the young socialising successfully and they may be excluded from the kind of group games in the primary-school playground which are so important to human development. In short, impulsive youngsters with impulsive parents may be more likely to commit crime in the future.

Track 2.18 (Unit 8, Speaking, Exercise 7)

1 I think it probably is. For example, my grandparents sometimes tell me they used to play ... um ... small tricks on teachers, for example. Certainly, you never used to hear about, er, about violence towards teachers like you do now.

***

Yes, they definitely help ... especially in younger children. However, parents and teachers need to apply rules regularly and, and, and ... fairly for them to work.

***

Both reward and punishments have their place in improving behaviour, but it depends on the, the, the ... individual child. For that reason, teachers and parents have to be ... um, flexible and adapt their methods to the child. For some, rewards are better, for others punishments.

Track 2.19 (Unit 8, Speaking, Exercise 8)

2 Times are different now. Well, I'm not sure things have changed that much. I know my dad was naughty at school. He used to miss classes regularly, he says. He was terrible. What was the question again?

***

Students have to understand what is acceptable and when it isn't. I'm not sure rules have to be strict. I disagree with hitting children. But people in a position of influence at home or school really must be fair. I hate it when teachers pick on individual students.

***

You can change children's behaviour quite easily. And young children who are easily influenced. You have to make it clear when behaviour is good or bad. So yes, basically.

Track 2.20 (Unit 8, Speaking, Exercise 11)

Let's talk about parks.

1 How often do you go to parks?
2 Did you live near a park when you were a child?
3 Do you prefer to relax in a park or in a garden?
4 How would you like to change your nearest park?

Now let's talk about games.

1 What games do you enjoy playing?
2 Did you play many outdoor games as a child?
3 Do you prefer indoor games to outdoor games?
4 Are there any games you'd like to try?

Track 2.21 (Unit 8, Speaking, Exercise 13)

Let's talk about rules.

1 Why do we need rules in society?
2 Do you think there are too many rules?
3 Are there any rules you would like to change?

Let's talk about children's behaviour in schools.

1 Are parents or teachers more responsible for children's behaviour?
2 Is a lack of discipline at home one of the main problems in schools?
3 Do you think parents are too lenient and need to be stricter?

Now let's talk about improving children's behaviour.

1 Do you think giving clear rules to follow improves behaviour?
2 Do you think punishments or rewards change children's behaviour more?
3 Do you think children should take responsibility for their actions?

Track 2.22 (Test file 4, Listening, Section 3)

You will hear a conversation between a professor and two students. You now have some time to look at Questions 1–7.

***

Now listen and answer Questions 1–7.

Professor OK, so to prepare for this tutorial, I asked you to read about a theory of motivation at work, called McGregor's X and Y Theory. Have you both had a chance to read the text?

Mia Yes, the main idea is an interesting one, that you can see motivation in one of two ways, X or Y, but I'm not sure I agree with the theory.

Harry Why not?

Mia Well, both X and Y theories seem to be based on two extreme views of employees. In theory X, employees need to be controlled and told exactly what to do all the time, whereas in theory Y, work is supposed to be natural, as natural as play or rest. But I'm not sure either way of looking at motivation is useful.

Professor So how would *you* go about managing someone who wasn't meeting their objectives?

Mia Well, I certainly don't agree with the idea of theory X that you need to be angry and raise the threat of punishments. Your workers aren't children.

Professor So perhaps your instincts lie with theory Y then, that people can direct themselves easily and that self-control is generally common?

Mia Not necessarily. Just because punishments aren't useful, it doesn't mean that you can just leave workers to do what they want.

Professor Hmm. Harry – where do you stand?

Harry I think I would side more with theory Y, especially when it comes to leadership. I think most people like to be in charge, and in fact I think most typical employees actually want to get responsibility. We like to be trusted.

Professor And which theory helps us understand workers' views on achievement better?

Mia Actually, I think I agree with theory X here. In my experience, some people don't have any ambition. They're simply motivated by doing what they enjoy outside of work.

Harry But theory Y here is also valid. Some people need to see their achievements recognised. They need some kind of reward. I mean, this is typical in sales – reach your goal and receive a bonus. For most, this is a key motivator.

Mia But for some people, they're happy with a low salary and a simple job. It gives them the balance between working life and leisure they want.

Professor OK, so are we saying that for some professions, theory X is a more useful way of understanding motivation than for others?

Mia Yes, it would work well in places like factories and on production lines – you just need hard work.

Harry But in an architect's office, for example, you need to use employees' intelligence. The less you control them, the more they will have the freedom and motivation to think.

You now have some time to look at Questions 8–10.

***

Now listen to the rest of the conversation and answer Questions 8–10.

Professor OK. I have some graphs here for you to look at. They're responses from an employee satisfaction survey.

Mia So what does this first one show?

Professor It's the overall level of satisfaction with your work. As you can see, in this company more people are satisfied with their work than dissatisfied.

Harry Just generally satisfied though. Only one in five are very satisfied. Did they investigate which factors were affecting their employees?

Professor They did, and their study largely supports the ideas of theory X and theory Y. So here in this next chart, a bar chart, you can see the factors that have the greatest impact on employee satisfaction. Employees were asked to rate each factor out of ten as to how important it was in impacting on their happiness.

Mia Interesting, not that many people are concerned about their career progression. That suggests money isn't that important.

Harry Yes, that's actually the lowest category. The feeling that you've achieved something seems to be the most important.

Professor Exactly. It highlights the importance of managers giving people targets to keep people motivated. Now, Mia, you mentioned the fact that money probably isn't that important; well, that was one of the factors that employees were asked about in terms of dissatisfaction.

Harry Oh yes, but it's not that significant when compared to other factors.

Mia That's interesting. Company rules and regulations have the biggest effect. I'm surprised by that.

Harry But if you think about it, if you're worried about environmental issues, for example, you won't want to work for a company that doesn't recycle.

Mia Mmm, that makes sense. Also, I can see how the second highest factor, how you're managed, would be important. Your manager can have a really positive or negative impact on how you feel about your job.

Harry Yes, that would definitely make me look for a new job!

Professor Well, if you're interested in these results, you can learn about them in tomorrow's lecture with Professor Simmonds.

That is the end of Section 3. In the test, you will now have 30 seconds to check your answers.

Track 2.23 (Test file 4, Listening, Section 4)

You will hear a lecture about a theory of motivation. You now have some time to look at Questions 11–14.

***

Now listen and answer Questions 11–14.

I'd like to look today at one of the key theories in motivating employees: Herzberg's two-factor theory, which is also known as Herzberg's motivation–hygiene theory.

The theory was developed from data collected by Herzberg from interviews with 203 engineers and accountants in the Pittsburgh area. They were chosen because of their professions' growing importance in the business world. They were interviewed and asked about times when they were very happy or unhappy in their work.

From the results, Herzberg saw that the factors that created job satisfaction and job dissatisfaction are not connected. It seemed that, to make the employees satisfied, it wasn't sufficient to improve lower-level factors such as a minimum salary or safe and better working conditions. By contrast, individuals get satisfaction from higher-level factors such as recognition and responsibility.

So, why is this result important? Well, it means that if you increase a factor linked to satisfaction, you don't automatically reduce dissatisfaction. So, to get better performance from workers, companies must address both sets of issues, guaranteeing good basic conditions and at the same time thinking of different ways to increase satisfaction.

You now have some time to look at Questions 15–20.

***

Now listen to the rest of the lecture and answer Questions 15–20.

Herzberg described the factors that give you satisfaction as 'motivation factors' and the factors that give you dissatisfaction as 'hygiene factors'.

But others have since argued that there should be a third factor. They argue that, for some aspects of work, personality or individual differences play a much more important role, and that there's no such thing as an average employee.

Let's take the concept of difficulty. Everyone is attracted to tasks that represent a challenge, so Herzberg would argue that this is actually a motivation factor – something that makes all people feel positive about their job. Easy and routine tasks become boring and ultimately unsatisfying. However, what about a demanding task that requires lots of hard work from someone? This is unlikely to be a motivator, because although everyone likes a challenge, not everyone enjoys working hard. So clearly here we cannot say that this will have a positive or negative effect on every employee.

Other employees are even more calculating when they consider how much time and energy to invest in a given task, and may consider motivation and hygiene factors together. If, for example, something is very challenging but in return they won't actually gain much reward, then they will be unwilling to invest much of their time and energy. Others, though, always love challenges and will give one hundred per cent, no matter what the possible gains are for them. In other words, it's very much dependent on who the person is.

However, in many aspects of work, Herzberg's neat distinction remains valid. Control over your work is a good example. Clearly, not everyone wants to be a managing director and make high-level decisions, but generally speaking, people always want control of their life and environment. If we take this at a very simple level of deciding when to start and finish work, when to take breaks or – on a higher level – the best way to complete a task, most people want to have this control. Being given this power will, in most cases, be a positive influence on employee productivity.

As I mentioned before, factors such as the salary paid and the level of security in a job can make employees feel very dissatisfied and so would be hygiene factors. Being under threat of redundancy is never going to be a motivator. But what about others sorts of financial benefit, like vacations? Well, whether we're talking about how many days you're allowed off or whether the company provides a pension or not, all will impact on levels of dissatisfaction.

There are other factors outside of these basics that can also have a negative effect. The other main area can largely be grouped together in a category of 'networks'. This can range from peer-to-peer to direct supervision. How well you get on with the people around you can make you feel very dissatisfied with your work, even when all other aspects are positive.

That is the end of Section 4. In the test, you will now have 30 seconds to check your answers and ten minutes to copy your answers to the answer sheet.

Track 2.24 (Test file 4, Speaking, Part 1)

Let's talk about going out in the evening.

1 Who do you go out with in the evening?
2 Where did you like to go out when you were younger?
3 Do you prefer going out in large groups or with one or two friends?
4 Do you think you'll go out more often or less often over the next year?

Let's talk about songs.

1 Do you have a favourite song?
2 Did anyone in your family sing songs when you were a child?
3 Do you prefer listening to songs or singing them?
4 Would you like to write a song one day?

Track 2.25 (Test file 4, Speaking, Part 3)

Let's talk about personal achievements.

1 Which has more impact on success: talent or hard work?
2 What's the best way to prepare before a test of your ability?
3 Why do people try to achieve things?
4 Some people think happiness is an achievement. Do you agree?

Let's talk about group achievements.

1 Which things are easier to achieve in groups?
2 Why do some teams perform better than others?
3 Which is more satisfying: achieving by yourself or achieving as part of a team?

Let's talk about national achievements.

1 What do people in your country feel proud of?
2 How do governments measure a country's success?
3 What can we do to impress visitors from other countries?
4 Do you think we should celebrate military achievements?

ANSWER KEY

Quiz: Get to know IELTS

Reading

1 1 thousand 2 general 3 eleven
2 5: 15 6: 23 7: 30 8: 35
3 1 False 2 True 3 True
4 1 facts; opinions 2 cannot
5 1 False 2 True 3 True 4 True
6 1 four 2 five 3 three
7 1 True 2 False 3 True
8 1 WP 2 P 3 WP 4 P
9 1 letters 2 may not have to 3 may
10 No (Only the Listening test allows time for transfer of answers.)

Listening

1 1 two 2 2 3 4 4 one
2 5: 18 6: 26 7: 30 8: 35
3 B
4 1 No 2 On a university campus 3 A tutorial
5 C
6 A
7 1 c 2 d 3 a 4 b
8 1 True 2 True 3 False
9 1 minutes 2 answer 3 mistakes 4 mark 5 band
10 Yes (You have ten minutes at the end of the test for this.)

Speaking

1 1 you 2 general 3 talk about 4 between one and two minutes 5 the topic from Part 2
2 1 linking words, speech rate
2 high-level words
3 complex sentences
4 word stress, speech rate
3 1 True 2 False 3 True 4 True
4 Band 6
5 1 (2 and 3 are descriptors for Band 8.)
6 1 False 2 False 3 False
7 1 Part 2 2 Part 3 3 Part 1
8 1 False 2 True 3 True
9 1 All parts 2 Part 2 3 Part 3
10 B (but only in complex sentences)

Writing

1 Task 1: 20 minutes, paragraphs not needed, including data, facts
Task 2: 40 minutes, an introduction needed, including examples, opinions
2 A
3 1 c 2 b 3 a 4 d
4 a) pie chart, bar chart b) line graph, bar chart
5 1 Yes 2 Yes 3 Examples
6 B
7 1 False 2 True 3 False (but you won't gain marks, and if you copy whole sections, the words will not be counted)
8 D
9 Band 6: B, C
Band 7: A, D, E

Unit 1

Topic focus

1 1 languages 2 physics 3 chemistry 4 maths 5 literature 6 economics 7 business 8 social science

Reading

3 1 b 2 a 3 c
4 a 2
b 1 and 3 (Scan to find correct section, then read intensively)
c 1 and 3 (Scan to find feature of text, then read intensively)

Strategy focus

1 The names (Although not all names are needed, answers may be matched more quickly by looking for the names first.)
2 No, there's one extra option.
3 1 Skills used while studying are key to academic progress.
2 Many business students make poor progress.
3 It isn't necessary to study some school subjects.
4 Business students don't make the most money.
5 Companies welcome non-business graduates.
6 Mental skills affect income significantly.
7 Some of what is taught has little connection with working lives.
5 1 B 2 G 3 A 4 E 5 C 6 D 7 F
6 8 B 9 D 10 A 11 I 12 E 13 C 14 G

Vocabulary extra

1 relevance 2 pay, income 3 programme 4 graduate 5 campus

Listening

3 1 a month when courses usually start 2 *a person's name* 3 a popular university subject 4 *a place name* 5 a normal price for a room 6 a useful facility in a student residence *7 a number or type of student 8 a noun describing something you can access from student accommodation* 9 a way of travelling in town 10 a way to contact someone
4 1 17 2 UAE 3 BPY 4 111 5 30th
5 1 January 2 Husham 3 global business
6 4 Westwood / West Wood 5 160 6 games room 7 (three/3) male/other 8 (high-speed) internet 9 (on) foot 10 text

Speaking

2 *Suggested answer*: language, culture and making friends
3 1 f 2 c 3 e 4 h 5 b 6 i 7 g 8 d 9 a
5 1 b 2 a 3 b 4 c
6 1 mostly enjoy doing 2 'd like to try 3 enjoyed doing 4 'd like to have a go at
7 1 Candidate 2
2 Candidate 2
3 Candidate 1 (Candidate 2's errors: *science-fiction movie**s**; local film festival**s** / **a** local film festival; we often **went** running; **It's** good to have; I'd really like **to join***)
4 Candidate 2 (*science-fiction, tournament, chill out, have a go*)
9 1 films 2 local cinema 3 every Friday
10 1 When do you watch movies?
2 How often do you watch movies?
3 Where/How do you watch movies?

Writing

1 The line graph shows a trend.
Suggested charts

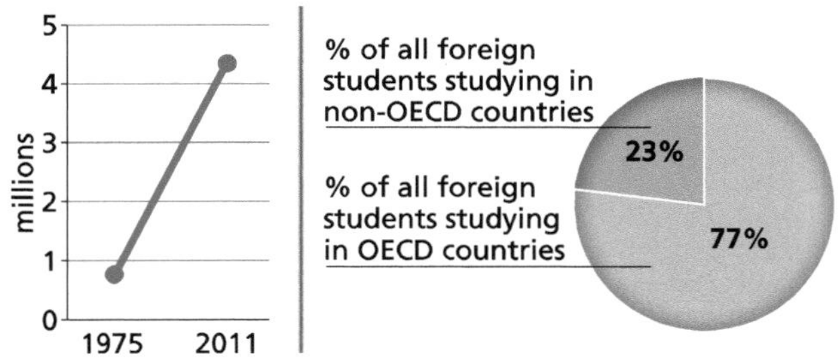

3 1 rising 2 2009–2010 3 Domestic students 4 Foreign students in this country 5 drop

4 *Suggested answers*
1 Overall, the data shows a rising trend in student numbers.
2 The number of foreign students peaked in 2009–2010.
3 The domestic student category saw the steadiest rise in student numbers.
4 The numbers of foreign students in this country showed the most fluctuation.
5 The percentage of students who are from other countries dropped in 2011.

5 1 Candidate 1 2 Candidate 2 3 Candidate 2 4 Candidate 1

6 1 students 2 left 3 grew 4 notable 5 peaked 6 fell 7 growth 8 more consistent 9 growing / to grow steadily 10 reaching 11 had overtaken 12 went

Unit 2

Reading

1 3 The author is worried that the internet is destroying communities.

2 1 F 2 C 3 D 4 B 5 A

3 *Strategy focus*
A 1 adjust; viewpoints 2 negotiate 3 division
B 1 Yes 2 No (The author says that the internet *hardly forces us to negotiate and compromise*, so the author is contradicting the idea that negotiation has become easier.) 3 Not Given

Questions 6–13
6 Yes (*Those with long shared histories, who have survived difficult circumstances together, form the closest bonds.*)
7 No (*The internet therefore hosts loose, limited-purpose and volatile communities.*)
8 Not Given
9 Not Given
10 Yes (*And people can join multiple online communities anonymously, without the fear of embarrassment ...*)
11 Yes (*... without having to pay membership fees or travel expenses.*)
12 No (*In other words, they are able to develop across the racial, geographical and even temporal divides that normally separate traditional communities from each other.*)
13 Not Given

Vocabulary extra
1 1 with 2 from 3 of 4 with 5 to
2 *Suggested answers*
1 When giving a presentation, it's important to interact with your audience.
2 Elderly people who live alone are often isolated from the rest of the community.
3 My father has membership of the local golf course.
4 Babies bond with their mothers when they are just days old.
5 People with mental health problems are vulnerable to being exploited.

Listening

3 1 Letters
3 B

4 1 I 2 F 3 E 4 H 5 G

5 6 (up to) 250
7 a playground
8 (the) public toilets
9 (their own) food
10 bikes / bicycles / cycles

6 at the bottom, directly in front, behind, leading off, to the north-west of, place, just south of here, just north of, in the bottom left, to the east of, between, in the bottom corner

Speaking

3 1 Her grandmother 2 His teacher

4 1 Candidate 2 2 Candidate 2 3 Candidate 1, because Candidate 2 is constantly referring back to the task sheet and is unable to extend answers naturally; Candidate 1 speaks more freely, adding more details.

6 *Suggested answer*
I've always admired my grandmother, partly because she **was (always) so selfless**. When I was younger, she **was dedicated to** me and **devoted herself to caring for me**. She **was (really) resourceful** when I couldn't do a school project. However, as I have grown older, I realise that there are many other reasons I admire her. I think to survive her childhood, she must have been very **determined**, and her efforts to sell things prove she was quite **enterprising**. Also, when my grandfather went off to fight in the war, she **was really courageous**. Now that I'm an adult, she **is passionate about** helping people who are less fortunate. She**'s (very) energetic** for someone who is 70. It **is (really) inspiring**.

7 Option B is best. You can't write on the question booklet, so Option A isn't acceptable. Option C doesn't cover enough ideas, and the candidate will start reading what they've written, which will reduce fluency.

Writing

1 1 b 2 a 3 c

2 a 3 b 1 c 2

3 1 c 2 a 3 b 4 a

4 a 2 b 1 c 3

5 1 Candidate 1 2 Candidate 2 3 Candidate 2

6 1 surviving 2 community members 3 argue 4 senior citizens 5 supported 6 close relatives 7 the State 8 accommodate 9 address 10 offer

7 See sample answer 2 on page 98.

Test file 1

Reading

1 C 2 G 3 E 4 H 5 F 6 D
7 No (*... scientists are discovering how much more of the key events in the brain are still happening through teenage years and into our early adult lives.*)
8 Yes (*So if a teen is doing music, sports or is busy studying, those are the cells and connections that will be hard-wired. If they're lying on the couch or playing video games or watching MTV, those are the cells and connections that are going to survive.*)
9 Not Given
10 No (*The gap between adolescence and full adulthood is becoming ever wider as more young people willingly, or because of economic necessity, prolong their education and postpone traditional adult responsibilities.*)
11 Yes (*For young adults, this period can be a stressful time. High rates of anxiety, depression, motor-vehicle accidents and alcohol use are at their peak from 18 to 25, trends that tend to level out by age 28, studies show.*)
12 Not Given
13 Yes (*This lack of development can actually be seen as a positive thing. The fact that the brain stays unfinished during early adulthood 'is the best thing that ever happened to humans' because it allows us to adapt to changing environments, says Dr Giedd.*)
14 No (*... abilities that are based on accumulated knowledge, such as general knowledge and crosswords, actually increase until the age of 60.*)

Listening

1 nineteen / 19 2 Wednesdays 3 7pm 4 Daryl Greene 5 07892 556250
6 Free 7 (hot) snacks 8 simple meals 9 Craft materials 10 comfortable shoes
11 G 12 A 13 H 14 B 15 C
16 second-year students 17 80% / 80 per cent / 80 percent
18 large organisations 19 language skills
20 (central) bus station

Writing

See sample answers 3 and 4 on pages 98 and 99.

Unit 3

Topic focus

1 Verbal communication involves words, either spoken or written; non-verbal communication is anything that doesn't involve words.
2 *Suggested answer*: the non-verbal pair
3 **Verbal**: phone calls, online chat, presentations
Non-verbal: clapping, photo messaging, hugs, emoji

Reading

2 A
4 1 No (*Laughter is rarely something we decide to do. Like crying, it is a natural instinct and one that is very difficult to control.*)
2 Not Given
3 Yes (*For example, we often smile after feelings of fear or confusion pass, or when people we perceive as more powerful than ourselves suffer a misfortune. Yet such moments often provoke a simple smile rather than a laugh.*)
4 Yes (*... real laughter is 30 times more common when we are with other people and it almost disappears when we do not have an audience.*)
5 Not Given
6 No (*Speakers apparently laugh over 50% more than their audiences ...*)
5 *Strategy focus*: 1 a verb 2 negative 3 elude
7 (a) reason 8 uncontrollably 9 social 10 initiate
11 sense of humour 12 (more) dominant 13 authority (relationships) 14 communication
6 *Suggested answers*
1 Which do you think is more important, face-to-face communication or communication via phone / email / etc.? / Why is face-to-face communication more important?
2 How could we stop people arguing?
3 Should parents and children always talk seriously, or should they also laugh?

Vocabulary extra
a laughter* b play a role, basic role, social roles, authority role c senior d audience(s) e giggles
* *Laugh* can also be a noun, but is not used as such in the text.

Listening

3 1 three
2 letters
3 *Suggested answers*
A sending an SMS
B useful websites, online information
C print media, journals
D adverts, commercials
E what the task needs
F ways of communicating that work
G books that tell stories, literary fiction
4 4 *Listeners* is not possible because it is followed by a singular verb (*is*).
5 *Put some punctuation* is not possible because you are allowed to use only one or two words, not three.
6 *To print* is not possible because *to* is already included before the gap.
4 1–3 (in any order) B, D, E
4 your audience 5 (to) pause 6 read
5 7 M 8 H 9 L 10 H
6 **Agreement**: OK, That's fine by me, She's right, Fine, Sure
Disagreement: I don't think so

Speaking

2 1 log off/out 2 Protect your privacy 3 Cyber crime
4 public network 5 digital footprint 6 share your passwords 7 internet security 8 bookmark
6 1 Candidate 3 (She should use the words *scammers* or *fraudsters* to describe people who try to access your data, and *hackers* to describe people who enter websites illegally.)
2 Candidate 2
I think it really depends. Not enough people **are** careful about who ~~do~~ they share photos with and what **people** **can** see in those photos. ... At the same time, this person is looking for a job and their potential employer **sees / might see** the photos. The photos ~~are~~ give a really negative impression of the person. You need **to** make sure you **are** happy for anyone **to** see them.
3 Candidate 1
7 If people can_access your password, they might_attempt to[w]access your bank_account_or buy things from_any[j]of your[r]online shopping_accounts.

Writing

4 1 False (The percentage bars drop consistently along the age range from younger to older.)
2 Not Given (There is no information about changes over time, so we can't say if there's a fall or a rise.)
3 Not Given (There is no information about changes over time, so we can't say if there's a fall or a rise.)
4 True (41% check their mobiles a few times an hour, and 11% check them every few minutes, making a total of 52%, which is a majority.)
5 Not Given (There is nothing to say what a 'dangerous level' is.)
5 1 Candidate 2 (Both candidates make some use of their own vocabulary, but Candidate 2 uses more (*over the age of 18, devices, mobiles*).) 2 Candidate 2 3 Candidate 2 (Candidate 1 does not refer to the fact that the survey relates to adults; note that Candidate 2 is correct in stating that the percentage of adults who check their phones at least a few times an hour is over 50% because this figu e must also include those who check their phone every few minutes.)
6 1 particularly 2 contrast 3 minority 4 accounts
5 pattern 6 suggests

Boost your band score
a **nouns**: make **use** of, frequency of **use**, **users**, phone **usage**
verb: are **used**, **use** their phones

Unit 4

Reading

1 *Suggested answers*
3 1 A 2 D 3 C 4 E 5 B
2 1 our genes 2 goals 3 over time 4 (German/college) students 5 two semesters 6 (personality) test 7 personal networks
3 *Strategy focus*
1 1 a 2 a
2 1 Travelling abroad for an extended period of time develops people's minds.
1a Long periods in another country have a positive effect on brain development.
2 People who are not open to new experiences do not like change in their environment.
2a Those that dislike doing new things often want a stable daily life.
8 A (*The study was interesting because it allowed researchers to first understand what kind of holiday different personalities choose before measuring how the experience changed them.*)
9 C (*... those who went on a one-semester trip tended to be higher in conscientiousness ...*)
10 D (*... those people who travelled tended to ... lose touch with people from their home country.*)
11 C (*Even students going from Germany to another EU country had to adjust to differences in language, food, and outlook.*)
12 D (*... it seems likely that adult personalities can be affected, if not by changes in social networks then at least by thought processes.*)
13 A (*It seems that travel makes us not only better people but cleverer people, too.*)

Vocabulary extra
1 a adapt, adjust, affect, evolve, influence
b maintain, remain
2 evolve, remain
3 influence

Listening

2 1 **Differences**: In Questions 1–3, you have to choose one answer for each question; in Questions 4–6, you have to choose three overall. You can also write the answers to Questions 4–6 in any order.
Similarity: All the questions require you to choose/write letters from a list of options.

3 1 C 2 B 3 A 4–6 A, C, E

4 7 D 8 F 9 C 10 E

5 1 Kenya 2 Costa Rica 3 Palau 4 Norway

Speaking

3 **Objects you look at**: d, h, i
Outdoor spaces: a, b, c, f, j
Buildings you enter: e, g, k*
* f may also be possible, as some markets and bazaars are indoors

4 1 Do you like walking / to walk around public gardens?
2 Have you been to a gallery recently? / Have you recently been to a gallery?
3 What famous statues can you look at in your town? / In your town, what famous statues can you look at?
4 Would you prefer to walk around markets or malls?
5 Do you enjoy looking at historic monuments?

6 a 2 b 1 c 1 d 2 e 2 f 1

7 1 Candidate 1 (The sentences begin with different subjects; not always *I*.)
2 Candidate 2 (Candidate 1's errors concern word order: ***Always it's*** *more relaxing; We* ***go usually*** *to Oman in the spring; I'd* ***love actually*** *to go somewhere really remote and peaceful.*)
3 Candidate 1 (*remote and peaceful; I love the idea of trekking through a jungle; isolated mountain range*)

8 1 a 2 c 3 d 4 b

9 *Sample answers*
1 Actually, I've never travelled abroad. Perhaps it's because I don't like flying.
2 I occasionally go for a walk in my lunch break, but generally I like to stay indoors and read a book.
3 I generally like travelling, but I rarely spend more than three weeks away from home.

Writing

3 B

4 1 Candidate 2 2 Candidate 2 3 Candidate 2

5 1 *Although* and *even if* can link two clauses.
2 *Admittedly* and *true* require a comma if used at the beginning of a sentence.

6 1 admittedly 2 although 3 True 4 maybe 5 even if

7 1 Bad
2 air passengers are admittedly useful for the economy; they generate income and create jobs; with air travel you can achieve a lot quickly; air travellers do have time to themselves.
3 b

8 See sample answer 6 on page 99.

Test file 2

Reading

1 order 2 male 3 territory 4 (song) recordings
5 nesting sites 6 effective 7 dominant 8 strength
9 C (*By producing song that requires a greater degree of effort, birds can therefore reveal how strong they are. Dominant cockerels, for example, produce higher-pitched sounds, which require more energy to create and sustain.*)
10 A (*Still others achieve success by having a repertoire of different tunes and indeed learn new songs each year to add to their collection. It seems this musical knowledge indicates an ability to survive for a long time …*)
11 D (*Generally, birds who have been neighbours for a long time are not as dangerous as new arrivals …*)
12 B (*In the latter scenario, the bird will match the tune of the new arrival as closely as possible in a process called 'song matching'.*)
13 A (*Young birds learn from other birds around them, mimicking parents, and despite some birds' habit of learning throughout their life, most species do their learning during a small period of time in their younger years.*)

Listening

1–3 C, E, F
4 D 5 R 6 T
7 B 8 B 9 C 10 A
11 symbols 12 twenty-two / 22 13 animal skin
14 a room 15 mass communication 16 (ballpoint) pen
17 (hard) point / tip 18 body 19 vent hole 20 spring

Writing

See sample answers 7 and 8 on page 100.

Unit 5

Reading

1 Positive: calm, joyful, relaxed, thankful
Negative: anxious, irritated, stressed, upset

2 The author thinks emotions affect our physical health.

3 1 B (*According to research published in the* International Journal of Psychophysiology, *the results can be long lasting, too.*)
2 C (*Your body would then be prone to the negative effects of anxiety, including weakened immunity, impaired memory and poor digestion.*)
3 C (*It also starts a calming effect on the body and mind.*)
4 B (*… oxytocin can initiate the release of DHEA, an anti-ageing, anti-stress hormone that triggers cellular restoration in the body.*)
5 A (*… that laughter relaxes tense muscles, reduces production of stress-causing hormones, lowers blood pressure, and helps increase oxygen absorption in the blood.*)
6 A (*He has found that, like love, gratitude and contentment both trigger oxytocin.*)

4 *Strategy focus*
1 But that is just one of several negative effects of anger.
2 **Anger**: irritated, disagreement, outbursts, tense
Effect: cause, increase, results, when
3 A
7 ii 8 viii 9 ix 10 iv 11 iii 12 v 13 vii 14 i

Vocabulary extra
1 a draining b irritated c outbursts d anxiety e calming f grateful

5 *Suggested answer*
You are most likely to have to describe your feelings in Speaking Part 2 when you talk about an experience, object, place or person that has a particular meaning for you. Other parts of the test may require you to give information or an opinion.

Listening

1 In a doctor's surgery

2 *Suggested answer*
1 register with the practice 2 make an appointment
3 report to reception 4 sit in the waiting room
5 have a consultation 6 lie down 7 pick up a prescription

3 a Question 4 b Three fifteen in the afternoon, three fifteen pm, (a) quarter past three c The information *in the afternoon* is already included in the notes, so writing *pm* is not necessary.

5 1 male 2 Qazwini 3 Tuesdays and Thursdays
4 1.45 / one forty-five 5 433 22 20

6 6 Form SA1 [capitals not important] 7 post
8 16 / sixteen (points) 9 (the) nurse 10 (photo) ID
(*Passport* is not correct because *any* form of photo ID is being requested.)

Speaking

2 A aerobics, yoga
B long jump, sprinting
C kite surfing, scuba diving
D judo, karate
E baseball, rugby

3 1 sprinting 2 long jump 3 kite surfing 4 rugby
5 scuba diving
5 1 Candidate 2 2 Candidate 2 3 Candidate 2
6 *Suggested answers*
1 Some people just do it (/) to get fit / but others do it (/) to protect themselves.
2 You need regular classes / and it takes a long time to prepare for the assessments.
3 Martial arts / such as karate, / judo / and taekwondo / are popular (/) in my country.
4 Anyone can do karate / but it's not popular with older people / because you get lots of injuries.
5 Lessons often happen in gyms / or sports halls / which have the special equipment we need.

Writing
3 *Suggested answers*
Similarities: Both processes involve heating; both processes involve mixing fat and alkali substances.
Differences: Ingredients come from different sources; the modern technique uses more industrial processes.
4 1 Candidate 1 2 Candidate 1 3 Candidate 2
5 1 is added 2 is fed 3 are mixed 4 has been cooled
5 are milled 6 is often added 7 has been completed
8 are pressed 9 is then stamped
6 First, Then, Once, After, then
(Relative pronouns also serve to add cohesion, but are not termed 'linking words'.)

Unit 6

Topic focus
1 1 species loss 2 air pollution 3 resource depletion
4 water pollution 5 extreme weather events
6 deforestation 7 soil degradation 8 waste

Reading
1 1 water pollution 2 no
2 c
3 1 vi 2 ii 3 v 4 viii 5 ix 6 i 7 iv
4 *Strategy focus*
1 A plural noun (because it follows *the growing number of*)
2 articles, disasters, problems
3 *... media stories on environmental topics have become increasingly common over the past 30 years ...* (para. A)
4 articles
8 E 9 C 10 K 11 I 12 J

Vocabulary extra
1/2 connect: connectedness (*abstract noun*), connection (*countable noun*), connected (*adjective*)
engage: engagement (*abstract noun*)*
environment: environmental (*adjective*), environmentalism (*abstract noun*)
urban: urbanisation (*abstract noun*)
* In the context of this reading passage

5 *Suggested answers*
- Using your car burns fossil fuels and produces harmful emissions.
- Flying emits CO_2.
- Showering daily uses water and energy.
- Buying imported food uses CO_2 in transport.
- Using plastic bags creates litter/pollution.
- Drinking bottled water creates pollution, and uses water and oil resources in manufacturing.

Listening
3 a Changes to a school and its surrounding area
b They concern the school's response to the plans.
c 6 different plan 7 plans to; use 8 Plants and animals; aren't very 9 to help produce; social media profile 10 Information; campaign
4 1 flats 2 nature area 3 projects 4 access road
5 running track
6 vote 7 count 8 rare 9 blog 10 5,000 houses

Speaking
1 Chart 1: 0.1% H_2O in atmosphere; 96.9% sea water; 3% water with no salt
Chart 2: 69% under the ground; 30% ice; 1% rivers and lakes
3 a rivers and lakes b ice c water with no salt d sea water
e under the ground f H_2O in atmosphere
4

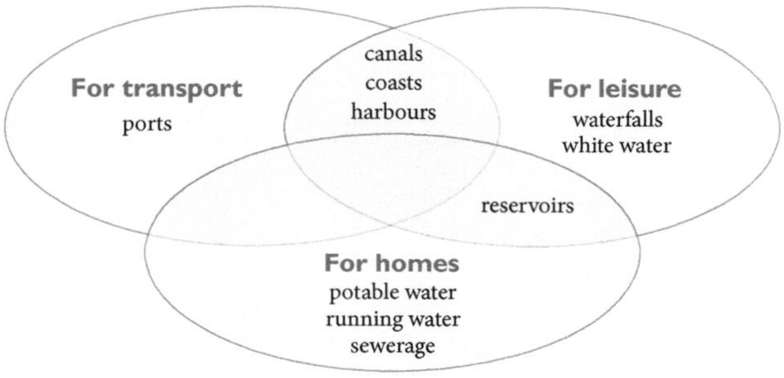

6 1 a 2 a 3 b 4 a 5 b 6 b
7 Candidate 1: question 3 Candidate 2: question 2
Candidate 3: question 6
8 1 Candidate 3 2 Candidate 2 3 Candidate 1
9 a Well, that's a good question; I mean; Um ... what else?; Actually; You see
b there are two key things; Most importantly; That way; Besides that
10 1 Most importantly 2 I mean; You see 3 Besides that
4 Um ... what else? 5 Actually 6 that's a good question
11 1 Without doubt 2 Generally speaking 3 for example
4 most importantly 5 What else 6 Well 7 I mean
8 um 9 Actually

Writing
4 Two questions
5 1 B, D 2 A, C 3 E, F
6 The topic
7 a consumer goods, individual item, new item, old one
b these, this, it, one
8 1 Candidate 1 2 Candidate 1 3 Candidate 2
9 1 They; one 2 Their; it 3 This 4 These
10 *Sample answer*
Finally, there is the issue with the changing lives of consumers. Firstly, personal wealth has increased in many countries. These richer shoppers have more disposable income and they can make more frequent purchases. Additionally, people often have extremely busy lives and they have little time to mend things, thus leading to a throw-away culture.
11 See sample answer 10 on page 101.

Test file 3

Reading
1 vi 2 v 3 ix 4 ii 5 iv 6 x 7 vii 8 viii
9 A 10 H 11 F 12 L 13 K 14 J

Listening
1 Sunday 2 90 minutes 3 blue (route) 4 sun cream
5 trainers
6 (legal) documents 7 (safety) equipment 8 (a) video
9 (short) test 10 surprise tasks
11 B 12 B 13 C
14 and 15 D, F (in either order)
16 honeymoon 17 (hiking) poles 18 ankle 19 torch
20 hotel manager

Writing
See sample answers 11 and 12 on page 101.

Unit 7

Topic focus

1 1 d 2 b 3 a 4 e 5 c 6 f

Reading

1 1 mining 2 manufacturing 3 medicine
2 1 Primary and secondary
3 No. The author believes that the nature of work will change, but does not argue that workers will be replaced by machines.
3 The task on page 60 has a word pool to select from. This task requires candidates to find the correct words in the reading passage.
5 1 connections 2 investors 3 quaternary 4 hubs 5 networking 6 self-publishers 7 digital goods
6 *Strategy focus*
1 Because they contain key content.
2 1 hobby: interests, pastimes
make money: earn money, have an income, get a wage/ salary, generate income / money / cash
2 Collecting things, doing sports, reading, playing games, making things ...
3 J (*... socialising, writing diaries or taking photos, once amateur pastimes, will become money-making activities.*)
8 C (*Certainly our ability to work with information, diagnosing problems, analysing trends or quantifying risks and so on are all skills that machines can almost certainly do better.*)
9 I (*But rather than taking their money, companies invite them to come in and try out their products so that they can gain feedback.*)
10 D (*Unemployment rates hover at just under 6% and are predicted to fall slightly.*)
11 F (*The 'internet economy' is larger in value terms than the agricultural sector, accounting for over 5% of the economy in richer countries, and will continue to help establish a greater number of economic connections between producers and buyers.*)
12 E (*Some of these, like logistics, may become increasingly automated, but others, like customer management and advertising, are likely to require a human touch.*)
13 G (*Scientific and IT hubs like Silicon Valley in California and Silicon Fen in Cambridge are providing jobs for an increasing proportion of their nation's citizens. The Osaka Innovation Hub accounts for a full 40% of new jobs in Japan.*)
14 H (*Any blog or e-book that becomes popular can generate income for the author if they agree to publish their content with advertisements, and many have grasped this opportunity.*)

Vocabulary extra
1 Workers: labourers, workforce, wage-earners, employees
Jobs: posts, employment, roles, employment opportunities, positions
2 The words are *employee* and *employment*.
Other words in the same family: *employer, employ, (un)employable, unemployment, (un)employed*
7 *Suggested answers*
a Creative thinking, communicating, all literacy skills, initiative
b Critical thinking, understanding and using information/ technology, flexibility
c Collaborating, communicating, initiative, social skills, leadership

Listening

2 1 Jobs; Advantages/Benefits; Disadvantages/Drawbacks
2 1 An adjective or adjectival phrase describing jobs
2 An adjective or adjectival phrase describing salaries
3 A singular or uncountable noun that takes a long time
4 A plural noun
5 A noun that can be difficult to make
6 An area of business
7 An adjective or adjectival phrase describing a profession
4 1 difficult to get 2 (very) high 3 Training 4 roles 5 decisions 6 Law 7 respected
5 8 C 9 B 10 C

Speaking

2 1 clients/customers 2 conferences 3 home 4 office 5 team 6 boss 7 bonus 8 account 9 company 10 pension
5 Candidate 1: zookeeper Candidate 2: telephone sales
6 1 Candidate 2 2 Candidate 1 3 Candidate 1 (Candidate 1 uses *would* to talk about a hypothetical situation; Candidate 2's use of the present simple makes his answer sound as if he is describing a job he actually does.)
7 1 It falls.
2 The important words that carry the meaning of the sentence
8 See audio transcript 2.15 on page 111 for intonation mark-up.

Writing

3 1 Circle: farmland and forest (Map A); spa hotel and golf course (Map B)
2 Box: port, farm, forest (Map A); shops, hotels, restaurants, golf course (Map B)
3 Candidate 1 has focused on one area first, whereas Candidate 2 has described the maps more thoroughly.
4 1 Candidate 1 2 Candidate 1 3 Candidate 2 4 Candidate 2
5 1 In 2 by 3 along 4 between 5 Opposite
6 1 extended 2 demolished 3 converted 4 relocated 5 replaced 6 cut down
7 See sample answer 13 on page 102.

Unit 8

Topic focus

1 **Positive**: community-minded, empathetic, energetic, engaged, enthusiastic
Negative: anti-social, apathetic, lacking respect, lacking direction, lazy

Reading

1 1 31 2 60 3 3 4 6
2 Men: c, e, f
Women: a, b, d
3 Lies told by defendants in court cases
4 1 B (*As a result of the test, the two men were found guilty of attempted murder.*)
2 H (*... some citizens made false claims on Twitter ...*)
3 D (*In courts around the world, the polygraph is now banned due to its inaccuracy.*)
4 G (*... women are much better liars than men.*)
5 E (*... it is much harder to tell a lie than the truth.*)
6 F (*Previously, it was thought that liars simply gave hesitant responses and tried to avoid eye contact. However, the software also showed that people usually look angry or pained ...*)
7 E (*People's brains often react quite differently according to the size of the lie or how far the subject believes their own lie.*)
5 *Strategy focus*
1 The questions on page 20 require students to write *Yes*, *No* or *Not Given* on their answer sheet. These are used for opinion texts. On page 80, students are asked to write *True*, *False* or *Not Given*. These are used for factual texts. Both types of question require the same strategy.
2 2 *Judge Van Pelt* <u>*believed*</u> *the two men were* <u>*guilty*</u>.
3 *Judge Van Pelt had* <u>*used*</u> *a* <u>*polygraph*</u> *in* <u>*court*</u> <u>*before*</u>.
3 1 False (They were arrested for *attempted* murder, so we know that no murder happened.)
2 Not Given (We don't know what the judge's belief was.)
3 False (We know he had *recently heard* of it, suggesting he hadn't used it before.)
8 True (*It worked by measuring blood pressure and responses in the skin while the person was being questioned.*)

9 Not Given (The text describes the current situation by stating 'the polygraph is now banned', but doesn't indicate whether the ban occurred recently or not.)
10 False (*While this can mean the tests are up to 95% accurate, it can also mean they are no more accurate than someone simply guessing.*)
11 True (*They work in different ways, but both analyse changes in the brain.*)
12 False (*... they have yet to be used in criminal trials.*)
13 False (*... people constantly move or fidget when they are telling lies.*)
14 Not Given (We are told that people have lied in social media, but we are not given any indication of how frequently they lie through this medium.)

Vocabulary extra

1 1 determine 2 decided 3 found 4 tell 5 made
2 All the verbs carry the meaning of 'to decide'.

Listening

3 1 nouns 2 won't
4 *Suggested answers*
1 theft / stealing / shoplifting 2 persevering / pursuing / making an effort / persistent 3 discipline / check / limit / curb 4 aggression / biting / hitting / punching 5 reactions / retorts 6 shouting / fighting / rowing / bad relations 7 visits / games / hanging out
5 1 plan 2 shouting (loudly) 3 control centres 4 (long-term) aims
6 5 T 6 A 7 C 8 A 9 T 10 C
7 1 c 2 a 3 d 4 e 5 b

Speaking

3 *Suggested answers*
Problems: being spoiled, lack of discipline, large classes, poor behaviour
Solutions: clear rules
Both: harsh punishments, large rewards, relaxed parenting, strict teaching
4 1 lack of discipline 2 poor behaviour 3 relaxed parenting 4 clear rules 5 being spoiled 6 strict teaching 7 harsh punishments / large rewards; large rewards / harsh punishments 8 large classes
5 *Suggested answers*
1 What's your favourite subject? / Who's your favourite teacher?
2 What did you like about school? / What was your worst subject?
3 Which was harder, maths or English?
4 What would you like to study in the future?
6 *Suggested answer*
Describe a school rule that you thought was unfair.
You should say:
what the rule was
what happened if you broke the rule
what rule you would have instead
and why you thought it was unfair.
7 Questions 2, 4 and 7
8 1 Candidate 1 2 Candidate 1 3 Candidate 2
9 1 However 2 Consequently 3 for instance 4 leads to 5 What's more

Writing

1 a 4 teaspoons b 9 teaspoons c 1 teaspoon d 13 teaspoons e 2 teaspoons
4 No. In 'discuss' essays, the structure usually means that you give both sides of the argument before giving your opinion in the conclusion.
5 Candidate 2, because it maintains a neutral style.
7 1 Candidate 1 (A complex sentence is defined as a sentence with a main clause and a less important clause.) 2 Candidate 2 3 Candidate 2
8 1 Others believe (that) a tax on sugary food and drink is a sensible solution.
2 Arguably, it's easier to tax products than force supermarkets to hide food. / It's arguably easier to tax products than force supermarkets to hide food.
3 Also, the money raised could perhaps be used for education campaigns.
4 The campaigns might try to teach people about the dangers of eating too much sugar.
9 In conclusion, the objections to a tax on sugary food are misplaced. While other measures may be more effective in the short term, a tax is a realistic solution that would provide a foundation for other measures.
10 See sample answer 14 on page 102.

Test file 4

Reading

1 F (*Cyber crime and online fraud in particular have witnessed steady growth.*)
2 B (*... epidemics of illegal drug use associated with the 1980s have ended ...*)
3 C (*... measures like the 1970 Clean Air Act in the USA, which removed lead from fuels, have been shown to ...*)
4 H (*... better policing, even inspiring political leadership have contributed to increasing levels of safety ...*)
5 D (*Ageing populations, they argue, have increased the presence of calmer moderating influences in families ...*)
6 False (*... rates of serious crimes have been falling across Europe since the turn of the millennium, despite some quite severe economic shocks and depressions.*)
7 Not Given (The text says *70% of prisoners have two or more mental health conditions*, but there is no suggestion of a decrease.)
8 True (*... it was during the 1980s that a particularly large cohort of young males started moving into middle age ...*)
9 True (*... inner-city areas (were) once breeding grounds for serious crime. As migration has accelerated ... many of these areas have been taken over by ambitious, hard-working migrant families.*)
10 False (*A 10% increase in prices is said to result in a 3.5% increase in crime ...*)
11 Not Given (The text says *The drop in prices of consumer goods has been matched by increases in our means of securing them*, but does not talk about increase in purchases.)
12 A (*... security cameras are deterring mugging and physical assault.*)
13 B (*... entertainment systems at home, far from inspiring violence, may be encouraging people to stay in safer indoor environments ...*)
14 D (*The more that plausible answers are put forward, the less it seems likely that we will ever arrive at a neat, satisfactory explanation.*)

Listening

1 play or rest 2 punishments 3 Self-control 4 responsibility 5 ambition 6 balance 7 intelligence
8 A 9 B 10 C
11 engineers and accountants 12 not connected
13 minimum salary 14 performance
15 M 16 P 17 P 18 M 19 H 20 H

Writing

See sample answers 15 and 16 on pages 102 and 103.